Humanistic Refclections in the Select Essays of Bertrand Russell and Aldous Huxley

Dr. K. Mahendran

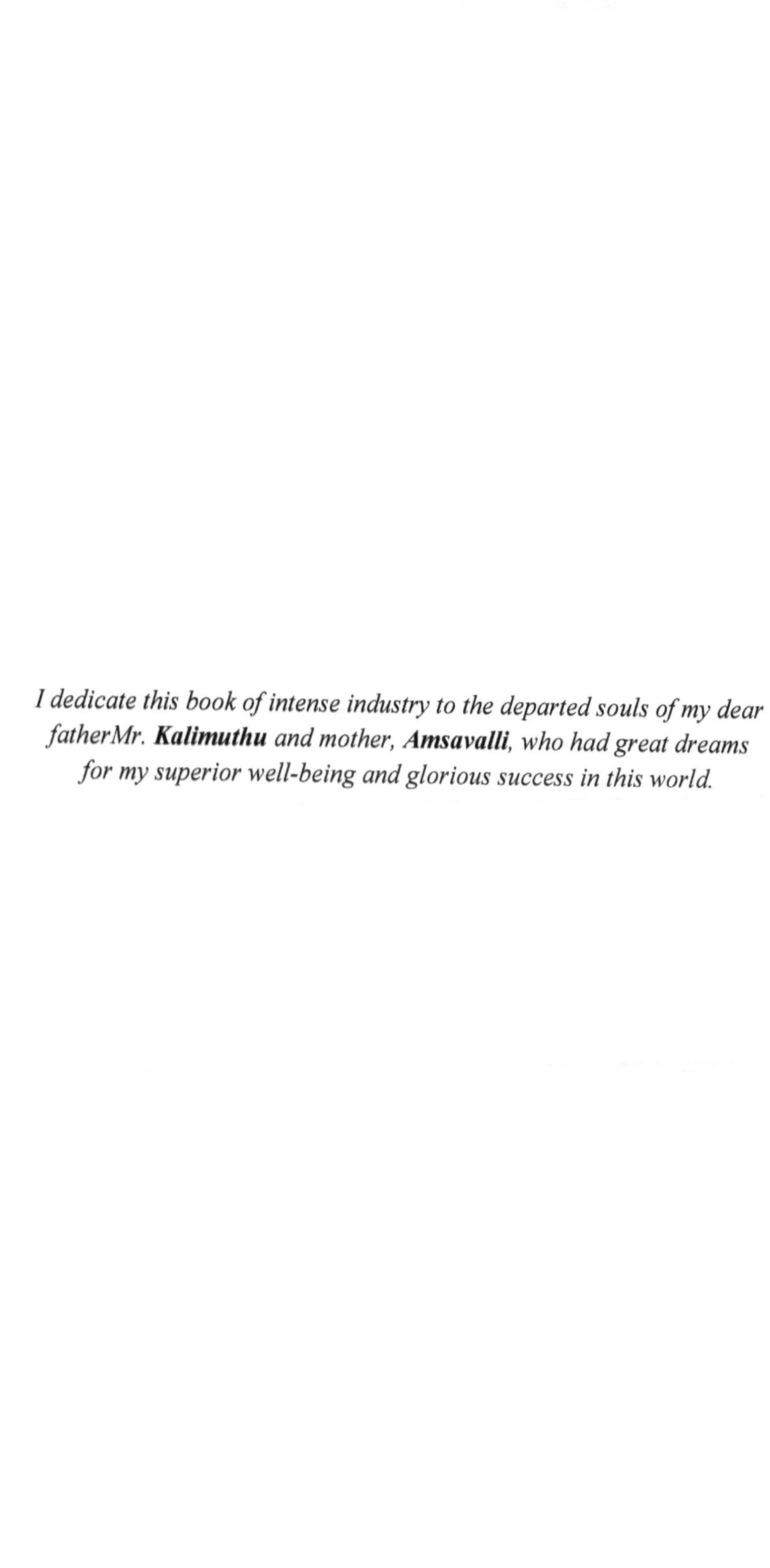

*I dedicate this book of intense industry to the departed souls of my dear father Mr. **Kalimuthu** and mother, **Amsavalli**, who had great dreams for my superior well-being and glorious success in this world.*

Contents

Preface

Literature is the most powerful preacher of human values, the ulmimate aim of all its propagations is to instil humanism in the mind of man. The idea of humanism is inseparable from the collective grievances connected with the modern world. The modern world, with all its cruelties, has necessitated the birth of many humanists to protect human values, the prosperity and peace of the world. This book is basically my thesis and it deals with the humanistic cogitations of Russell and Huxley to quell all the socio-political problems existed during the first and second World Wars. Bertrand Russell and Aldous Huxley are the prominent intellectuals and socio-political critics of the twentieth century, who were well-known especially for their humanistic speeches and writings, and anti-war activities. They have written essays to reflect on so many subjects and ideas, besides their other forms of writings.

The international socio-political atrocities, speaking against power politics, war, political imperialism, nationalism and its destructive consequences, capitalism leading to the madness to rule the world, political dishonesty, hunger for superpower, totalitarianism, world government, poverty, social and class oppression, humanism and freedom, the privileged, under-privileged and private education are some of the most prominent themes that they dealt with. Humanism is the core of their identity as thinkers and writers, which is greatly shimmering through their writings, especially essays. This thesis deals with the select twenty essays from both Russell and Huxley to explore the humanistic perspectives of these writers on the areas of social reformation, education, ethics, politics, anti-war.

Russell and Huxley say that the collective attitude of the human society is not so refined as to have a qualitative and peaceful life in general. It is with many negative emotions that hamper the prosperity and well-being of the world. They admonish the self-destructive habits of the modern people like being after entertainment, being indifferent to the time-honoured ideas, being selfish and being ignorant about the contemporary socio-political problems. They talk of how the modern people have gone away from the basic ethics for healthy life and give suggestions to set right their ways to become responsible and healthy citizens.

They talk of the present pathetic condition of the field of education that fails to produce strong individuals. They say that the education of the modern world is very mechanical and does not make students become creative in their chosen field. It makes students competitive to become wealthy and powerful but does not contribute towards their leadership and human qualities. Russell and Huxley talk of the pathetic condition of the modern students with the heavy syllabus and the difficulties of the professor due to many academic irrelevant works.

They talk of the true responsibilities of the students to learn and grow vital as the most productive individuals in the society and the teachers' responsibilities that they must devote careful and affectionate attention to all the students in achieving their dreams to become achievers in the respective fields that they love and respect the most. They are very emphatic that this state of education must be changed so as to enrich not only human brain but also heart so that the world will be prosperous and peaceful. Russell and Huxley talk of individual, social and institutional ethics, with which the individuals in the world can be transformed as to construct a strong humanistic society. They talk of the condition of the modern politics and the characteristic qualities of politicians and the future of the international political scenario.

Russell and Huxley, being humanists, are very intensely against war and blood-shed and talk of how war is basically cruel and inhuman. They announce that war is barbaric and self-destructive and so man has to understand the convincing masks of the vicious intentions to make war against a race, country, a particular area of a country etc,. Russell and Huxley talk of the first and second World Wars and the regrettable destructions caused. They talk of the condition of the world during their time that could lead to the third World War. Russell and Huxley bring out the possible unthinkable destructions of such a war in the future due to the scientific advancement and the modern lethal weapons that could wipe off human species from the world.

They say that the first step towards extirpating war from the world is to create awareness among the common people about how irrational and animalistic war is and make the important politicians, scientists and other decision-making authorities realize that war springs from human ego to dominate and be the most powerful, curtailing of which can water humanism that can offer enjoyable and secured life. Russell and Huxley recommend the much-discussed idea of World Government, which means one government for the entire world so that there will not be any necessity to wage war against any country and say that the heads of and the important people of all the countries in the world must think of the possibilities to be unitedly live under a single government.

Thus, this book sheds light on how humanism is strongly recommended as the last resort to resolve all the socio-political problems of the times of Russell and Huxley in their select essays. The readers are sure to be benefited with my insights into the carefully chosen essays of the two greatest thinkers of all time, with the help of which not only the cross section of terrible socio-political atmosphere the past can be understood but also the judicious decisions can be taken, having an eye on the glorious future that the international community would like to build for the posterity.

Dr. K. Mahendran
Professor of English
SRM Institute of Science and
Technology, Kattankulathur

Acknowledgments

I express my heart-felt gratitude to my research guide, **Dr. T. Murugavel**, who, besides being a responsible and exemplary guide, has been my friendly mentor.

I am very much indebted to **Dr. K. Chellappan**, former **Head, Department of English, Bharathidasan University** and **Sahitya Akademy Prize** winner, for the inestimable privilege of getting insights on my research through the discussions and guidance.

I am deeply grateful to **Dr. P. Maruthanayagam**, Former **Head of the Department of English, Pondicherry University**, who, as my professor, introduced me to the world of literary criticism and inspired me to dwell in the field of research.

I express my love, respect and gratitude to **Dr. Clement Lourdes**, Professor of English, **Pondicherry University,** for suggesting the area of my research.

I thank **Dr. Jeyagandhi**, former Head of the Department of Chemistry, **Poombukar College of Arts and Science**, for his unforgettably significant help for the emergence of this work.

I thank **Dr. Balasubramaniam**, the Head of the Department of Nanotechnology, **Bharathiar University,** Coimbatore, for his timely support for the launch of this book.

I happy to bear a very deep gratitude to my friend
Dr. Neelakandan, Professor of English, **Sri Ramakrishna Mission Vidyalaya College of Arts and Science**, Coimbatore, whose great help broke the obstacles to the peaceful birth of this work.

I thank **Dr. Aiyapparaj**, Associate Professor of English, **Annamalai University**, Chidambaram, for offering clarity and guidance for my doubts on this research work.

I am extremely grateful to my dear friend,
Dr. Sivaraja, Assistant Professor, **Poombukar College of Arts and Science**, for his constant moral support and guidance to the completion this work.

I am thankful to my dear friend, **Dr. Sathish**, Assistant Professor of Tamil, **Dr.M.G.R. College of Arts and Science,** Sirkazhi, for his relentless support and wish for the successful completion of this work.

I am very grateful to **Dr. Sathiyamoorthy**, Assistant Professor of English, **Dr. MGR College of Arts and Science**, Sirkazhi, for the timely help with useful material.

My joyful thanks to my friend, **Dr. Immanuel**, Dean, Academics, **Bharath University**, Chennai, for his constructive guidelines for the effectiveness of this research work.

My sincere thanks to **Dr. P. Madhusoodanan**, Head, CDC, **SRMIST**, Kattankulathur, for his moral support for the speedy emergence of this research work.

I thank my colleague, friend and well-wisher, **Dr. Jeyapragash**, Assistant Professor, CDC, **SRMIST**, Kattankulathur, for the very good material and encouragement for this work.

I am thankful to my colleague, **Dr. Padmapriya**, Assistant Professor, CDC, **SRMIST**, Kattankulathur, for her help with useful material for my research.

I am very thankful to my dear intellectual and humorous friend Mr. **Roland Rencewigg**, Assistant Professor, CDC, **SRMIST**, Kattankulathur, for his help in formatting this work in its initial stage.

I thank **Dr. Balamurugan**, Assistant Professor, CDC, **SRMIST**, Kattankulathur for the constant moral support for all my intellectual endeavours.

Above all, I am eternally thankful to my **Gurus, Ragavendra Swami and Korakkar** and the collective forces of the **Divinity** I am associated with.

Chapter I

The distinct identity of man:

The universe stands as the mightiest stretch of the all-encompassing and ever- inspiring source of enquiry to man. Its immeasurable vastness, the incomprehensibly complex functions, the impenetrable might that it reflects and the profundity of its blatant and hidden meanings have an inbuilt connection and impact on everything under the sky, especially on human dissecting and enquiring intellect. Human beings are very special and distinct because they are endowed with thinking ability with which they are decisive about their actions and become responsible for the consequences of their actions. Great qualities and lofty ideas are associated only with man. Man realizes the responsibilities of his distinct state on this planet as he makes an enquiry on his true identity and its connection with the universe. The great Indian philosopher Dr. Radhakrishnan, in his essay, *Transform the Nature of Man*, exhibits this significant truth:

> The laws of nature point out to you that there is something deeper than the world of space and time in which you live. If you open your eyes, you will discover that this progressive unfolding of the universe from matter to life, from life to animal mind, from animal mind to human intelligence, from human intelligence to God-man, to the spiritual soul, there has been a law governing this whole universe working in this devout consummation, namely turning over this earth into a true Kingdom of God, into a Brahma Loka, whatever you may call it (7).

Man's intellect perceives the inbuilt law and order in any structure from atom to the unfathomable stretch of the universe. So, man, both intuitively and through painstaking intellectual enquiry, comprehends that there is an inbuilt discipline that operates and administers everything including himself. The reasoning capacity of man leads to the richness and sophistication of refinement and principles, which make him think of leading life with peace, joy and significant significations that naturally demand the construction of a very long-lasting structure called family, community and society and the rules imposed become the governing principles to ensure safety, peace, well-being and enrichment in general, which are the cradle of humanism.

The primitive history of human beings has recorded two great events, the construction of society through civilization and culture, and the hunting and fighting spirit either for food or both for broadening territory and defending it. The advancement of science and arts has made life more comfortable and easier, but unfortunately the spirit for fighting to prove one's physical and mental might in the barbaric culture still remains deep-seated. The intelligentsia of the world has not only rummaged and attained clarity on the cross-section of the material world but also the world of philosophy and spirituality. Science can only discover the nature, positions and operations of the heavenly bodies, the milky- way and the universe, but it cannot think on what is behind the creation of the system and the mystic governing principles of the structure and its operations, which are dealt with in the glorious branches of philosophy and spirituality, the distillation of which is humanism, without which literature cannot stand so tall as the epitome of life.

It is not a comparative study, but a thematic analysis, since a comparative study is a matter of comparing and contrasting.

In the above-mentioned works, the respective writers have dealt with the select essays of Bertrand Russell to explore his ideas on the areas of his writing style as an essayist, education, politics and culture. The researches on Huxley indicate that it is the combination of both some of his essays and the popular themes of his novels. So, some writers have written on the essays of both these writers separately, but to have a twofold increase in the effect and its impact of all these essays, due to the affirming similarity among the critical views of Russell and Huxley on various ideas, a thematic analysis in the essays of both the writers in the light of humanism is necessary.

This study analyses the themes of the Social Reformative Concerns, Ethical Views, Educational Views, Political Views and Anti-war in the select essays of Bertrand Russell and Aldous Huxley. The objective of this research is to showcase the fact that Bertrand Russell and Aldous Huxley talk of many vital contemporary issues of their times with the advocacy of humanism as the only resort to resolve all the issues. It highlights the contemporary burning socio-political issues of their times, the suggestions to wipe off all the issues and how their humanistic perspectives are predominating in the select essays. The analysis concludes that both Bertrand Russell and Aldous Huxley have similar views on all the five themes taken for the research, with very strong humanistic perspectives.

This study comprises five chapters. The introductory chapter begins with an introduction to humanism and famous humanists and their might as humanists. It is with an introduction to essay as a genre and its significant role in literature. The hypothesis and the objective of the study are explained in the chapter. The list of select essays of Bertrand Russell and Aldous Huxley are given in this chapter, followed by a short introduction to the authors.

The second chapter deals with the five themes from the select essays of Bertrand Russell, The third chapter deals with the five themes from the select essays of Aldous Huxley and the fourth chapter deals with the analysis of the five themes of both Russell and Huxley so as to bring the similarity between their socio-political observations, criticism and recommendations with humanistic intentions. The conclusion of this study is presented in the 'summing up,' the last chapter.

The primary sources used for this research

Unpopular Essays (1950), Human Society in Ethics and Politics (1954), The Basic Writings (1961), Mortals and Others (1975), Fact and Fiction (2009), Collected Essays of Aldous Huxley (1960), Between the Wars (1994) and The Complete Essays of Huxley (2000)

The select essays used for this research is enlisted below:

The select essays of Bertrand Russell

The social reformative concerns

1. Is the world going mad? 2. The decay of meditation 3. Whose admiration do we desire?

4. Marriage 5. Children 6. On Mental Differences between Boys and Girls. 7. Equality

Russell's Ethical views

8. On optimism 9. Illegal? 10. Flight from reality.

Educational views

11. Education

Russell's Political views

12. On politicians 13. On National Greatness

Russell's political views

14. The world I shall like to live in 15. Psychology of East West Tension. 16. War and Peace in my lifetime. 17. The social responsibility of scientists. 18. Three essentials for suitable world. 19. Can war be abolished? 20. Do governments desire war?

The select essays of Aldous Huxley:

Huxley's social reformative concerns

1. Science and civilisation 2. Pareto and society 3. The horrors of the society

4. How to improve the world 5. Work and leisure 6. Babies --- the state property

Huxley's Ethical views

7. On not being up-to-date 8. Pleasures

9. Talking of monkeys

Huxley's Educational views

10. Education Huxley's Political criticism: 11. Follow my leader

Huxley's political views

12. Words and Behaviour 13. Total war and pacifism 14. Politics and religion

15. The psychology of suggestion 16. The prospects of fascism in England

17. The scientists' role 18. Artists against fascism 19. What can we do about it

20. Decentralisation and self-government

Humanism:

The term 'humanism' has its root in the German word 'humanismus', so says Tony Davies, in his book, *Humanism*. He says, "Well firstly, as we have already seen, the word itself is a German coinage; and secondly, its credentials are Greek. *Humanismus* was a term devised, probably by the educationalist Friedrich Immanuel Niethammer, in the early nineteenth century" (10). Reason is glorified in the field of intellect and emotions are considered inferior even though art and music are the much glorified superior human emotions. Reason has a superior stand over emotions not only in the field of logic and philosophy but also in social justice, ethics and politics. According   to *The Sage Dictionary of Cultural Studies*:

> 1. Humanism- the doctrine that people's duty is to promote human welfare humanitarianism doctrine, ism, philosophical system, and philosophy, school of thought a belief (or system of beliefs) accepted as authoritative by some group or school. 2. the doctrine emphasizing a person's capacity for self-realization through reason; rejects religion and the supernatural. 3. the cultural movement of the Renaissance; based on classical studies cultural movement – a group of people working together to advance certain cultural goals (88).

Types of Humanism:

Liberal Humanism: The first type of humanism philosophy is Liberal humanism. Liberal humanists believe that the sacredness of humanity lives in every individual. Therefore, the most important thing is to protect each individual's sacredness and freedom. This is where our modern idea of "human rights" comes from. For instance, because liberal humanists believe in the sanctity of every individual, they object to the death penalty. They'd rather put murderers in prison and help them rediscover their sanctity than kill them.

Socialist Humanism: The second type of humanism philosophy is socialist humanism. Social humanists believe that the sacredness of humanity lives in the collective, the Sapiens species as a whole. The most important thing is to protect the equality of individuals in the species (rather than the individual freedom favored by liberal humanists). Inequality denies our sanctity because it privileges unimportant qualities like wealth or skin color. When we favor the rich over the poor, for example, it shows that we value money over the sanctity possessed by all humans, regardless of their net worth.

Evolutionary Humanism: The third type of humanism is evolutionary humanism. Evolutionary humanists believe that we need to actively direct the evolution of our species, making sure we evolve into super-humans rather than sub-humans.

Globalization does include not only multi-dimensional approach but also multi-directional. Reason and emotions are inseparable and socio-political justice and effective beneficial activities grow in the world, only when emotions are advocated and supported by reason. Justice is an emotional reason or reasonable emotion fundamentally needed for the well-being of social structure, the rudimentary monument of civilization and culture. For Plato the highest exercise of the mind was the grasp of that which was purely intelligible, "which the reason lays hold of by the power of dialectic" (Republic, VI, 511b).

The tradition of humanism in the Western world has its roots in the Enlightenment. Carrington says, "A variety of thinkers, critical of the scholastic tradition of transmitting speculative theology to passive students, proposed an alternative account concerned with studies of human beings living well in the world" (293). In the western philosophy, many inter-connected 'isms' are associated with humanism, which eventually has received a collective opinion from great thinkers and philosophers that it is difficult to be clear about the definition of humanism, but in the Indian philosophical and cultural context it means being humane in one's thoughts and activities.

In the Indian moral philosophy, it is about being very lovable, loving, caring and defending the comfort, dignity and rights of not only human beings but also animals and vegetation. To have feeling heart for the suffering of others, irrespective of nation, religion, language, caste and creed. It is only in this meaning the term 'humanism' is dealt with in this thesis. R.C. Jebb, when talking about the characteristic qualities for which the period of Renaissance is highly regarded, announces that the quintessence of the nature of the period is reflected in the idea of Humanism:

> The classical literatures which were being gradually recovered, were the supreme products of the human mind; that they were the best means of self-culture; that there alone one could see the human reason moving freely, the moral nature clearly expressed, in a word, the dignity of man, as a rational being, fully displayed. All this is implied in humanism, when we speak of humanism as the direction in which the Renaissance chiefly tended (5).

There are associations to protect animals, trees and forest like Blue Cross and Anti-deforestation Bodies. Indian philosophy stands for the culmination of humanism that preaches of sacrificing one's life for the sake of other's well-being is the most meaningful life. But the western philosophy says that humanism is the concept of affirming the independency, ability and responsibility of man to lead a life of fulfilment with the ethics that he has formulated without being dominated or governed any thoughts, ideas and rules in the name of religion and God. It is a pragmatic approach to life in general that actually revolves around the supremacy of man and not God or Heaven. It is a rational bent of mind, offering the prime importance to human beings rather than divinity and anything supernatural. Tony Davies says that humanism is about, "…the dignity and freedom of man, individualism, wide intellectual curiosity and a refusal to submit to the constraints of clerical orthodoxy" (97).

It is the concept that embraces man as the beginning of any moral and philosophical enquires and so it basically advocates a complete human freedom, autonomy and the free will to ramify through sheer labour, experiencing challenges and difficulties. David E. Cooper says, "Humanists, as the first great historian of the Renaissance explains, tended to emphasize the uniqueness and 'subjective side' of the individual, together with a daunting sense of moral responsibility" (242). Lee Spinks, in his book, *Friedrich Nietzsche*, says that even truth, the ultimate reverential idea and the value of anything can be discovered only by the human mind. He says, "The key idea of humanism is that truth and value can be discerned by the human mind directly" (117).

Humanism is the anthropocentric approach to quell not only the basic inbuilt predicaments of life but also the man-made socio-political problems. Self-love is the basis, but it does not serve the purpose of being a human, it is the reason for selfishness and the spirit to own whatever is the best in the world. So self-respect and love should give into humanistic maturity and richness as to be noble in perception on others with the help of the bundle of emotions and thoughts with which one's mind or ego is embellished or honoured. *The Oxford Companion to Philosophy* records that the nucleus of humanism is its rational approach to the socio-political views of many things in the world, including religion:

> Humanism, often called scientific humanism, then becomes associated with rationalism, not in

its philosophical senses but in that of an appeal to reason in contrast to revelation or religious authority as a means of finding out about the natural world and the nature and destiny of man, and also as giving a grounding for morality; the term 'ethical humanism' is sometimes used in this last context, though the outlook can also be called scientific humanism in so far as it claims that science can provide a basis for morality.

Humanists may also reject the implication in the title 'scientific humanist' that science can at least ultimately answer all questions. (Naturalism, positivism) Humanist ethics is also distinguished by placing the end of moral action in the welfare of humanity rather than in fulfilling the will of God (402).

The questions on the purpose of doing anything is the most important and fruitful enquiry of the human mind. The purpose of living in this world is invariably associated with many lofty idealism and doctrines. The construction of the society and world for peaceful and productive life is due to doctrines, ideologies, rules and disciplines. The term 'Humanity' has become synonymous with being benevolent to not only other fellow human beings but also all living and non-living beings. Being a human being is not physical in the world of morality, it is qualitative, the measuring scale of the standard of an individual and the quality of life also. Friedrich Nietzsche, the German philosopher, who has taken an inspiration from Charles Darwin to think on man, says in his much-celebrated work, *Thus Spoke Zarathustra*, "man is something to be overcome" (12). by which he does not mean anything physical, but the admirable standard of mental, emotional and intellectual evolution.

Existentialism and humanism:

There is an interconnection between existentialism and humanism. Jean Paul Satre, in his book, *Existentialism is a Humanism*, says:

There is no other universe except the human universe, the universe of human subjectivity. This relation of transcendence as constitutive of man (not in the sense that God is transcendent, but in the sense of self-surpassing) with subjectivity (in such a sense that man is not shut up in himself but forever present in a human universe) — it is this that we call existential humanism. This is humanism, because we remind man that there is no legislator but himself; that he himself, thus abandoned, must decide for himself; also because we show that it is not by turning back upon himself, but always by seeking, beyond himself, an aim which is one of liberation or of some particular realisation, that man can realize himself as truly human (14).

The roots of humanism are with existentialism that deals with the existential struggles, pains, challenges and experiences to survive and live with peace, security, dignity and contentment. The history of the world, including the prehistoric period, has recorded the need for individual and socio-political discipline and order. The literatures of the world have spoken primarily for humanism through almost all genres.

Famous humanists:

The list of writers, holding up the flag of humanism is very lengthy. A very famous group of poets and writers known as war poets like Wilfred Owen, Rupert Brooke and Robert Graves and novelists like Leo Tolstoy, Earnest Hemingway and William Faulkner, have gained universal attention and appreciation and anti-war associations and movements have their significant contribution towards the spread of humanistic values across the world and peace keeping actions and plans. They censured war deeply by bringing the cruelties of war into spot light. Movements for children, orphans, women, aged and downtrodden people are the living symbols for the necessity of advocating humanism. Mother Teresa was a very prominent humanist to gain the international reverence for her relentless service to the sufferings and pains of many orphans especially in

India. Carl Marx's, Dos Capital, which killed feudalism, was launched to spread communistic ideas against the common people's oppression in the hands of wealthy landlords and the irresponsible king.

The Gandhian Non-violence has become the recently discovered invincible weapon against all sorts of oppressions and the victimizing and swindling attitude of the strong and cruel, trying not only to be comfortable, sapping the strength of the weak but also taking pleasure in oppressing them. Human conscience beyond a point and in spite of any sort of strong masks and negative influences, leaps out with its true nature of being humanistic, the promise of which is epitomized by the War Poets. Martin Luther King the junior and Malcom X were the unstoppable forces, fighting for the freedom and dignity of the black Americans. Gautama Buddha, who was the vibrant fountain of humanistic ideas like peace, renouncing desire, forgiving and altruism, and swami Vivekananda, who focused on human mental, intellectual and spiritual development, are the best examples for Indian spiritual humanists. The socio-political revolutionists and the freedom fighters of all the countries of the world from the British Colonialism are with the sword of humanism.

The essay and humanism:

Literature is the most powerful preacher of human values and life in general. Literature is on par with religious moral prescriptions for healthy and purposeful life to the accomplishments of spiritual aspirations, which at least achieve bringing the common people to be serious about certain basic principles in life. It talks of philosophy, beauty, discipline, spirituality etc., but the ultimate aim of all the propagations is to instil humanism in the mind of man. British literature has done this noble task excellently well through all its genres, and essay is not an exception in trumpeting to the world of the most important idea of humanism. The word essay derives from the French infinitive essayer, "to try" or "to attempt". In English essay first meant "a trial" or "an attempt", and this is still an alternative meaning. One definition is a "prose composition with a focused subject of discussion" or a "long, systematic discourse". Most readers know that the word "essay" comes from the French *essai*. The verb form, *essayer*, means to attempt, to experiment, to try out.

The standard definition of the genre holds that an essay is essentially a way of trying on a thought or an idea like a hat. Essay has never been an insignificant genre in being productive and contributing to the human welfare and society. It has been a very powerful bombshell in the hands of many brilliant writers to devastate many social ills, since essay is a simple medium to project both simple and great ideas. Essay is the most powerful, simple and not time consuming like the other forms of writing.

Many great thinkers and writers across the world, besides writing novels and criticism, have written essays to convey their thoughts. Bertrand Russell and Aldous Huxley are the two prominent advocators of humanism. These two humanistic thinkers have promulgated their ideas, through their speeches, books, poems, novels and essays. The essays written by them are so special in their forms and the themes that they could not have handled with the other genres like novels and poems. Scot Black says that this is the genre which is the most effective to preach humanism to the world as the simplicity of which is very compatible with common people.

Scot Black affirms that a simple content with a simple dress of communication is the most suitable. He says, "Essay was the name for a tool of reading that enabled a certain competency and skill – a kind of commonplace book where the work of selection and collection that is key to humanist reading is practiced and undertaken" (21). The essence of humanism is compatible with the features of 'essay'. If a socially responsible person or an organization or the head of a state or even country wants to announce, create an awareness or to preach something important during an emergency period, essay is the only form through which the content can be effectively communicated. Scot Black says, "Essays here are synonymous with moral philosophy, and are organized by different exigencies than knowledge (arts and science)" (24). It denotes the role and responsibilities of this genre with the different spears of the society.

The essay occupies a very special place among the genres of writing, in spite of its deceptive appearance of seeming very rustic and inchoate. It is the most comfortable form that fundamentally welcomes and necessitates a natural flow of thought through its simplicity. In its directness and intimacy, the essay is the ideal literary form for the twenty-first century. The form or the structure of the essay is very simple and natural that it is compatible with any reader without taking through any difficult structure and infused features. The essay is the primary shape of the thought process of any thinker or writer, including the genres of writings that demand deep meditation to arrest thoughts into difficult measurements, aesthetic forms and expressions. At the same time, the essay is not about penning down the wandering thoughts of a writer. *The Essay Review* records:

> Though still marginalized academically, the essay has benefited from the popularity of literary nonfiction in general, which has thrived since the 1960s, thanks in large part to the appeal of New Journalism, that daring mix of ethnography, investigative reportage, cultural criticism, and fiction that rocked magazine culture during the heyday of radical chic and political activism in America. Today's essayists, who are savvy about the genre's history and formal possibilities, have pushed the envelope of the essay in any number of ways, from forays in prose poetry to experimental writing and the essay film. The essay as currently practiced is a place to act out one's engagement with a world that grows stranger each day. The best essayists do that by returning to the key developments in the essay's history, taking advantage of its subjective, place-oriented way of dramatizing thought (15).

Essay is the simple but disciplined expressions of a writer's thoughts that stand as a concrete proof for the distinction between an eloquent speech and a well-thought over, well-knitted and well-written ideas. It is not, like Samuel Johnson, in his *Dictionary of the English Language* (1755) defines, "...a loose sally of the mind; an irregular indigested piece; not a regular and orderly composition." There is a subconscious intimacy with the essay for the readers as it speaks out with the voice of a responsible simpleton, with a nonlinear narrative or expressive technique. Scot Black talks of the freedom that the readers have, since they feel an intimacy with essay, to think and interpret the text as expressed by Francis Bacon and Montaigne. He says "It's within the genre of the essay that the reader's freedom is most audaciously worked out. In the commonplace method the reader 'performs a very individual reading and interpretation, and an act of power "over" the text, an act which makes what he writes and thinks his own" (18). Jeff Porter, when speaking of the distinction between the pleasure of reading a novel and an essay, he glorifies the essay:

> Yet getting lost in an essay is not the same as getting lost in a novel. Novels have plots; the essay is famous for rambling, its paratactic structure favouring breaks and digressions over continuity—the kind of disjointedness criticized by Johnson. What Johnson didn't like appeals to us now. It is the mindful-ness of the essayist, no matter how digressive, that offers us a refuge from the hullabaloo of the world, the discursive slippage from one thought to another (22).

The function of essay:

The function of essay does not have any complexities but runs directly to the readers and fulfils the purpose of bringing an idea or issue with a judgment or plea to the people, institution and government concerned. An inclination to compose an essay springs from a moral responsibility to declare something vital, promote ideas, criticize a socio-political condition or decision, teach an important moral or social idea or lesson, warn the society or government on some doings, create an awareness to bring about order or rectification etc,. The place of essay in world literature has gained increased significance in the modern world. It is the modern thinker's and writer's weapon to wage a war on the socio-political ills. The articles on the newspapers and magazines are the modern faces of essay.

Essay as a form of writing was used by different writers for various purposes. For example, Francis Bacon, the father of English essay, used it to epitomize his wisdom, William Hazlitt embraced it to launch his critical excellence, Joseph Addison took it to shed light on the foibles of the aristocratic society, Steele used it to expose the false arts of life, to pull off the disguise of cunningness, vanity and affectation, and to recommend a great simplicity in our dress, our discourse, and our behaviour, EM Foster handled it to deal with the class differences, George Orwell possessed the genre to speak out his views on imperialism, nationalism, capitalism, political dishonesty, power, totalitarianism, privilege and private education and James Baldwin used it to write on racism, classism, white privilege, homosexuality, bisexuality, nationalism, fundamental Christianity, and social alienation. Charles Dickens wrote his novels only as periodical essays which brought many social ills to the notice of the government that took steps to quell and later on they were composed to be novels, especially the novel, *Oliver Twist,* which was not only the reason for the refinements in Juvenile Prisons, but also pushed juvenile delinquency into a different light.

Bertrand Russell and Aldous Huxley, the good friends, had essay to reflect on so many subjects and ideas. The international socio-political atrocities, speaking against power politics, war, political imperialism, nationalism and its destructive consequences, capitalism leading to the madness to rule the world, political dishonesty, hunger for super power, totalitarianism, world government, poverty, social and class oppression, humanism and freedom, the privileged, under-privileged and private education are some of the most prominent themes that they dealt with. Humanism is the core of their identity as thinkers and writers, which is greatly shimmering through their writings, especially essays. This thesis deals with the select twenty essays from both Russell and Huxley to explore the humanistic perspectives of these writers on the areas of social reformation, education, ethics, politics, anti-war and peace and world government. The list of the essays is given in the bibliography under primary sources.

Bertrand Russell (1872 – 1970) was born in Monmouthshire into one of the very prominent British aristocratic family. He was one of the most prominent man, who was in the spot light for his various meritorious activities. He was a twentieth century British academician, a chief philosopher, social critic, political activist, a prominent mathematician and a very prolific writer and a dynamic speaker, whose knowledge and contribution to the respective fields are astonishingly vast, varied and immense. Russell possessed philosophy as a guide to life itself. P.T. Raju, in *The Concept of Man, A Study in Comparative Philosophy*, remembers Bertrand Russell's understanding of the function and the practical utility of philosophy as a guide. He says, "The aim of philosophy to be a guide to life is tacitly recognized by thinkers like Russell, who, speaking of logical analysis, says at the end of his book, *A History of Western Philosophy* that it also is meant to suggest and inspire a way of life" (30). His *Principia Mathematica*, which he produced with the help of his teacher, A N Whitehead, is a milestone in the branch of logic, which tries to connect the nucleus of mathematics to logic.

A *History of Western Philosophy, Introduction to Mathematical Philosophy, The Problems of Philosophy, My philosophical Development and Power: A New Social Analysis* are his very famous books. Russell's article, "On Denoting" is revered very much as a prototype of philosophy. Jalalul ha, in *Bertrand Russell's Philosophy of Perception*, says, "Russell's uniqueness among his contemporaries, lies in the fact that he was not only fully conscious of the graveness of the problem but also tries to resolve it by employing all his abilities as an erudite scholar and ingenuous philosopher" (19). He was not only an armchair critic, but also passionately participating in trying to solve the burning political issues of his times.

Russell, along with Gottlob Frege, his friend and colleague G. E. Moore and his student and protégé Ludwig Wittgenstein, founded Analytic Philosophy that stood for the revolution against the prevailing British Idealism. Being a pacifist, he promulgated anti-imperialism and his advocacy of anti-nuclear war is the height of his concern for the international society and the manifestation of his humanistic affection. *The Oxford Companion to Philosophy* reflects:

> After the Second World War, he was the prominent member of the campaign for Nuclear Disarmament and was arrested for participating in one of their protest demonstrations), and helped initiate the Pugwash conferences, international gatherings of distinguished intellectuals, mainly scientists, devoted to discussing ways to achieve and maintain world peace (825).

Russell was one of the voices for the independence, as a part of the India League that articulated the independence and self-governance of India. He came out with the idea of World Government when he was against the atomic monopoly and a proponent of nuclear disarmament, and went to the prison for his pacifistic ideas during World War I. He was against both Adolf Hitler and Stalin and admonished America for Vietnam War. He was an essayist, political adviser, pacifist and a humanist, who talked and wrote on innumerable subjects through which, he made a huge impact on the different sections of not only the international community but also the political intelligentsia, which eventually honoured him with the prestigious Nobel Prize in 1950.

Russell's critical views on whatever he wrote and spoke of had a special attention among the people of the world because they were uttered and written with the selfless benevolence of the well-being of humanity. He was a veritable bomb shell in the field of criticism and political decision-making to which his contributions, out of his humanistic personality, was remarkable. His works have greatly influenced the fields of mathematics, logic, set theory, linguistics, artificial intelligence, cognitive science, computer science and analytical philosophy, especially philosophy of mathematics, language and epistemology and metaphysics.

Aldous Leonard Huxley (26 July 1894 – 22 November 1963) is a respectable name in the refulgent fields of English Literature and Philosophy. He is a novelist, non-fiction writer, essayist, poet, socio-political critic and above all a great humanist. He was a pacifist and an active anti-war propagandist like his friend Russell. Being a startled witness of both the first and second World Wars, Huxley was greatly disturbed by the international political atmosphere, which became his major preoccupation. Charles M. Holmes in the book, *Now More Than Ever: Proceedings of the Aldous Huxley Centenary Symposium*, says, "But for most of his writing career he watched closely the political world, and more than once took a definite political stand" (187). Huxley was unflagging in being about the proximity of the political activities of his time.

Huxley, wrote extensively and spoke dynamically against the cruelties of war in general and associated himself with many supporting groups. Petre Firchow in his book, *Aldous Huxley, Satirist and Novelist*, says, "He joined canon Shepard's Peace Pledge Union, began to lecture on pacifism, conferred with Gerald Heard on practical ways and means of preventing war, and in 1937 came out with Ends and Means, a closely reasoned, forceful analysis of the motives and futility of war" (23). His novels are much celebrated, non-fiction works were well appreciated and essays deserve a respectful attention. Huxley was a voracious reader of interestingly varied subjects. T.S. Eliot, In *AldousHuxley, A Memorial Volume*, says, "His reading was immense, his taste impeccable, and his ear acute – I remember his pointing out to me once that the metre of Tennyson's Catullus was identical with that of Edward Lear's Yonghy-Bonghy-Bo" (31). He graduated from Balliol College, Oxford, with an undergraduate degree in English literature.

Early in his career, he published short stories and poetry and edited the literary magazine Oxford Poetry, before going on to publish travel writing, satire, and screenplays. *The Perennial Philosophy, The Doors of Perception, Point Counter Point, Brave New World, Crome Yellow, Antic Hay, Those Barren Leaves, Time Must Have a Stop, Ends and Means* and his final novel *Island* are his much-celebrated works. Donald Watt in his book, *Aldous Huxley, The Critical Heritage*, says:

> In numerous essays and isolated passages in his novels, he has clearly set forth his attitude. A true understanding of Mr. Huxley's philosophy indicates, contrary to the common American conception, that his novels are genuinely significant works; the unit of his thought, his intellectual acumen, his humanity, above all, his morality (for he describes immortality only to condemn it) become crystal clear. Mr. Huxley than stands out as one of the important social thinkers, as well as critics and creative writers, of our time" (239).

It was during the First World War that Huxley met several Bloomsbury Group figures, including Bertrand Russell, Alfred North Whitehead, and Clive Bell. Huxley's works during this period included important novels on the dehumanising aspects of scientific advancement, most famously *Brave New World*. In Brave New World. Huxley began to write and edit non-fiction works on pacifist issues, including *Ends and Means, An Encyclopedia of Pacifism*, and *Pacifism and Philosophy*, and was an active member of the Peace Pledge Union.

Gerald Heard introduced Huxley to Vedanta (Upanishad-centered philosophy), meditation, and vegetarianism through the principle of ahimsa. In 1938, Huxley befriended Jiddu Krishnamurti, whose teachings he greatly admired. Huxley and Krishnamurti, many a time, had heated discussions and arguments on various philosophical ideas. Krishnamurti represented the more rarefied, detached, ivory-tower perspective, but Huxley was with pragmatic concerns, the more socially and historically informed position. Huxley very proudly provided an introduction to Krishnamurti's quintessential statement, The first and Last Freedom 1954. Huxley became a Vedantist with Hindu Swamk Prabhavananda and wrote the much respects book for its spiritual values and ideas, The Perennial Philosophy that contained the teachings of renowned mystics of the world. This book was much appreciated by George Orwell for its profundity and importance in the subject. He was nominated for the Nobel Prize in Literature nine times and was honoured with the awards, James Tait Black Memorial Prize, American Academy of Arts and Letters Award of Merit and Companion of Literature.

Huxley's book affirmed a sensibility that insists there are realities beyond the generally accepted "five senses" and that there is genuine meaning for humans beyond both sensual satisfactions and sentimentalities. A.E. Dyson, when talking of his writing style, in his book, Aldous Huxley and the Two Nothings, says, "I shall argue later that Huxley specialises in ironic traps from which there seems to be no way out; that he has a genius for locking us in Doubting Castle and demonstrating that all the keys have been lost" (293). The writing styles of Russell and Huxley are thus unique and produce a combined impact for the readers to understand the issues they deal with in a better light.

Huxley was a theist and was much into philosophical mysticism unlike his friend Bertrand Russell, but both joined hands to fight against the international military oppressions and violence against innocent civilians across the world, with the most powerful shield of Humanism. Donald Watt in his book, *Aldous Huxley, The Critical Heritage*, says, "The salient difference between the humanism of Mr. Huxley and that of the humanists of the school of the late Professor Irving Babbitt is found in Mr. Huxley's modernity, at the centre of which is his reconciliation of the psychological and humanistic points of view. He can best be described as a 'psychological humanist" (241). These valuable distinction of Bertrand Russell and Aldous Huxley necessitates this research on their select essays to discover their intense humanistic intentions behind their socio-political views and aspirations for the eternal peace of the world.

Chapter II

Bertrand Russell's Humanistic Perspectives

2.1 Russell's social reformative concerns

Russell says that the present condition of the world is really pathetic and it is suffering from two kinds of misfortunes. The first problem is that there are people who genuinely think that the world has to be peaceful and all the people of the world should be comfortable and happy, but cannot purchase any good to offer those who suffer and the second misfortune is that there are people who have what those who suffer terribly are in need of, but do not sell. Russell says that the second type of people want to make a huge profit out of their surplus goods.

Russell says that the surplus of coffee in Brazil is used as a fuel on the railways and it is burnt in large funeral pyres in the lonely valleys of the county. There is a gut of rubber due to the fact that the workers of the country cannot help taking rubber from the trees and that it was actually stopped by the pest attacked the rubber trees. He says that in the past the weevil that affected the cotton production is now regarded a heaven-sent gift or cure for the human carelessness in producing the surplus amount of something, which is not properly planned for the usage, but wasted by using for unproductive purposes of out a touch of indifference. He says:

> The world at the present day is suffering from two misfortunes: there are people who desire good which they cannot purchase, and there are people who have goods which they cannot sell. Those who have goods which they cannot sell are adopting various ingenious means of disposing of their surplus. IT would be demoralizing to wage earners to pay wages for work not done; therefore, they continue to produce the good that they cannot sell but adopt various means of destroying them after they have been produced. Brazil, which suffers from

a surplus of coffee, has taken to using it as fuel on the railways and to burning it on large funeral pyres in lonely valleys. There is a glut of rubber, which is unfortunately made worse by the fact that the natives cannot be restrained from tapping the rubber trees. Fortunately, rubber trees are subject to a pest, which has hitherto been combated but which is now about to be encouraged. The world's cotton crop has, in the past, been threatened by the boll weevil, but now the boll weevil is welcomed as a friend, since it helps to prevent overproduction of cotton (MO: 54).

Russell says that anything very significantly useful, which is produced out of the sheer toiling and human squandering of energy, must not be either wasted or misused so as to get a false gratification that it is after all used for some purpose. He says that the habit of doing some productive tasks is deeply instilled in the human psychology that man cannot not but find pleasure in involving himself in some productive activities, which he associates with a sense of pride and usefulness. He not only has this inclination towards doing some work, but also the most efficient ways of doing it, since the clear display of efficiency in doing something sets forth the doer at a supreme level and his endeavour to do something in a special way is greatly wondered and appreciated. Others are also deeply inspired by the height of capacity at which some productive assignment is dealt with.

Russell says that every producer of some products must think of the truth that it going to be both fruitful and bring joy for the user or consumer. Russell says that the morality of work, throughout the world, is very intense and the world follows it strictly, since it considers work as something divine, which actually has established a world system that has witnessed half of the world being poor because of its overproduction and the other half is also poor, since it consumes little. He says:

> The habit of work has become ingrained in the greater part of the human species and not only the habit of work but, what is worse, the habit of looking for ways by which work can be made more productive. Nobody has thought for a moment that it might be a good thing if somebody could enjoy the produce of human labour. Our morality is ascetic, which makes us regard work as a virtue; it follows that production is good and consumption is bad. This ascetic twist has produced a world system in which half the world is poor because it produces too much and the other half because it consumes too little (MO: 54).

Russell says that this attitude of being not careful about the limit of the production of something, which is the intelligent way of avoiding regrettable wastage and improper usages, is insane and therefore it must be seriously strategized in order to preserve what has been produced by hard labour and to prevent destroying life-giving resources of Nature. Russell in a very funny way says that the boll weevil that eats at cotton would say, if asked, that the purpose of cotton production is misunderstood and that it is not for the production of dress material for human beings, but for giving nourishment for their species and that it would even go to the extent of complaining that cotton is a very velvety and delicious substance and it is unfortunately spoiled by the nasty perspiration of human beings.

Russell adds with his humanistic perception that the boll weevil here does not wage war against human beings with police force and does not teach that human beings are to be destroyed completely and boll weevil must replace man on this planet, if they, the weevil, are to get enough nourishment, happiness and freedom, which are severely hampered by the nasty human attitudinal cruelty. He says:

> What is the cure for this queer insanity? If we could ask the advice of the boll weevil and the rubber pest, they would have a ready answer. The boll weevil would say: 'you have radically

misconceived the purpose of cotton; it does not exist to clothe human beings but to supply nourishment to the boll weevil. Human beings', so I am afraid it might continue, 'have in any case not much to be said for them, and it is unworthy of a pleasant substance such as cotton to be condemned to absorb their perspiration. The boll weevil, on the contrary, fights no wars, has no police force, and does not teach the multiplication table to its young. Clearly, therefore, the sum of sentient happiness in the terraqueous globe will be increased if the boll weevil replaces man (MO: 55).

Russell says that there is enough logic and intelligence in the argument of the weevil and man may reject the argument out of his partiality, pride and selfishness. Russell says that if man is to refute the logic of the insect, he has to behave sensibly like the insect at least. The insect consumes the cotton, whenever it wants and does not think of hiding it for other benefits and profits like human beings. Human beings keep the goods in one place and the future customers in another place, calling it a bad trade to overcome this huddle and to improve trade, the gap between the goods and the want of the customers must be beneficially bridged, with the understanding and acceptance that each operation at each moment may not be profitable. Russell says:

Perhaps we, as human beings, may be allowed enough partiality for our species to reject this argument. But it is not enough merely to reject it, we ought not to be outdistanced in logic by this humble insect. If we are to refute him, we must behave at least as sensibly as he does. He consumes the cotton when he wants it whereas we keep the cotton in one place and the would-be customers in another; we then complain of bad trade. It seems clear that to improve trade, we must find some way of bringing goods to those who want them. So far, however, the collective wisdom of mankind has not been equal to this effort (MO: 55).

Bertrand Russell comes out with his profusion of humanism through the exhibition of his worry that many downtrodden, unemployed and forsaken population of this world are into starvation and the concern that they must be given enough food to the languishing population to make them feel that they are also living in this world at least with the basic requirements to be joyfully alive. He says that the rotting food in the West America and Canada could be given to those people of starvation around the industrial regions so that the world would be really richer and this can be achieved at the cost of the inhuman profits of the individual capitalist. This is possible only by an organized public endeavour and the humanistic motive of which will be unstoppably undeniable. Russell recommends:

> There is food rotting in the West of the United States and Canada; there are unemployed populations starving in all he industrial regions throughout the world. If the food were brought to the starving populations, and they were set to wok such as would satisfy the wants of Western farmers, the world would be the richer even I no individual capitalist made a profit. The motive of individual profit has apparently broken down, and only organized public effort will restore the economic life of the world (MO: 55).

Bertrand Russell talks about the pathetic condition of the world due to the mental, emotional and intellectual decay, which the majority of the modern population is least bothered about. Russell says that a hundred and fifty years ago, the rich people were truly civilized. A rich man of those days, he says, was expected to quote Latin poets, to judge Italian Renaissance pictures and appreciate classical music and so a man of the period had a considerable knowledge about the literature of his country and France. In the modern times, such expectations are only with professors and it is so awful that it is restricted to departments.

Russell says that these are not very serious nowadays because he does not find any necessity to know the names of muses or the signs of the zodiac, but they were taught to his grandparents, which they remembered even at their eighties. He says that the modern world does not find any leisure because their sense of pleasure has become very tiresome as their work, resulting in the increase of cleverness and decrease of wisdom, because modern man does not find time to meditate on a thought so intensely as to have distilled wisdom out of it. He says:

> The result is that while cleverness has increased, wisdom has decreased because no one has the time for the slow thoughts out of which wisdom, drop by drop, is distilled. A problem such as the prevention of war, the urgency of which is obvious to everyone, is dismissed with a shrug of the shoulders in the hope that circumstances will solve it without the aid of human thought. But circumstance, unaided, are not likely to be so kind (35).

Russell says that it is the reason why the majority of the people of the world is indifferent to the greatest thought like the prevention of war, the most urgent idea to be executed. Mere circumstances will not solve it without the serious and careful human efforts. Russell mocks at the quakers stating that they instilled in the minds of the people that the practice of half an hour of silent meditation will give people enough physical and mental strength to do their personal, national and international works efficiently. He says, "Two minutes a year, on Armistice Day, are given to silence, and all the other minutes of the year to largely futile bustle. The proportion is wrong; if the silence were longer, the bustle would be less futile" (MO: 35). Russell aims at bringing in a sea-change in the minds of the people of the world to be sensible and clear about their personal, social and political responsibilities, through pointing out both their petty and inexcusable mistakes.

Russell has chosen the frailty of the modern people to seek admiration in other people in the society to shed some intellectual light on. He wants the people of the world not to seek their comfort and peace of mind outside of themselves, since the secret of joy and peace lies with their state of mind. He says that though many people are under the impression that they are living only to the contentment of their conscience and do not pay attention to the opinion of others, the majority of the people of the world seeks to impress others and tries hard to get their admiration. Russell says that only a few do not care for the opinion of others and they are the real heroes. He says that it is really important to observe whose admiration people desire to attain. An average man has the aspiration to get the respect from his colleagues, wife, children and subordinates. He is so strong that his business associates must think that he is very special and capable that they must have an eternal respect and admiration for him, but he never minds knowing how well his wife and children love him and tries to persuade himself that during a crisis his children would come to him to seek his advice. He says:

> The average man desires the respect of his colleagues, of his wife and children (if possible), and of his underlings. He hopes that his business associates do not consider him a simple fellow whom anybody could take in. He takes pains not to realize how well his wife knows him. He tries to persuade himself that in a crisis his children would turn to him for advice. The average married woman tries to impress other married women. She tries to persuade them that her husband is richer than theirs and her children more successful. If she is well-to-to, she tries to display better taste than her neighbours in the management and decoration of her house. As they are playing the same game, this requires great skills and much thought (MO: 50).

The spirit to impress these people does not yield even if it encounters difficulties in impressing many or some. He comes out with the example of the writers, Bronte sisters and says that even though their books have attained acclaim and love, their personalities are such that they never try to impress their neighbours. Russell comes out with some examples of great men who were driven by the spirit of impressing others. Anatole France's Pontius Pilate convinced himself that the posterity will understand him and get him justice after his death, when he incurred the ranker of the Emperor. Julius Caesar had Alexander the Great as his rival in his mind, in spite of the glorious victories he had. The eminent men of the past lived with the intention of living forever in the minds of the people of the world even after their death.

Russell remembers an Italian business magnate, who was on his death bed under the impression that he had not enough fame or place in the pages of history said that he missed the chance of murdering the Pope and the Emperor at once that would get him a place in history. He says that such a desire to be immortalized in the pages of history of the world has been decreased thanks to the newspapers of the present days. The contemporary fame and the possibility of being famous through newspapers is more intense and greater than the expected fame of a person in the pages of the history and so today's world knows that the possible admiration from the readers of history is less than the contemporary fame that one could possibly get now. Russell indirectly expresses his discontentment and amazement when he says that the fame of a film star, at the height of his career, in the present day exceeds even Alexander the Great and Julius Caesar's. He says:

> The fame of a film star at the present ay far exceeds that of Alexander or Caesar at the height of his career. Probably more people know the name of Einstein now than have known the name of Archimedes in all the centuries from his day to our own. The effect of all this is that admiration is sought in more ephemeral forms than those formerly desired. Men's work becomes less statuesque and there is more effort to make it appeal to all and sundry (MO: 51).

He says that the possibility of getting instant fame throughout the world is very much and that is the reason why the number of people who know Einstein is more when compared with how many know of Archimedes in all the centuries from his days and says that the admiration of the modern world is ephemeral than how was it in the past. The desire for posthumous fame lingers in almost all very prominent men along with the fear of having something bad in their biography and so they are afraid of their biographers and as a result, in the life of eminent people hypocrisy has replaced spontaneity. Bertrand Russell says that admiration is not offered to what is truly admirable and those who are admired do not deserve it.

Marriage is an interesting subject to all throughout the world and Bertrand Russell recollects the driver of the car he was travelling by turning back and asking whether he was Bertrand Russell and said that he used to listen to his lectures and has stopped such intellectual activities since his marriage. Russell says that marriage, which is expected to make anyone become complete and fulfilled, unfortunately attributed to unhappiness. He says that the actual reason lies partly both with economics and social custom. He says that the conventional idea that husband and wife should spend their leisure time together is not an intelligent idea. He continues to say that his taxi driver's wife does not have any taste for intellectual lectures and does not like him also to enjoy the lecture without her company. Russell says that many husbands and wives are ready to sacrifice their pleasures on the jealousy of the pleasures of their partners and calls it dangerous to object and prevent other people's pleasure out of jealousy than to be selfish about pursuing one's own. He says that if a husband and wife are to be compatible and happy, there must be some sort of social separateness. Russell says:

> The convention that husbands and wives should spend their leisure hours together is a bad one. No doubt my taxi driver's wife does not care for lectures and also does not like him to go to them without her. Many husbands and many wives will forgo their own pleasures out of jealousy of their pleasures that they imagine that their partners as desiring. It is much more harmful to object to other people's pleasures than it is to be a trifle selfish in pursuing one's own, and a

certain amount of social separateness of husband and wife is necessary if they are not to become dull and incapable of finding anything to say to each other (MO: 36).

The second reason, economic difficulty, is more serious, he says and that an unmarried man, unlike a married man, is free to be lavish about his money for his leisure time and amusement, including searching for a wife. He says that well-educated and intellectual married men will find that their freedom and leisure time for intellectual pursuits have vanished and educated and intellectual women are bound to feel the loss of freedom and time to explore the world of intellect more intensely than men do, if they remain childless and as a result both have some feeling against the institution of marriage. Russell says that this problem cannot be cured unless the state undertakes the entire expense of children.

Russell says that this condition can be effectively changed with the adoption of an intelligent attitude towards childrearing. Bertrand Russell says that child-rearing is a very responsible act, since it is a calling for cultivating a great set of skills, giving chance to interesting observation and taking them to the world of science. He says that when compared with affection, science and other skills and intelligence are of no use and nothing can replace affection and that science and the acquired skills should supplement affection. If not, it will produce unexpected dangerous results. He says that he is sure that intellectuals will never see marriage in an admirable light, if they come to realize the scientific interest of infancy.

Russell declares to the world that an ignorant person blessed with a rich affection is better than a very intelligent and knowledgeable person with no heart, but a well-informed person being fond of children, is the better state to have children. Russell impliedly says that a man with an enriched heart is more desirable than a man with an enriched brain. He says, "The ignorant person with affection is perhaps better for an infant than a well-informed person who has no heart; but a well-informed person who is fond of children is much better than either" (MO: 37). He embraces and reflects the ideas of the Greek philosopher,

Aristotle, "Educating your mind without educating your heart is no education at all." The societal well-being depends on the human qualities of the people ultimately, though a society becomes advanced with the help of human brains.

Russell talks about the modern parenting and the incompatible method of teaching children at schools and colleges. Russell says that he is against the popular belief that all parents love their children, because they show their love through being very strict about their activities and expressions. In the name of teaching discipline, they are told that whatever they do are wrong. Children are not allowed to be children and they are given the feeling that whatever is taught does not permit them to be free and happy. Russell says that majority of the parents are very strict with their children because they know not of the modern child psychology. He says:

> Now character is mainly determined before the age of six, when schooling begins. If the state understood modern child psychology it would make all children go to nursery school from the age of two onward. There the child would find an environment composed of other children, with a grown-up in the background who would unobtrusively give a sense of safety. There would be no prohibition of noise and movement; there would be a minimum of dangers to be guarded against; and there would be as few things forbidden as a carefully arranged environment would make possible (MO: 43).

Bertrand Russell talks of the deceptive appearance of the American Society that it gives importance to women's emancipation and that women have achieved equality. He says that the ideal of America is equality from the beginning of the history of the declaration of American Independence. He says that manufacturers, land owners, railway mines and oil trade have made some people so rich that they have become very important persons to influence the important affairs of their countries. They are blessed with technology and immense knowledge and technique about the economy in general that no force against inequality can possibly defeat them. Even though America brags about its ideal of equality, it has used its ideal only in some compatible political directions and not in the society. Social equality is the basic necessity that every citizen of a country needs in order to experience the fundamental freedom and joy of life. This American ideal has not been experienced by the people, especially Negro men and women. Still they are considered inferior to the white race and the black Americans undergo insults and oppressions in the society, even though, the political ideology of the country strongly condemns such oppressions.

Russell says that women have political equality with men, but not economic equality, which is very important for women in the modern world to be independent and feel confident about their constructive sides. The wife of a rich man will have enough money to spend, but the women of others classes depend on their earning husbands for money. The women, according to the law, have their rights to share the income of their husbands, but still it is unfortunate that the true emancipation, economic independency, of women has not been attained. Russell says:

> Although equality was, from the moment of the Declaration of Independence, proclaimed as a principle, it was only applied in such directions as were politically convenient. For a long time, nobody thought of it as including Negroes or women. Even now, although women have political equality with men, they do not, as a rule, have, economic equality, which is in many ways more important. Among the rich, a wife normally has money of her own, but in other classes she depends upon her husband's earnings. The law gives her a right to a share of his income, and to alimony when she gets tired of him or he of her; but it does not give her the economic power that belongs to the person who earns money (MO: 269).

Russell says that the American women seems to be more powerful than men to the foreign onlookers, when they look at the rich people of the country, but it is deceptive because women are more powerful than men only in the fields in which men are not given the first preference. He says that the power of love of a business man finds its outlet in his office itself and so, he can be free of his business plans and strategies, when he is at home, reserving them all to himself and enjoy the home atmosphere, which is more important to the country than his dependency of his wife, when it comes to the household activities. Women do not like this attitude and so they are of the opinion that business is for those who are not so refined and for very sensitive men. Women, as they think of business in this way, tend to underestimate the significance of earning money, without understanding that the economic reality is at war with the pretention that women enjoy economic equality and they are superior to men.

This attitude leads to the psychological satisfaction about their superiority complex and imaginary status. This pretention leads to giving superficial importance to feminine culture, in the name of respecting or even regarding them as superior parts of the society. Russell says, "With this goes, quite naturally, a tendency to underestimate the importance of the economic side of life, since the economic reality is at war with the social presence of women's equality or even superiority. Acceptance of this pretence gives, as acceptance of pretence always does, a certain superficiality and unimportance to much feminine culture, besides having a regrettable effect upon the psychology of women" (MO: 270). Russell says that the concept of democracy is not very clear, when there is a confusion between quality among classes and equality between men and women. This inequality will continue to exist as long as it is political and not economic. The right to vote against someone politically is just a consolation given to women.

Russell says that political democracy has to exercise its power to suppress any evil force in the society, causing imbalance and must execute the distribution of economic power. He says that political justice cannot be achieved, without achieving economic justice and neither of them is complete without the other, which was recognized by the founders of the country, but their plan of creating a number of independent economic units is not available in the industrial age. He says:

> Democracy, whether taken as equality between classes or as equality between men and women, has not much reality so long as it is merely political and not also economic. It is small consolation to be able to vote against a political programme, if its advocates have the power to make you starve. Political democracy has its importance, since it prevents certain extremes of oppression, and is a necessary step towards the more equitable distribution of economic power. But without economic justice, political justice is incomplete. This was more or less recognized by the founders of American Democracy, but their method, which was the creation of vast numbers of independent economic units is no longer available in our industrial age (MO: 270).

Russell, in the pretext of talking for the economic equality of women in the western world, talks for it for the women of the entire world. He makes a very strong statement, "The battle for economic democracy will be the next great struggle for justice in human affairs" (MO: 270). The society that Russell aspires to establish has the characteristic qualities of an ideal society. He wants the people to be free from any sort of fear and grow confident and brave. People should be well-educated, rational and humanistic with free operations of intellect so that they will be courageous enough to be revolutionary, whenever they find any obstacle for the healthy function of the society. Peter Stone in his book, *So You Want to Read Bertrand Russell*, says, "A society dedicated to Russell's radical liberal principles required citizens who were fearless, thoughtful, ready and willing to challenge authority, sceptical of dogma, respectful of other human beings regardless of nationality or creed" (22). Peter stone has encapsulated the major socio-political ideas of Bertrand Russell in all these words.

2.2 The ethical views of Bertrand Russell

A man without ethics is neither a trustworthy man nor driven by self-respect. Albert Schweitzer, in the book, *Albert Schweitzer: An Anthology*, says, "Ethics is nothing else than reverence for life" (78). Bertrand Russell talks of optimism, not for intellectualizing the idea of optimism, but to reflect the core issues with the optimistic attitude towards anything, which he brilliantly associates with the problematic times he was living in. Russell says that optimism is very pleasantly acceptable, when it is credible and when it is incredible, it causes irritation. There are people who share our troubles with other people and are very optimistic that the problems shall vanish soon. Such people cause so much of emotional disturbance to those who are in trouble, since they do not operate within the limit of the cultural freedom given to them by the person concerned.

Russell says that one has to be extremely careful about being optimistic about other people's troubles and says that in such a situation all that is necessary is the concrete strategy as to what to do in order to quell the problems efficiently or at least to reduce their intensity. He cites the example of a doctor, who is optimistic about curing an ailment, with the prescription of an effective medicine for the ailment and says that a friend, who has the mere words of cheering a person with some disease, is quite an annoyance. Russell says that the optimism of a doctor with a cure is an acceptable optimism unlike a cheering friend's. He says:

> The fact is that optimism is pleasant so long as it is credible, but when it is not, it is intensely irritating. Especially irritating is the optimism about our own troubles which is displayed by those who do not have to share them. Optimism about other people's troubles is a very risky business unless it goes with quite concrete proposals as to how to make the troubles disappear or grow less. A medical man has a right to be optimistic about your illness if he can prescribe a treatment which will cure it, but a friend who

merely says, 'Oh I expect you will soon feel better', is exasperating (MO: 70).

Russell says that there were many people, who talked so optimistically about the past two years, but the time span has shown the world all possible negative spectacles. They are like the cheerful friend, who has no moral freedom or right to make any such expression, and not like the medical man, who is a contributor basically and so he hopes his patient to get well soon. A mere cheerfulness has nothing to do with improving the poor condition of those who are starving, Russell says, since he prefers reason to emotion. He says:

> Most of the people who have talked optimistically thought the last two years about the bad times have been in the position of the cheerful friend rather than of the medical adviser, and I doubt whether their cheerfulness has added much to the happiness of those who were starving.

> In every kind of trouble what is wanted is not emotional cheerfulness but constructive thinking. This fact is gradually being borne in upon the world by the world-wide depression, and in this I perceive the only basis for optimism that our present troubles afford. These troubles can be cured by constructive thinking, not by ballyhoo (MO: 70).

Russell comes out with the prescription that it is only constructive thinking that will safeguard people at their worst times and not being emotional or expecting moral and emotional support from other people. The ultimate distinction between man and animals is man's possession of reasoning capacity and therefore it is no wonder that a humanistic writer like Bertrand Russell propagates the significance of using the head rather than heart even during exigencies, which make people have an optimistic approach towards life in general.

Bertrand Russell being a humanist, is against killing human beings in any way, including a person killing himself, suicide. He strongly condemns suicidal tendency and calls it irresponsibility towards life and incapability to withstand the inbuilt challenges of life. Russell, by pointing out certain facts and examples, indirectly attacks the encouragement and justifications that people with suicidal tendency give themselves. Russell is not a philosopher who deals with the subject of suicide merely to intellectualize it to show his knowledge or critical analysis of the subject or a futile philosophizing. His deep humanistic concern that no one should suffer in this world and find life intolerably painful to that extent that the person wants to leave this world. His natural sympathy and mercy towards human ordeals and distress disturbed him to the maximum extent that he made such confessions on private and public platforms.

Russell brings out the anecdote of an Australian farmer, after the country was badly injured in a war, tried to hang himself from a tree but was saved by a neighbour, but the farmer sued a case against the neighbour that he prevented him from escaping the cruel state of his life and inflicted further pain on him. The court understood the condition of the farmer due to the destroyed condition of the country, even though it released the neighbour on some other grounds. A true humanist not only has an interest in the prosperous life of all human beings, but also has the capacity and tolerance to listen to the just reasons of the people who has a lot of grievances and complains against life in general. Russell talks about how true are the reasons of the people, who try to commit suicide at the same time comes out with the roaring announcement that it is not only a personal stupidity but also a social negative tendency.

Russell says that attempted suicide is equal to attempted murder in England and America and anyone who tries to commit it on the reason that his or her life is insufferably painful, is imprisoned with the intention of making them love life. Russell says that it is irrational to think that the attempt to kill oneself itself is a crime. The understanding that to kill oneself is equal to killing others seems idiotic to Russell. He gives the example of throwing one's wristwatch into the sea and says that there is a difference between throwing someone's watch and one's own watch into the sea on any ground and to consider them on equal light is not intelligent and logical. He says:

> To say that it is as bad to kill yourself as to kill someone else seems to me absurd. If I take someone else's watch and throw it into the sea, I'm a criminal, but if I throw my own watch into the sea, I am at worst foolish, and if the watch is worthless, I may even be quite sensible. What applies to my watch applies also to my life. When I take another man's life I am taking what does not belong to me, but the question of taking my own life is clearly one that concerns me more than it does anyone else (MO: 67).

Russell gives a logical justification for suicide, because he believes in the emancipation of original and unhampered thinking and not in any sort of authoritative thrusting of ideas or orders. He believes that through producing clear logical evidence to justify the just reasons behind an action, the doer of the action will understand the logic, which will eventually make him capable of thinking on his own in a logical way about the other side of his deeds, if it is negative and self-destructive. Russell has a deceptive appearance of being an advocate of the suicidal tendency. Russell says that the subject of suicide is to be considered in relation to human sacredness.

Russell talks of different kinds of readers and their purposes behind their act of reading and his humanistic concern that everyone must read to extirpate their ignorance and prejudices to be clear and knowledgeable. He wants to promote a serious type of reading that makes people with strong intellect and original thinking. Russell says that the majority of people does not read and that the majority is not serious about reading but fleeting through pictures. The readers, who know the real taste of the habit of intense reading of all kinds and branches together, make a small number, says Bertrand Russell. Only these people read with the intention of acquiring knowledge and only young people belong to this group. This group reads in order to fly away from all sorts of mental conceits and prejudices, and it is really mature. Russell says that it is unfortunate that a great number of readers reads to have neither knowledge nor opinions, but for the sheer pleasure of escaping into the world of imagination, avoiding the hard reality of life. He says:

> The majority of mankind red nothing at all; of the remainder, the majority red only the picture papers. Of those who read something more than picture papers, the majority never gets as far as books. All the readers of books – grave and gay, profound and superficial, scientific, literary or lurid – all put together are a very small fraction of the population. Nevertheless, they differ among themselves in all sorts of ways. There are those who read in order to acquire information; they are generally very young. These are those who read in order to acquire confirmation of their prejudices; these people are what is called mature. But the great bulk of readers are seeking neither knowledge nor support for their own opinions, but an escape from reality into the world of imagination (MO: 65).

This act of escaping from reality to dwell in the world of imagination takes all kinds of forms. Novelettes and films offer the crudest form of slipping into the utopian world for unreal and vicarious pleasures. They are living an unreal world, where an obscure young man or woman achieves splendid success or experience a rich and joyful married life and this happens at a greater level with those who slip into the past history and imagine the abundance and glory of the past ages. A next stage is with the subject of astronomy wherein the aspects of the world of colourful imagination can be found. Russell says that the stars in the book, *Jeans and Eddington*, are very fortunate to lead a quiet and undisturbed life. They are not troubled by the problems of the people in the actual world like the tax collector, the illness of their children and business depression. Unlike the real life, the life of the characters in the utopian world sooths the readers like the imagination with the stars or nebula. People not only need soothing experience but also excitement. Russell confesses that it is only excitement that prompted his desire for reading. He says that reading detective stories is his most favourite activity. Russell says that detective stories, poetry and astronomy represent different forms of escaping from reality.

He says that according to psychoanalysis the inclination to escape from reality is bad, which Russell partly disagrees with. He says that if imagination makes a person neglect his or her responsibilities, it is destructive and so deplorable, but if it nourishes a person to become constructive, it is highly preferable and appreciable. He says, "The desire to escape from reality becomes a bad thing when it produces delusions or cause a man to neglect his business" (MO: 66). Russell cites some examples. A poor man harassed by his creditors can find a relief, imagining that he is the President of the Bank of France, which is utterly stupid and the person can be punished for escaping reality. A young woman who forgets herself being into the romantic tale of King Cophetua, neglecting her duty, finally loses her job, also can be punished. But there are other forms of forgetting the real world, fleeing into the world of imagination, which are very much desirable.

Russell actually talks of the role of the power of imagination in making a person be gifted with a creative bent of mind. Mozart, one of the greatest music composers of the world, escaped reality to reach the pleasure dome of creative imagination not to be affected by the worries of his debts, which gifted him with the rarest of music talent and genius. Had Mozart taken the words of the psychoanalysts, he would have been very careful about his balance sheet, but the world would have lost his ever-inspiring symphony. Russell says:

> But there are other forms of escape from reality which are wholly desirable. Mozart used to compose music in order to forget his duns and his debts by escaping into a world of phantasy. If he had followed the advice of eminent psychoanalysts, he would instead have drawn up a careful balance sheet of receipts and expenditures and set to work to devise economies by which the two could be made to balance. If he had done this, he would have lost

his income, and we should have lost his music. Escape from reality, as this instance shows, is not undesirable when it is into a world of imagination recognized as such and used as a means of making reality itself more tolerable (MO: 66).

Russell says that to escape this reality for the world of imagination to get something very precious with which the hard realities of life can be tolerated and accepted is not deplorable, because such an effort with the world of fancy brings a great boon to the world to soothe 'the fret and fever' of life. Russell says that the most useful inventions would not have been possible without this sort of attempt and so he encourages this sort of reading that ultimately makes readers create something valuable, which they return to the reality with.

2.3 The educational views of Bertrand Russell

Bertrand Russell talks of the purpose of education, the present condition of education, the responsibilities of a teacher, the present lamentable condition of teachers, the responsibilities of students and what should be done to resolve the existing problems in the field of education. Russell's humanistic observations and recommendations to resolve the problems of the field of education and improve its standard are very significant. He says that the role of education in forming and shaping the character of children and their opinions is admirably powerful. Russell says that education is a powerful force that stands for fundamental changes in the world. He says that education makes children think originally and does not make them think like their teachers. Bertrand Russell says that education does not make children merely choose a political party to be a member of it, but enables them to choose intelligently between parties. He says:

Education would not aim at making them belong to this party or that, but at enabling them to choose intelligently between the parties: it would aim at making them able to think, not at making them think what their teachers think. Education as a political weapon could not exist if we respected the rights of children. If we respected the rights of children, we should educate them so as to give them the knowledge and the mental habits required for forming independent opinions; but education as political institution endeavours to form habits and to circumscribe knowledge in such a way as to make one set of opinions inevitable (BWBR: 380).

He says that it makes children think originally and does not make them think like their teachers. He says that if it is true that we respect the important fundamental rights of children, we must educate them as to make them become knowledgeable and cultivate the habit of constructing independent opinions so that education as a political weapon shall perish. But a political institution wants to instil a set of opinions to be respected and followed without any question. Russell says that the two great principles of Justice and Liberty, which play a vital role in the construction of the society, are not enough in the field of education. Education must essentially impart many useful ideas on what makes a good life. He says that the teachers do not have freedom to be the guardians and mentors of the children at their own sought after freedom and desire. Authority in education is understandably unavoidable, but Russell says that it must not go to the extent of damaging liberty, which is the soul of educating children. Russell talks of showing respect and cultivating the nobility of respecting others.

Russell goes on to reflect the present condition of the field of education, including the plight of teachers due to the work-load that they straddle with. He says that the rules to be followed come from the government to the field of education. Teachers struggle with their large classes, fixed and stagnant curriculum and overwork and they can only produce students with mediocrity, without any reverence for the child. He says that such a reverence is possible only with imagination and affection that they are foolish, tender, weak, tender children, who are yet to learn, implement and achieve and that the teachers are strong and wise. If this is not the attitude, the teachers will have an indifference and contempt for the children for their inferior status of being beginners. He says:

> In education, with its codes of rules emanating from a Government office, its large classes and fixed curriculum and overworked teachers, its determination to produce a dead level of glib mediocrity, the lack of reverence for the child is all but universal. Reverence requires imagination in respect of those who have least actual achievement or power. The child is weak and superficially foolish, the teacher is strong, and in an everyday sense wiser than the child. The teacher without reverence, or the bureaucrat without reverence, easily despises the child for these outward inferiorities. He thinks it is his duty to 'mould' the child: in imagination he is the potter with the clay. And so he gives to the child some unnatural shape, which hardens with age, producing strains and spiritual dissatisfaction, out of which grow cruelty and envy, and the belief that others must be compelled to undergo the same distortions (BWBR: 380-381).

Russell says that reverence to children does not come out of a sense of duty to shape them, but it feels itself in all living creatures. A true reverence is natural and does its activity of educating, shaping and launching them towards the pursuit of their goals that they have formed for themselves. He says that children are sacred, tough to define, vast, unadulterated purity and individuality and very precious, the growing principle of life. A teacher with real reverence for the children feels accountable with humility that exhibits something noble that is not synonymous with the self-confidence of teachers and parents. Such an accountable person knows that they are superficially weak, dependent and helpless and becomes rally trustworthy to the children, and he will have imaginations about the growth and strength of the children and their accomplishments and powerful positions in future, by means of excavating their strength and potency. He says:

> The man who have reverence will not think it is his duty to 'mould' the young. He feels in all that lives, but especially in human beings, and most of all in children, something sacred, indefinable, unlimited, something individual and strangely precious, the growing principle of life, an embodied fragment of the dumb striving of the world. In the presence of a child he feels an unaccountable humility --- a humility not easily defensible on a rational ground, and yet somehow nearer to wisdom than the easy self-confidence of many parents and teachers (BWBR: 383).

The teacher will have such dreams about the children and will be longing to help them win the battles of their aspirations. He will do it not for satisfying any institutional expectations or authority but to help the children explore their potentiality and operate at its height, and experience the fulfilment of self-actualizing and reaching inspiring heights in their life. Russell says that only such a concerned teacher will be omnipotent and heroic to his authority, without invading the actual principles of liberty about educating children. He says:

> The outward helplessness of the child and the appeal of dependence make him conscious of the responsibility of a trust. His imagination shows him what the child may become, for good or evil, how its impulses many be developed or thwarted, how its hopes must be dimmed and the life in it grow less living, how its trust will be bruised and its quick desires replaced by brooding will. All this gives him a longing to help the child in its own battle; he would equip and strengthen it, not for some outside end proposed by the State or by any other impersonal authority, but for the ends which the child's own spirit is obscurely seeking. The man

who feels this can wield the authority of an educator without infringing the principle of liberty (BWBR: 381).

In the modern education system, the focus is on the capacity of students to amass material wealth and reach lucrative positions, which ultimately make them very ordinary. He says that almost all educational systems have a political motive, the aim of which is to support and strengthen some national, religious and social group, competing with other groups. This competitive spirit to be superior to the other groups that decides which subject should be taught, the knowledge to be imparted and the knowledge to be hidden from them, including the intellectual and mental habits that these students have to attain and follow throughout their life, as a result, this system does not do anything to nourish the internal growth of the mind and spirit of the pathetic pupils. Russell says that the more a person is educated, the less is the impulse for original thinking to be decisive and creative in life and they live with the mechanical aptitude taught in schools and colleges.

Russell emphasizes on education for all and says that the world needs very talented doctors, advocates and engineers and wants the student's community, when they aspire for higher education, to be careful about their preference for a branch of study and its compatibility with their personality and personal and professional goals. He says, "All children must continue to be taught how to read and write, and some must continue to acquire the knowledge needed for such professions as medicine or law or engineering. The higher education required for the sciences and the arts is necessary for those to whom it is suited" (BWBR: 382). Russell says that the subject of history is the most controversial, since it is taught in all countries to exaggerate their bright side to give an impression to their citizens that their country is the best in all possible ways, hence superior to the rest.

Children learn to believe that their country has never been truly defeated by any country and those who attacked their country are unrefined and the most dangerous people in the world and this impression becomes inseparable from their mind. Russell says:

> History, in every country, is so taught as to magnify that country: children learn to believe that their own country has always been in the right and almost always victorious, that it has produced almost all the great men, and that it is in all respects superior to all other countries. Since these beliefs are flattering, they are easily absorbed, and hardly ever dislodged from instinct by later knowledge (BWBR: 382). This cunningly made impression is the fundamental reason to become eternally prejudiced on people, culture and religion.

Russell says that education must bolster the instinct and desire for truth and not for creating the conviction that a particular creed is the truth. Russell says that inactive children with mere beliefs become prejudiced, cynical, intellectually hopeless and they become hyper-critical about everything to make all look foolish, being unable to be operated by any creative impulse, thereby destructing it in others. He says that a strong rational attitude is the only virtue to escape from this misleading forces. He says, "In those whose minds are not very active the result is the omnipotence of prejudice; whole the few whose thought cannot be wholly killed become cynical, intellectually hopeless, destructively critical, able to make all that is living seem foolish, unable themselves to supply the creative impulses which they destroy in others" (BWBR: 384). It is advocated that free and creative intellectual enquiries must be cultivated to be with clarity and truth about anything.

Education is conceptualized as a drill to achieve unanimity through slavishness and is convincingly stated that it is the path to victory and prosperity. There are many important practical affairs that require the power of human intellect and intelligence and not inactivity. Russell says that education that produces gullibility in children brings them to the stages of mental decay very quickly and that at least, a minimum of indispensable development can be achieved only through a spirit for free enquiry. He says, "And in the modern world so much intellect is required in practical affairs that even the external victory is more likely to be won by intelligence than by docility. Education in credulity leads by quick stages to mental decay; it is only by keeping alive the spirit of free inquiry that the indispensable minimum of progress can be achieved" (BWBR: 384). The slavishness and gullibility vanish with the true light of education, an unbridled, fresh and liberated state of mind for rational rumination on anything.

Russell says that certain mental habits like obedience and discipline, being ruthless for worldly success, acceptance to the wisdom of the teachers without any question are instilled in the minds of students by the teachers and the educational system, which is against life itself. Independence and impulse are more important than obedience and discipline and the ethics of education is that it should show the seeds of justice in the minds of students. Contempt should be replaced with reverence and the capacity to understand the ideas and opinions of others. It should stop forcing children to embrace credulity and encourage them to doubt constructively. The education which is wanted presently must cultivate the love for mental adventure and being bold in thoughts. Getting satisfaction out of reaching a status and feeling superior about having subordinates are the immediate evil effects of an undesirable system of education, which promotes only acquiring material power and richness. He says:

Certain mental habits are commonly instilled by those who are engaged in educating: obedience and discipline, ruthlessness in the struggle for worldly success. Contempt towards opposing groups, and an unquestioning credulity, a passive acceptance of the teacher's wisdom. All these habits are against life. Instead of obedience and discipline, we ought to aim at preserving independence and impulse. Instead of ruthlessness, education should try to develop justice in thought. Instead of contempt, it ought to instil reverence, and the attempt at understanding; towards the opinions of others it ought to produce, not necessarily acquiescence, but only such opposition as is combined with imaginative apprehension and a clear realization of the grounds for opposition. Instead of credulity, the object should be to stimulate constructive doubt, the love of mental adventure, the sense of worlds to conquer by enterprise and boldness in thought (BWBR: 384).

Russell says that obedience and discipline are important and indispensable when there is an order to be maintained or instruction is to be given to a class, but when compared with the ulterior motive of the system of education to produce only obedient servants to obey orders without letting them to think on their own, the significance of obedience and discipline in the class is to be rethought of. Obedience, according to Russell, is yielding one's will to an outside direction and it is the counterpart of authority and blind obedience to authority hampers the natural growth and function of the intellect of the children.

Russell talks of the plight of teachers also by their authority. He says that the authority thinks that the teachers can work like bank clerks for hours, which will produce intense lassitude and lack of interest out of irritation of nerves and shall eventually be mechanical in their speaking and activities with the children. Teachers should be given enough freedom to have natural love for teaching. Russell talks of how teachers should be and function with children, while teaching them. He says that a class, having children small in number is highly preferable, which is compatible with not only pleasurable teaching but also the feasibility to have an eclectic teaching methods. Russell says that teachers should not think of dealing with as many ideas as possible in a day. They should think of teaching a subject and the extent to which it can be taught should be under consideration according to the mental needs of the students in the class. This leads to a friendly relationship between teachers and students instead of the intense hostility, which extirpates the misunderstanding that education does take away their pleasurable time and joy.

He priscribes:

> A teacher out to have only as much teaching as can be done, on most days, with actual pleasure in the work, and with an awareness of the pupil's mental needs. The result would be a relation of friendliness instead of hostility between teacher and pupil, a realization on the part of most pupils that education serves to develop their own lives and is not merely an outside imposition, interfering with play and demanding many hours of sitting still (BWBR: 385).

Russell says that the kind of discipline desirable is that which comes from within, which one acquires through the power of devoting consistent attention and endeavour, experiencing many sufferings and ordeals in the intellectual task. This task involves submitting minor impulses to Will, which is directed by the conflagration of a creative desire, without which accomplishing a serious ambition is not possible. This necessary discipline is out a strong desire for the end and not out of anything immediately attainable and a true education must nourish such desires. Russell says that it is one's will that begets such a desire and not any outside authority and that this does not happen with the presently existing system of education. He says:

> The desirable kind of discipline is the kind that comes from within, which consists in the power of pursuing a distant object steadily, forgoing and suffering many things on the way. This involves the subordination of minor impulses to will, the power of a directing action by large creative desires even at moments when they are not vividly alive. Without this, no serious ambition, good or bad, can be realized, no consistent purpose can dominate. This kind of discipline is very necessary, but can only result from strong desires for ends not immediately attainable, and can only be produced by education if education fosters such desires,

which it seldom does at present. Such discipline springs from one's own will, not from outside authority. It is not this kind which is sought in most schools, and it is not this kind which seems to me an evil (BEBR: 386).

Russell says that the true success of the traditional higher education is to produce mental discipline and that it can't be achieved through compulsion. Russell talks of the nature of children and the way they prefer to learn their subjects. He says that children are spontaneous and enjoy acquiring knowledge only spontaneously and they do not want to learn anything that they do not desire to learn and that this is the best method of education according to him. He says, "The child's attention is wholly spontaneous, as in play; it enjoys acquiring knowledge in this way, and does not acquire any knowledge which it does not desire. I am convinced that this is the nest method of education with young children: the actual results make it almost impossible to think otherwise" (BEBR: 386). Russell talks of the importance of giving prolonged attention to something and says that it is not found naturally, but acquired through outside force. He says that some children, who have enough intellectual desires, do have the capacity for devoting their attention continuously in learning something, through exercising their free will. For others an external inducement is a must to make them learn something entirely.

Russell says that children are afraid of receiving official commands about taking great efforts in their fields and that should be done through stimulating advice and not through forcing them to use their potential. A good teacher does it to any student of a remarkable mental capacity, who is capable of great achievements. Russell says that to enrich the mental capacity of students to achieve many things, education, attained through books, is not the best method and that teachers are to be strictly informed that they must succeed in this method of capacitating the students to become achievers. If not it is easy for teachers to be sluggish and blame their children for not functioning efficiently, when the fault is actually with them. Here Russell talks of talking to the students as mentors and not as mere traditional teachers, associated only with the act of mechanical teaching. He says:

> A good teacher ought to be able to do this for any boy who is capable of much mental achievement; and for many of the others the present purely bookish education is probably not the best. In this way, so long as the importance of mental discipline is realized, it can probably be attained, whenever it is attainable, by appealing to the pupil's consciousness of his own needs. So long as teachers are not expected to succeed by this method, it is easy for them to slip into a slothful dullness and blame their pupils when the fault is really their own (BWBR: 387).

Russell is against the act of advertising the successes of pupils and says that a negative competitive spirit is watered by the act. Russell is very deep about his comment that it actually encourages competitive spirit that comes to be in the forefront of the decision taken in all spears of life, including socio-political areas. Instead of nurturing the competitive spirit, Russell says that the latent inclination for knowledge in young children has to be nourished. The talented minds of children, in being competitive, learn certain ideas and concept by heart, which are very disinterestedly supervised and examined by the teachers for the purpose of awarding diplomas and degrees.

Russell condemns this system stating that it is, for the abler students, nothing but a long tiresome task of giving and receiving examination tips and textbook facts because there is no time for the indulgence in intellectual taste. The most intelligent students are ultimately disgusted with their learning, which they try to forget to get into a life of useful actions and these children also get into the trap of running for money, which seriously affects their spontaneous desires in life. He says:

> For the abler boys there is no time for thought, no time for the indulgence of intellectual taste, from the moment of first going to school until the moment of leaving the

university. From first to last there is nothing but one long drudgery of examination tips and textbook facts. The most intelligent, at the end, are disgusted with learning, longing only to forget it and to escape into a life of action. Yet there, as before, the economic machine holds them prisoners and all their spontaneous desires are bruised and thwarted (BWBR: 387).

Russell says that the examination system makes the children think of knowledge from a utilitarian point of view that it is a road to money-making and not the truth that it is a gateway to wisdom. The examination system affects those who have a strong intellectual interest and so they feel the pressure of being compelled to prepare for mere examinations. Russell says that almost all children consider education as a means to attain the status of being superior to others. This system is corrupted and putrefied with ruthlessness and social inequality. Inequality is contrary to justice and those who succeed are benefited by it.

Russell says that accepting the wisdom of a teacher passively does not take independent thought and looks deceptively rational because of the belief that the teacher knows whatever he teaches more than his pupils. This passive acceptance is a way to get into the good books of the teachers also. Russell talks of how dangerous is passive acceptance. He says that students of passive acceptance cannot become leaders and they will be in search of leaders, instead of taking the position of a leaser, since they have been accustomed to being only followers. Russell says that this is want is found with Churches, Governments, party caucuses and all the other organizations, where these types of people are supporters of the old system, which are detrimental to the nation and even themselves. He says that there cannot be any room for independence of thoughts, even though promoting this is a part of an educational system. So, the students must be given the freedom of thinking and articulating their opinion freely through conducting various activities that necessitates critical thinking and being expressive, connecting with others. He says:

> Passive acceptance of the teacher's wisdom is easy to most boys and girls. It involves no effort

of independent thought and seems rational because the teacher knows more than his pupils; it is moreover the way to win the favour of the teacher unless he is a very exceptional man. Yet the habit of passive acceptance is a disastrous one in later life. It causes men to seek a leader, and to accept as a leader whoever is established in that position. It makes the power of Churches, Governments, party caucuses, and all the other organizations by which plain men are misled into supporting old systems which are harmful to the nation and to themselves. It is possible that there would not be much independence of thought even if education did everything to promote it; but there would certainly be more than there is at present. If the object were to make pupils think, rather than to make them accept certain conclusions, education would be conducted quite differently: there would be less rapidity of instruction and more discussion, more occasions when pupils are encouraged to express themselves, more attempt to make education concern itself with matters in which the pupils feel some interest (BEBR: 388).

Russell says that the power of original thinking comes to a person who has travelled beyond the daily routines of the mundane life and from the practical life's triviality and wearisomeness, breaking down the prison walls of the commonplace. Russell says that the pleasure and the supremacy of creative thoughts and original criticism are not known to the majority in the world. He says that the power of the world of creative thinking is an incomparable adventurous spirit, which men can experience instead of welcoming war to show their thirst for adventurous activities, since creative thinking has nothing to do with cruel thinking, blood-shed and destroying our own species, but increases one's self-worth and dignity and brings peace of mind as a result of creative splendour, due to which the education of the mind is be valued so high. He says:

The powers of thought, the vast regions which it can master, the much vaster regions which it can only dimly suggest to imagination, given to those whose minds have travelled beyond the daily round an amazing richness of material, an escape from the trivial and wearisomeness of familiar routine, by which the whole of life is filled with interest, and the prison walls of the commonplace are broken down. The same love of adventure which takes men to the South Pole, the same passion for a conclusive trial of strength which leads some men to welcome war, can find in creative thought an outlet which is neither wasteful nor cruel, but increases the dignity of man by incarnating in life some of the shining splendour which the human spirit is bringing down out of the unknown. To give this joy, in a greater or less measure, to all who are capable of it, is the supreme end for which the education of the mind is to be valued (BWBR: 388).

Russell says that it is the young people in the world who know the joy of mental adventure when compared with the grown-up people. A natural spirit for mental adventure is quite common in children and it grows rampantly out of living in the world of imagination and creative thinking, but it education in their later life kills it. Russell says, "The joy of mental adventure is far commoner in the young than in grown men and women. Among children it is very common, and grows naturally out of the period of make-believe and fancy. It is rare in later life because everything is done to kill it during education" (BWBR: 389). He says that there is nothing in the world like fear that every man is afraid of, which is more than their fear for devastation in generation and even death.

Russell aims at refining human mind and psychology through creative thinking to become rational beings with the right kind of education. He talks of the nature of fear and how men are afraid of many things, especially to think on various concepts that they follow so as to have their opinions. He says that an institution inspired by fear cannot give us hope for life. Hope is the creative principle of human activities, he says. It is only the spirit of safeguarding anything good that has made man great and modern education is not inspired by hope and so does not achieve great results, since careful desire to preserve the past than the hope of creating future is the dominating force of the administrators of the field of teaching. He says that the purpose of education is not to be teemed with dead facts, but to create. It should be out of inspiration and not like the wish to restore the old and shimmering beauty of something valuable after it has vanished. He is optimistic and has a vision that in the future, the world of creative thoughts will dominate and become the ruler of the world and says that those who are taught with the aim of creating such personalities, shall be with the true essence of life. They will be suffused with hope and joy and become great contributors to the unshakable faith in the glory that human endeavours can create in this world.

Russell discusses what is naturally suitable for men and women to excel in the selected branch of study or interest. Russell says that it is utterly stupid and highly piteous to impose the kind of education that has made men worthless on women in the name of enriching them. The education that is mostly masculine does not have anything to do with arousing feminine interest. Russell makes a fundamental difference between men and women and says that the true emancipation of women is not in the mere influence that they have to become like men. Men have certain natural traits and interests, which they develop through their education and self-interested activities and the same is applicable with women, if they are to achieve true emancipation as women. He says:

> As regards intelligence, the attempts to ignore native differences are beginning to seem a mistake. A great deal of the scholastic education of men is worthless, and it is a pity to inflict it on women. The most important part of men's education is the most masculine, namely, that concerned with science and machinery, and it is

this part especially which almost always fails to arouse feminine interest (MO: 75).

Russell says that it is insane to think and conclude that female intelligence is inferior to masculine intelligence. Men have set a standard of intelligence and \made it very suitable for themselves and created a mechanical civilization, which does not have any room for human values. Even if women had been left to the freedom of being themselves, they would have never invented machines. If they had been asked to contribute effectively for human civilization, they would not have forgotten to preserve human values, shinning mechanical ingenuity totally. He says:

> It would be foolish to draw the inference that female intelligence is inferior to that of the male. Men have set a standard of intelligence and have instinctively set it to suit themselves; they have created a mechanical civilization which largely ignores human values. Women left to themselves would, I believe, never have invented machines. But if they had been able freely to contribute to the sum total of civilization, they would not have forgotten to preserve what is valuable in human life and would not have been led astray, as men have been, by a blind worship of mechanical ingenuity (MO: 76).

Russell announces that the real contribution that the true characteristic qualities of women could make, have not been made so far, because of lack of freedom for women. Since women have been receiving the education compatible with men, their prudence to acquire what is suitable for them to make substantial and the most productive contributions has been debarred. Russell comes out with a humanistic and optimistic note that this condition will soon disappear to see women to reach their true empowerment. He says:

> Contribution which women's nature would enable them to make, they have not yet been able to make, because they have not been free.

They have been exposed to an education designed for men, and they have been debarred by prudery from the kind of education which would have most developed their faculties. This state of affairs, however, is rapidly improving, and I think we may hope that before many decades have passed women will be in a position to be no longer either restrictive or imitative but genuinely creative in important ways for which their faculties are more adapted than those of men (MO: 76).

2.4 The political views of Bertrand Russell

Bertrand Russell talks about the present state of democracy, the pitiable state of the citizens of democratic countries, the field of politics, politicians and their image in the minds of the people. Russell says that democracy is a beneficial form of government, but a democratic country must have an evidential display of democracy only to some extent. He says that it is painful that the citizens of many democratic countries in the world have insufficient resect for its rulers, because they are too democratic to be respected. Russell makes a brave statement, "It is a curious fact that the more democratic a country becomes, the less respect it has for its rulers" (MO: 44). Russell says that the indifference of the citizens of a country to democracy depends on the intensity of its democratic nature. He says that aristocratic people and foreign conquerors are to be hated but unfortunately, they are not despised.

Nations, which select men, who have gained universal admiration and love, to govern them, expect them to be the best and wisest so that they can deal with the delicate and responsible act of managing other people's affair. Bertrand Russell reflects the bitter facts about being in politics and the typical identity or characteristic qualities of a politician in the modern world. He says that in most of the democratic countries of the world, to call a person a politician is to associate many unpatriotic emotions. It is implied that the word 'politician' has become synonymous with being a criminal.

Russell talks of the unfortunate international political atmosphere that does not have a comfortable room for good politicians and the good people aspiring to become politicians. Russell says that a good person who is popular in his area or community would never think of getting electoral votes and even if he endeavours, he would be a miserable failure and that those who win vote are not of admirable kind. Russell says that this problematic paradox was not foreseen by the pioneers of democracy, because it was not the case with their time. Great men come to power to rule a country, when the country meets democracy for the first time and it becomes stultified, when this form of government is well-established. He says:

> In most democratic countries to call a man a politician is to say something derisive about him. The men who enjoy the good opinion of the community, with few exceptions, do not seek to win its votes and would be unsuccessful if they did, while the men who win votes are apt to be professionals of a not wholly admirable kind. (I am not thinking of those who obtain the highest offices)

> This is a paradox which was not foreseen by the pioneers of democracy. Indeed, it was not true in their day. When democracy is new it usually brings great men to the fore, but it loses this merit as it becomes well established. Why is this? (MO: 44).

He asks why Archangel, as an independent candidate, would not be selected in the election, if Satan and Beelzebub were nominated as official candidates? He says, "Why is it that, if Satan and Beelzebub were nominated as the official candidates and the Archangel Gabriel stood as an independent, the Archangel would have no chance of being elected? For that is the fact, strange as it may seem" (MO: 44). Here he talks of something universal, representing people's mind-set and at the same time being critical about the collective inferior attitude and indifference towards individual, societal and political governance. The implied statement is that the field of politics has become extremely corrupted and the aboard of scoundrels as Plato and Abraham Lincoln said, "politics is the last resort of scoundrels". People are of the opinion that independent candidates can never win because they are just new-comers, which is also a reason why individual candidates do not get enough votes to win and reach power.

Russell talks of the political irresponsibility of not caring to be well-informed of the contemporary political scenario so as to be clear about who has to be selected to rule them. Russell knows that the majority of the people of the world still does not know the true value of their wright to vote, because they don't know their socio-political importance in being decisive about the construction of a government for a better society and well-being in general. Russell says that the majority of the people in this world votes to a particular candidate without making any reasonable inquiry into the character, ability and merits of the person, because they are used to vote to the person, which is shockingly mechanical and irresponsible.

Russell says that they vote for the person mechanically because they have seen their fathers voting the person and the fathers did it because their fathers did it. Russell's anguish is very deep that they know not how precious is the democratic right to vote. Their ordinary and ignorant life has distanced the necessary political knowledge and responsibilities. He says, "The ultimate reason, I believe, is nothing more recondite than habit. Most men, without inquiring into the merits of the particular candidate, vote as they always have voted, and always have voted as their fathers have always voted. This applies to reformers just as much as to conservatives" (MO: 45).

Russell says that until this abominable habit is broken, good people will have no place in politics. Russell says that the force of habit from a very long distance of ancestral attitude has to be mitigated at least, though not uprooted and that people should understand that the sort of criticism that they have on politicians in democracy is actually a criticism on ourselves, because they ultimately have the politicians they deserve to be ruled by. Russell says:

No one can free himself from the force of habit, and if he could, he would be reduced to such a condition of doubt that he would achieve nothing. Yet so long as habit holds sway, good men will have little chance in politics.

Is there, then, no solution? Yes, but it is a matter of degree; we must be dominated by habit to some extent but we might be less so than we are. And that lessening might make all the difference. Meanwhile, let us remember that in a democracy criticism of our politicians is criticism of ourselves – we have the politicians we deserve (MO: 45).

Russell advocates the necessity of understanding how important it is to know about politics and administration in general and exercise the basic right of being a citizen of a country by having knowledge about the historical, social and political condition of the land. He also says how important carefulness and responsibility are in choosing our leaders to rule us. Russell says that people must know everything about the political system and those who compete with themselves in ruling them so that they can decide, based on their capacity and personal character and personality on the heads of the administration of their country.

Bertrand Russell talks about the role of a nation in shaping individuals and individuals' efforts to bring laurels to their country by bringing their latent talent out to that extent that they become exemplary personalities in their respective fields. Russell says that the greatness of a country lies in creating powerful individuals. He says that a nation that stands majestically among other countries of the world has its superior impact on its citizens also. The citizens are very proud and confident that they belong to a soil that is highly respected in the international community, which acts as a stimulus to the individual's talents, pursuits and achievements. He cites examples of the birth of great individuals in many fields of a few countries whenever they succeeded in wars. He says:

There can be no doubt that national success is a stimulus to individual achievement. When the Athenians had beaten the Persians, they built the Parthenon and produced Aeschylus. When the English had defeated the Spaniards, they produced Shakespeare. The victories of Louis XIV were associated with the great age of French literature. Instances of this sort of thing could be multiplied indefinitely (MO: 52).

Russell talks of the individual productivity also, which has no connection with the success and greatness of a nation. He says that Bach, Mozart and Beethoven became musical genius which has nothing do with the greatness of their countries. Spinoza belongs to an oppressed race and the country he belongs to was about to be defeated, when he raised to greatness. Russell says that the architecture of a country and its achievements in building majestic and colossal buildings do have an influence on the pride of its citizens and so it is said that the great men in various fields and their achievements are the pride of many citizens.

2.5 The anti-war perspectives of Bertrand Russell

Russell was one of the eminent western humanists greatly disturbed with the insecure state of the world after the World Wars. He started spending much of his life time only in propagating humanism and solid ideas to prevent human brains from strategizing a full scale nuclear war, which would result in the total annihilation of lives on the globe. Russell desires to extirpate war from the world and the glorious state of mutual love and care to be rampant, promising the joy of eternal security and prosperity to human beings. Bertrand Russell, being a startled witness of the two World Wars, their unspeakable cruelties and irrecoverable devastations, is a vehement attacker of the very idea of being pugnacious to dominate and make a nation or the world being subservient to one or a group of nations. He reproaches fight in any form and war in particular that stamps on people mercilessly. Russell carries the ever benevolent flag of humanism and is against the merciless act of waging war against any country that ultimately results in killing of innocent lives.

Russell says that his adult life has been in utter gloom and shaken at the terror prevailing all over the world due to the World Wars and that the world has seen the start of the decomposition of human values and civilization, since the eruption of the first world war. He says, "The world since 1914 has been one in which civilized ways of life and humane feelings have steadily decayed; and there is, as yet, little sign of a contrary tendency" (FF: 223). This confession is supported by Jo Vellacott in his book, Bertrand Russell and the Pacifists in the First World War, says, "Russell was shocked when Europe plunged itself into full-scale war in 1914" (11). He says that war has been the basic instinct of the primitive man, but man has crossed many levels of his cultural evolution and become civilized, but still the push to be pugnacious and blood-thirsty remains inextinguishable. Barbaric culture was superior in its culture when compared with the morality of the modern civilization. The modern world is a slave to the developed ego to dominate others and be destructively mighty.

He says that there was an advent of powerful machines and a huge production in America and Britain, which the other countries wanted to follow and as a result, a considerable part of human capacity of advanced nations was spent to produce machines to destroy the other advanced nations. Russell says that so long as the attitude to destroy the competitors, every brilliant improvement in the field of science is fatal to the very existence of human beings. Russell says, "The older competitive doctrines which have come down to us from the times of tribal warfare are no longer true. Two powerful groups can always prosper more by co-operation than they can by competition" (FF: 135). In the modern world, two countries which are powerful try to be superior to the other through armaments. The rash and insurmountable hostility of increasing military strength and lethal weapons has pushed the present world to the limits of insecurity, restlessness and hopelessness, and the only reason for this unfortunate state is the tension between the East and the West.

The Indian humanist Dr. S. Radhakrishnan, in his book, *Science, Culture and Man, Impact of scientific progress on culture and human evolution,* talks of unity among the countries and universal peace and prosperity. He says, "It is not possible for us to build universal brotherhood unless you transform the nature of man, unless you are able to depend not merely on external structures but on the inward soul, unless we are able to feel in the pulse of our being that we all belong to one human race; unless we are able to transcend our group loyalties and acknowledge the primacy of the human race". (6) Russell says that the existing enmity between the East and West is capable of bringing the catastrophic possibility of ending in nuclear war that would reduce both to ashes. He unleashes a didactic command that America and Russia must stop their fight for power and stay in agreement not to be nightmares to the rest of the world, but unfortunately, the endeavours taken to achieve friendly relations have failed many a time and aggravated only the negative impacts.

The hatred for each other is so deep-seated for generations with thoughts about each other's wickedness that even a slight flexibility from any side would be surrendering to absolute evil. The recollection of destructive activities, news spread and speeches against each other are the major damaging factors of the tenuous possibility of falling into a bond of affability. Russell says, "Each of these speeches is a mixture of truth and falsehood. Each produce furious vituperative retorts from the other side. Both speeches are made by eminent statesmen at meetings of the United Nations, but, to everybody's astonishment, they do not generate friendly feelings between East and West" (FF: 211).

This clearly indicates that the predominating fear, hatred and suspicion from each side do not necessitate the possibility of amicable smiles. The hatred is due to the clash between the Western freedom and the communist menace. Russell gallantly declares that the governments of both US and USSR are criminals. He says, "I do not mean either East or West is impeccable. On the contrary, I think the governments of both are deeply criminal" (FF: 218). Russell says that he is not completely a pacifist since he accepts that a war can be beneficent also like the American War of Independence. He accepts that evil in any form should be devastated by military power to maintain peace, but he is against the unreasonable and merciless war that takes place to quench man's animal instincts.

Russell, in one of his articles, 'The Ancestry of Fascism', says that the founders of fascism surprisingly have the collective attitude of not preferring anything constructive, good and peace-giving. He says, "The founders of the school of thought out of which Fascism has grown all have certain common characteristics. They seek the good in will rather than in feeling or cognition; they value power more than happiness; they prefer force to argument, war to peace, aristocracy to democracy, propaganda to scientific impartiality" (5). Russell says that men who possess dominating power are stupid enough to think that the devastation of mankind is better than submitting themselves to someone inferior or equally powerful.

Russell says that such people are intoxicated with the pleasure of fanaticism and are blind to the fast-approaching human excellence to be tasted. Humanism that takes its roots from strong morality is the strength of Bertrand Russell. A.J. Ayer says, "While he has an extensive knowledge of history, of which he makes effective use, Russell's approach to social questions is more moral than historical" (21). Russell says that the problem to be quelled does not exist in the outside world, but with the mind of man. Men should realize that they are not only drifting towards the internal command of their animal instincts but also that their actions are suicidal. Russell says:

> What I do say is that the way of the trouble is psychological and consists in making men realize, on both sides of the Iron Curtain, that neither side can hope to win any good thing until there is mutual rapprochement. And, in bringing about such a lessening of tension, I can think of nothing more effective than the realization of the happiness that the whole human race might enjoy if only it would allow itself to do so (FF: 135).

Bertrand Russell advocates toleration as the backbone of constructing a trustworthy agreement to defend world security and peace. "The evil lies in the dogmatic temper, not in the particular character of the dogma. Since modern weapons leave us with no choice except all to live together or all to die together, the preservation of human species demands a greater degree of mutual tolerance than has ever before been necessary" (FF: 275). Russell says that there should be freedom for thinking and expression of opinions throughout the world so that people shall fight for peace and universal security for human life. Russell insists on being rationalists to avoid being quarrelsome and be peaceful in life. Russell says that man should think honestly to make the existing indignation and fear less virulent with the sharp intellect developed over the period of time, which itself is the cradle of this danger. He says:

> If however, the reign of fear can somehow be made to cease on both sides of the Iron Curtain – or, if not to cease, at any rate to grow less virulent – intelligence and skill, which have never before been as great as they are at the present moment, and which are, in fact, the very cause of our present dangers, may be ruined into fruitful channels, and our grandchildren may look back to our time as the last moment of the dark ages from which, as from a long tunnel, mankind will have emerged into the sunshine and happiness of mutual harmony (FF: 136).

Russell says strongly that unless there is a strong collective force from the people all over the world against the weapons of mass destruction, a nuclear war is unstoppable. He says that an invincible opposition from the people is the strongest force against which no weapon can operate. They should realize that the military and political men of the strong nations who are the minority, decides to wage war due to which the majority of people who are the innocent are victimized. So it is fundamentally the citizens of every nation who are to honestly ruminate and take action against safeguarding their life and the posterity. Russell says, "Although many of the people who take this extreme view profess to be democrats, they nevertheless consider that a small percentage of fanatics have a right to inflict the death penalty upon all the rest of mankind" (FF: 216). Russell says that modern democracy and the methods of popularizing something are not ethical but deeply affect public opinion. He says that it is the moral responsibility of the media to present the actual information about the cruelty and the possible level of devastation of the war using weapons of mass destruction, and should make a silent revolution through the people of the world against nuclear war. He says:

> The consequence is that what ought to be known widely throughout the general public will not be known unless great efforts are made by disinterested persons to see that the information reaches the minds and hearts of vast numbers of people. I do not think this work can be successfully accomplished except by the help of men of science. They, along, can speak with the authority that is necessary to combat the misleading statements of those scientists who have permitted themselves to become merchants of death. If disinterested scientists do not speak out, the others will succeed in conveying a distorted impression, not only to the public but also to the politicians (FF: 230).

Russell says that the role of scientists in quelling war plays major role. Men of science should not think that their responsible role in the society is not just to offer knowledge and create efficient machines but should be operated by the basic moral responsibility of making life easy and comfortable to the people. The ultimate responsibility of scientists is to contribute effectively towards the security and peace of the world. So they should not invent anything that would become a potential peril to human existence at any time. They should know the value of life and its beauty and should bear great respect for them more than anything else. Scientists should be humanistic in their perception of the world and people and should operate compatibly. He says:

It is impossible in the modern world for a man of science to say with any honesty, 'My business is to provide knowledge, and what use is made of the knowledge is not my responsibility'. The knowledge that a man of science provides may fall into the hands of men or institutions devoted to utterly unworthy objects. I do not suggest that a man of science, or even a large body of men of science, can altogether prevent this, but they can diminish the magnitude of the evil (FF: 230-231).

He says that scientists, who play one of the vital roles in building a national power, should be productive and not destructive with their eminence. They ought to spread the value of using certain branches of science for the well-being of the people such as increasing food production to wipe off poverty and poor lifestyle in their respective countries rather than just producing weapons to nourish barbarous instincts. They should proclaim that it is an utter waste to spend so much of money on military power and other inventions for destruction, which is out of human toil, to spend on activities to turn lives and marvellous constructions to ashes, but to spend on productive plans to make their citizens' life fertile and satisfactory. This is possible only with humanistic love for oneself, people, country and the world of which a country is a dependent part. The significance of interdependency, which has made nations and people come together and learn the truth that unity rules peace and prosperity, must be understood. Russell suggests:

There is another direction in which men of science can attempt to provide leadership. They can suggest and urge in many ways the value of those branches of science of which the important practical uses are beneficial and not harmful. Consider what might be done if the money at present spent on armaments were spent on increasing and distributing the food supply of the world and diminishing the population pressure. In a few decades, poverty and malnutrition, which now afflict more than half the population of the globe, could be ended. But at present almost all the governments of great states consider that it is better to spend money on killing foreigners than on keeping their own subjects alive. Possibilities of a hopeful sort in whatever field can best be worked out and stated authoritatively by men of science; and, since they can do this better than others, it is part of their duty to do it (FF: 231).

Russell suggests that there should be some governing body to control and monitor the activities of the powerful nations. There should be some eminent men and neutrals from East and West. Russell is of the opinion that these men should spend much time in talking to each other with the intension of understanding each other so that mutual respect and concern as human beings can be achieved. They should involve actively in the noble act of becoming human beings to each other, destructing the already existing bitter thoughts and grievances about each other. Such a committee should be formed by the United Nations. In the beginning of the associations no definite and concrete proposals are to be achieved. They should try their level best to develop a positive attitude to the necessity for reaching an amicable stipulation and towards the possibility of mutual agreement for world peace. He says:

> What I should like to see is the establishment of a very small body, which might be called the Conciliation Committee, consisting of eminent men from East and West and, also, certain eminent neutrals, who should spend some time in each other's company until they had become accustomed to thinking of each other as individuals and not as emissaries of Satan. This committee could be appointed by the United Nations, given the previous admission of China. I should wish these men in their early stage of their association, to make no attempt at concrete and definite proposals. I should wish them, at

first, only to arrive at a state of mind in which agreement seemed possible and the necessity of reaching agreement had become evident. After the mellowing influence of propinquity had proceeded to the tackling of questions as to which agreement is difficult (FF: 218-219).

Russell says that the lethargic and pessimistic people may think that achieving security at this exigency is not possible. He thinks that the fundamental change in the attitude of the people will produce a benevolent move towards security. He says that he is only an optimist and not a prophet to foretell the future condition of the attitude of the powerful people and the world. Russell suggests three important ideas for a stable world. He suggests:

The first of these is that all the major armaments should be under the control of one single authority, so that great wars should no longer be possible. The second is that there should be a continual approach in the poorer parts of the world towards that level of prosperity which has already been achieved in the West. And the third is that the habits of populations everywhere should be such as to prevent a rapid increase of population. Given these three conditions, fear might cease to dominate our daily lives, and, with the disappearance of fear, other more generous and more creative emotions would take its place. If once these political problems were solved I should expect an extraordinary renaissance in art and literature, in thought and science. I should hope to see man at last come into his kingdom – the kingdom that he has deserved by his intelligence, and hitherto forfeited by mutual suspicion (FF: 134).

Russell is optimistic about the implementation of a peace treaty, muting all the weapons of mass destruction, since he is confident that not only the people of the world, but also the proud men of the powerful nations will understand the necessity of showing their humane side for the existence of the world. He says that it takes some time to achieve the real blissful state before 1914, but if the world realizes the existing emergencies, such a revival of hope is reachable and the presently existing terrible state is exterminable. He says:

> It is obvious that the first necessity is the creation of a system in which attack by either side will be no longer a pressing danger. But this is only the first step. Asia and Africa will remain to be dealt with and the aim must be to find ways of admitting them to equality without anarchy. I do not suggest that this is easy, but it will become gradually possible when both East and West have ceased to be a menace to new freedom.   For   it
>
> will then be possible, in spite of propaganda to the contrary, to persuade Asia and Africa that we have both the power and the will to benefit them (FF: 237).

Russell knows how serious and painstaking are the efforts involved in the ideas he suggests, but creates confidence through recollecting a worth-remembering productive achievement of the past. An amicable handshake was possible through relentless efforts to bring a half-century of enmity between Russia and Britain to a temporary end at least. He says, "All the disputes that caused a half-century of enmity between Russia and Britain were solved by a month or two of negotiation, and from then until 1917 any criticism of the Czarist Government was frowned upon" (FF: 214). The untiring cogitations of a true care and affection might sound impossible and even preposterous, which is very much applicable to the conception of World Government by Russell. Brian Carr informs:

> Russell felt that the one hope left of escaping a world holocaust was the emergence of a single World Government, more urgent than ever since the bombing of Hiroshima and Nagasaki in

1945. He made a number of broadcasts during 1953, emphasizing the dangers inherent in the possession of nuclear devices, and followed them two years later with an appeal, signed jointly with Albert Einstein and a number of other leading world scientists, for government action to avert the dangers (20).

Bertrand Russell says that the people of the world can agree that the world will be annihilated, in case of another war. Russell talks about the terrible effects that could possibly be experienced by the people, if another war breaks out. Russell says that aeroplanes and poison gas have strengthened the evil intentions of the powerful nations and that if there is a war between England and France, within a few seconds of its outbreak, all the people of the cities of London and Paris will be dead and within another few days, all the industries of the cities will be pulverized, the railways would be destroyed and the terrified population would fight with each other for food and kill each other and the left over people will be without any culture. Russell says:

> Aeroplanes and poison gas have made the attack much stronger than the defence and have made it easy to attack civilian population behind the lines. If there should be a war (say) between England and France, it is to be expected that, within a few hours of its outbreak, practically all the inhabitants of London and Paris would be dead. Within a few days, all the main centres of industry would be destroyed and most of the railways would be paralysed. The population, maddened with terror, would fight with each other for stores of food, and those who were most successful would retire into lonely places, where they would shoot all who approached them. Probably within a week, the population of both countries would be halved, and the institutions which are the vehicles of their culture would be destroyed forever (MO: 113).

Russell is very angry that the governments of all the nations of the world, despite knowing this bitter truth, oppose any possible force to stop the possibility of such a cruel war. He says that the Disarmament Conference was of no use because it was about renewing some old futile agreements. Russell says that there is neither intelligence nor an emotional care that the people should be safe and comfortable. The people of the conference seem to have thrown of their intelligence and decided not to present anything that could possibly lessen the possibility of a war. He says:

> All this is well known, and yet, incredible as it may seem, the governments show a rooted opposition to all serious attempts to prevent war. The Disarmament Conference, after long deliberation, decided merely to renew certain futile agreements which, as everyone admits, will be broken on the day that war breaks out. The assembled governments decided to flout the intelligence of the civilized world and to make it clear that they would do nothing whatever to make war less likely or less horrible. (MO: 113-114).

It is very clear that no country that could play a vital role to play to convince the superpowers to achieve the historical event of getting into a reconciliation to stop any further fight, spoke constructively in all the peace conferences, meetings and discussions, which indicates their arrogance to perpetuate war as powerful people.

Russell says that Einstein, with his friends, with an intention of establishing peace, went to Geneva Conference to find out some hope to do something about it, but the conference did not reach any productive agreement. Then they wanted to have a congress to discuss what should intelligent people do to save Europe from being self-destructive, but the Swiss Government did not accept to conduct a meeting at Switzerland, in the pretext of stating that it must be done by communists. The French Government was also did not co-operate with the noble intentions and even the British Prime Minister did not even reply. He says:

> Einstein, who is universally recognized as the greatest man of our age, went to Geneva during the conference to find out whether there was hope of anything being done. The conference having proved futile, Einstein and various other friends of peace, many of them eminent and highly respectable, attempted to hold a congress that should consider what intelligent people could do to save Europe from suicide. The Swiss Government refused them permission to meet in Switzerland, on the pretext that friends of peace must be Communists. The French Government proved equally unfriendly. The British Prime Minister, personally appealed to, did not even reply; apparently, he is now ashamed of his honourable record in the Great War (MO: 114).

Russell says that from the way all the heads of the important countries are behaving, it can be concluded that even though they are not for the war, they do not want to do anything to obstruct any measure that would possibly prevent war, like they did before 1914. It shows the insensibilities of the modern man towards anything precious and irrecoverable, including time and human life. Russell very optimistically says that before they would make such productive measures, the common people of the world would take the necessary steps to save themselves and their children from any horrible death. The first step is universal compulsory disarmament and the second step to save the world is the creation of an international government. He says that powerful armies and soldiers are not to protect us and so the only way to bring protection and peace for the world is not to have any means to fighting. He says:

> The conclusion to be drawn from such facts is that the governments of the world, while not positively desiring war, are just as determined as they were before 1914 to obstruct every measure that is likely to prevent war. It is to be hoped that

ordinary citizens will, before it is too late, acquire the common sense required to save themselves and their children from a horrible and futile death. The first step should be universal compulsory and complete disarmament, the second the creation of an international government. Armies and navies do not make for safety. The only way to be safe in the modern world is not to have the means of fighting (MO: 114).

Russell says that a scientific society can be strong and stable with certain conditions. There must be a single government constructed to govern the entire world so that there will be one strong army with which a permanent peace can be established. Presently there are many countries and armies with which the top officials of the respected countries take a decision to wage war against a country and get attacked by their enemy country, but having a monopoly of army force quells this fundamental problem. The second condition is that there must not be any further development in their military strength of any country, hereafter so that it does not kindle envy in anybody's mind. The third condition Russell puts forth is that every country must have an eye on their population rate so that they can ensure a low birth rate. Creating a conducive socio-political atmosphere for the individual initiative for work and play, which is possible by maintaining the necessary political and economic framework, is the fourth condition. Russell quotes his own words:

My conclusion is that a scientific society can be stable given certain conditions. The first of these is a single government of the whole world, possessing a monopoly of armed force and therefore able to enforce peace. The second condition is a general diffusion of prosperity, so that there is no occasion for envy of one part of the world by another. The third condition (which supposes the second fulfilled) is a low birth rate everywhere, so that the population of the world becomes stationary, or nearly so. The fourth condition is the provision for individual initiative both in work and in play, and the greatest diffusion of power compatible with maintaining the necessary political and economic framework (HSEP: 221).

Russell says that the importance of implementing these conditions must be realized, otherwise, a scientifically organized society will continue to run certain risks, of which the most dangerous risk is the possibility of the human race to be wiped off the earth in a large scale of war, using the most detrimental weapons ever fought with. He says that if those conditions are followed as soon as possible, the world will collapse into an anarchy and civilization will also be affected considerably, followed by violence, starvation and other unthinkable sufferings, affecting at least the fifty percentage of the world. Russell is sorry and disturbed that the present world does not care to consider the true steps to be taken for the global peace and so he wants all the powerful and sane people to think on these lines with an intention of making productive contribution towards the most wanted state of peace for the world. He says:

> Until these conditions are realized, a scientifically organized world will continue to run certain grave risks. Of these, the most catastrophic is the extinction of the human species in a large-scale war. Short of this, there is a danger of collapse into anarchy and a general lowering of the level of civilization. Such a process must inevitably be accompanied by appalling suffering, since it will involve the death by violence or starvation of about half the population of the globe. Sane men must therefore which to see the world moving towards the fulfilment of the conditions required for stability. It cannot be said that at present the worlds travelling in this direction. What hope is there of a more constructive movement in the not-too-distant future (HSEP: 222).

Russell is much concerned with the rivalry of not only the US and USSR but also the East and West in being powerful in their military capacity. He says that those who are against the game of power-politics must see to it that the presently existing problem between the East and West is resolved as soon as possible by making them realize how futile it is basically and how irrecoverably destructive and unthinkably detrimental if any explosion takes place with the most vicious intention. So they must decide to come forward to a mutual determination to take the deep-rooted fear off their comfortable lives and well-being, preserve the people of the world and give assurance for peace. He says:

> War, as was argued in the preceding chapter, does not appear to be a road towards better things, no matter what may be its outcome. Those who place the future of mankind above the game of momentary power-politics must therefore hope that, before an explosion occurs, bothside sinthe present conflict of East and West will realize its futility and will become willing to give and accept convincing assurances of their mutual determination to preserve the peace (HSEP: 222).

Russell says that presently the East and West are governed by fanatics obsessed with the imagination that the competitive spirit to be the most powerful in the world has come to an unavoidable climax that they must destroy the other to bring about a new millennium. Russell condemns the Soviet Government stating that it is driven by an ideology that hatred is the vital moving force in human affairs. It has an unworldly and monstrous fervency of dogma that it is the force of economic determination that has ordered the fierce fight between Capitalism and Communism. They are so confident about winning this fight to be the most powerful in the world, since the Scriptures of the Marxist has already foretold that it is only Communism which is going to be victorious throughout the world.

Russell says that this foretelling is a mere myth and no rational man in the world can embrace this concept. Bertrand Russell says that this fanaticism has to be prevented from taking its full operation to execute its evil intentions and that unfortunately there is a view among the common people of America that fanaticism must be fought with fanaticism only and the only way to combat communism is to declare the wickedness of the followers and start spreading how terrible and a potential threat for the peace of this world are they basically, and making use of all sorts of public and socio-political strategies to prevent the people from understanding the communist ideologies and outlooks. He says:

> The soviet Government accepts an ideology according to which hate has always been, and still is, the moving force in human affairs. It believes, with the superstitious fervency of unquestioned dogma, that an internecine struggle between Capitalism and Communism has been decreed by the blind forces of economic determination, and that this struggle, when it comes, must end, as the Marxist Scriptures foretell, in the world-wide victory of communism. All this of course is a myth which cannot be accepted by anyone capable of rational thought (HSEP: 222-223).

Russell says that the solution for this problem of the ever-increasing tension is not to be found in war, but in conciliation in the gradual diminution of mutual hatred and fear. The commencement of this arm-race was due to the foolish belief that it is only an increase in armaments that provides and ensures their safety, for which both Russia and America spend so much of their wealth on their military capabilities, which otherwise, could well be utilized for the proper development of the infrastructure and the rich well-being of their people, there by being exemplary, in how to develop one's country out of a true nationalistic spirit, to the rest of the world.

Russell is utterly fearless in stating openly that the main reason for not attaining any reconciliation so far is the superpowers' low-level rationality. They don't rationalize the dangerous condition and the selfishness involved between themselves for superiority and that the rest of the world shall be affected, which is neither ethical not intelligent. Each side firmly thinks that they need to be stronger than the other side to defend themselves, in case there is a powerful attack. If there is an announcement that one of them has increased its armaments to certain level, the other side also cannot help increasing its power to be at least capable of protecting it. Neither side thinks of going for a reconciliation because they think that a declaration for a peaceful reconciliation will give an impression that they are afraid of the other. Russell compares this comical state with the pathetic condition of the two men in duelling, not wanting either to hurt or get hurt and says that such private duelling is dead, but not the international duel with the same stupid psychology. He says:

> One of the things that make this situation so apparently hopeless is that it has on both sides a certain low-level rationality. Each side believes that the other will attack if it has a good hope of victory. Each side is therefore persuaded that its armaments must be strong enough to deter the other side from attack. When either side increases its armaments, the other side's fears are increased, and therefore the other side's armaments are still further increased. Neither side dares to start the conciliatory movement or to emphasize the evils to all mankind that would result from war, for if it does so, the other side, it is thought, will take such action as a proof of fear and will therefore be encouraged in bellicosity. The situation is exactly like that which used to arise in the days of duelling, when two men, neither of whom wished to kill or be killed, were driven on by the fear of being thought cowardly. Private duelling has died out, but the international duel remains, with exactly the same absurd psychology (HSEP: 223-224).

Russell says that it is difficult for any Communist or Anti-communist association to do something to lessen this mutual suspicion. The only way to settle this issue is that the governments of countries of Neutral Power must think of talking to both the countries, which can neither be taken for cowardice nor will it be suspected for hostility. Russell says that the public opinion has much influence on anything, but it has nothing to do with talking to the Russian Government and that is why other countries with a very friendly attitude must approach these two super-powers to help them talk it out and come to an agreeable pact that actually increases the respect for each other's supremacy and humane intelligence. He says:

> The first step, I think, be taken by neutral Powers. They have two advantages: one of these is that they cannot be accused of cowardice, the other, which is even more important, is that they can speak to Governments without being suspected of hostility. In Western countries, public opinion is still a force. But to have any influence upon Russia, it is necessary to be able to persuade the Russian Government --- and only Governments can hope to do this with any effect (HSEP: 224).

Russell strongly thinks that India is a land of spiritually and non-violence and it stands for pacifism as the core of its doctrine and so he wants the Indian government to appoint a commission that consists of eminent Indian politicians, economists, scientists and military personals, the purpose of which is to bring the possible devastation that a full scale war could bring not only to the superpowers, but also the neutrals. He says that India should make such a detailed and meticulous report and present it to all the governments of other powerful countries, inviting them to freely be critical of the prediction. Russell is so sure about any disagreement from any country on such a presentation. The victory of such a presentation so as to get the frank opinion from the other powerful countries is with both the presentation and the reaction of the superpowers, when they are involved in a careful observation on the existing enmity and the impending unimaginable and unjust destruction due to the inherent fear and ego between them. It shall definitely make them rethink their negative attitude towards each other for the benevolence of mankind in general.

Russell says that neither USSR nor US is very aggressive on each other, but the one suspects the other being too aggressive about suppressing the other and this suspicion is enough to cause any tangible harm. Russell says that the neutrals must persuade both the countries in such a way that the suspicion disappears, and a joyful, humane and respectful understanding replaces it. There must be a common consensus that one can fight only when the other comes forward to attack due to which both will be waiting for the other to make the first move, which will never happen. He says:

> I should like to see the Government of India appoint a Commission, consisting solely of Indians, who should be eminent politicians, economists, scientists or military men, the purpose of the Commission being to investigate in a wholly neutral spirit the evils to be expected if the cold war became hot, evils not by any means confined to the belligerents but affliction neutrals also, though probably in a lesser degree. I should wish the Government of India to present this report to be Governments of all the Great Powers, and to invite them to express either agreement or disagreement with its forecasts. I think that, if the work of the Commission were adequately performed, disagreement would be very difficult. It might in this way become possible to persuade government on both sides that neither side could hope to gain by aggression. I do not myself believe that at the present moment either side contemplates aggression, but each side suspects that the other may do so, and this suspicion does almost as much harm as if it were well-founded. What neutrals would have to achieve is to allay this suspicion and to persuade each side to a

genuine belief that the other side will only fight if attacked (HSEP: 224).

Russell says that such a peace treaty is not possible in the near future unless an authoritative neutral investigation demonstration with no bias comes to unite both the superpowers. If so, it will be trustworthy and genuine, in spite of the fact that it is going to be tested with many questions out of selfishness, fear and pride. Russell says, "I do not know whether, in the immediate future, it would be possible to bring about this belief on both sides, but I think it would become much easier to bring about if it were backed by an authoritative neutral investigation demonstrating without bias how little either side could hope to gain by aggression" (HSEP: 224-225). Russell says that when the two countries become one in understanding that what is presented by the neutrals is true and war is not the solution for their problems, negotiations would be possible soon and the existing tension will rapidly diminish, which will redeem the traditional courtesies in diplomatic intercourse.

Russell says that the presentation must lead to the decision-making of a Congress on what solutions to be made to achieve stability rather than committing the mistake of giving a diplomatic victory to one of them or both. He talks about Germany in the divided condition and the invading attitude of Hitler and the refusal of recognition to the Government of China and says that the problems of Germany could be resolved only by Russian concessions and the problems of China could be resolved only by American concessions. The concessions expected to be comfortable is possible only with the wish to reduce the risk of going for war to prove one's might. Russell says that the state of mind necessary for the two sides to come to a realization and then to an agreement is to be brought about by the neutrals. He says:

> If once it were agreed and acknowledged on both sides that war is not the solution, negotiations would soon become possible and the tension would rapidly grow less. The first step would be to diminish the asperities of official propaganda and restore traditional

courtesies in diplomatic intercourse. The next step would be a Congress to consider all the points in dispute, and to seek such solutions as should give stability rather than such as involved diplomatic victory for this side or that. If each side were genuinely actuated by the wish to diminish the risk of war, such mutual concessions would no longer be so difficult as they are at present. And I think that in bringing about the necessary state of mind on both sides, neutral powers can play a beneficent and decisive part (HSEP: 225).

Russell says that the first resolution should be internationalizing of the administration and supervising of atomic energy. Russell says that it was America, which was ready to get into a peace treaty in the beginning, but the suspicion of Russia broke the possibility and even now the suspicion remains unsuspended or not even diminished, after which American suspicion became intense on Russia. Russell says that the reversal of this situation is possible now because both the countries have the most dangerous atom and hydrogen bombs. He says:

Of these, the first to be tackled would probably have to be the internationalizing of the control of atomic energy. America made a wholly praiseworthy endeavour in this direction at the end of the last war, but Russian suspicions made the endeavour abortive. Since that time Russian suspicions have not grown less, and American suspicions have hardened. We must hope for a reversal of this process, and I think that a reversal has become more possible since both sides have possessed atom and hydrogen bombs (HSEP: 225-226).

Russell is sure that unless Russia or America has to lose its national independence, the world will never be at peace. So, rapprochement, which obliterates the fear of war, is the best that could be expected out of this stiff and untiringly egoistic struggle between these two countries. When this achieved reconciliation grows stronger and stronger, both the countries will realize that not everything is possibly attainable in life and that certain kinds of liberty is not possible in this scientific era that has made the glob very small like a hamlet. He says:

> It is not easy to induce either Russia or America to surrender absolute national independence, but until this is done the world will not be safe. I think the best that can be hoped is a détente during which the fear of war is not imminent, and a gradual growth, while the détente lasts, of a realization that certain kinds of liberty, which have seemed very previous, are no longer possible in a planet which technique has made small and over-crowded (HSEP: 226).

Russell says that the possibility of establishing an international government depends on the attenuation of fanaticism and the habit of viewing communities in the world scientifically and not passionately. The fanaticism of both Russia and America depends on the curtailment of fanaticism that they bear for each other. He says, "If Russian fanaticism is to grow less, it will not be because American fanaticism has grown greater. On the contrary, American fanaticism is a product of Russian fanaticism, and its only probable effect is a reverberation which still further increases the Russian fanaticism that caused it" (HSEP: 226).

Russell says that it is only the spreading of the application of a scientific spirit that will make the world united and survive. Russell, by 'scientific spirit', means not anything related to scientific technology, but to judge and accept anything based on evidence and to reject that which does not have a substantial evidence. Fanaticism in all forms must be suspended. It can be Hindu or Muslim or Catholic or Communist, are a legacy of the Middle Ages. He says that after the much-awaited reconcilement, the governments of the countries of the world must stop encouraging the blindness of fanaticism and the hatred that it unstoppably gives birth to. Robert D. Worley says,

"Russell predicts a path from anarchy through despotism to democracy" (9).

Russell says that even though man has a tremendous strength to endure suffering, he is so powerful as to curtail, to a great extent, the possibilities of the sufferings and miseries of the world, which is not possible unless man is not driven by irrational beliefs and ideologies to take pleasure in dividing human race into intensely and mutually hostile groups and associations. Sufferings and miseries of the world are the very strong indications and stamp of the miserable failure of human wisdom and humanism. The principles and ideologies of the rulers of their respective countries and territories must not be abstract, but concrete like the typical affection and care of parents for their children. Russell says that the divine combination of wisdom and humane warmth is the most essential, which is lacking presently and concludes with a rejoicing optimistic stateliness that this awful condition will not leap into eternity.

Chapter III

The Humanistic Spirit of Aldous Huxley

3.1 The social reformative concerns of Aldous Huxley

The Huxleyan social reformative ideas are for the individual refinements of the people of the world to be strong and responsible about their socio-political contributions for their countries. Huxley says that there are many definitions of an ideal society and he wants to give a humanistic definition of an ideal society, which all men and women would find acceptable. He says that a humanist is the one who believes that human nature as a whole should be harmoniously developed and that the sacrifices man makes should be done out of his highest interest for the well-being of the entire humanity and not due to anything supernatural or out of anything humane. He says:

> The humanist is one who believes that our human nature can, and should be, developed harmoniously as a whole – that the sacrifices which man must always make should be made in his own highest interest, and not in the interest of something external to himself – not in the name of any less or any more than human cause. (BW: 107)

According to a humanist, Huxley says, the members of an ideal society are superior in quality physically, intellectually and morally. The society is impeccable in establishing morality in all possible realms that no one will be treated unjustly and no talent goes unrecognised. It becomes the embodiment of personal liberty and at the same time garlands and eulogises any altruistic efforts, it is not stagnant, but purposefully dynamic, drifting towards the realization of lofty human aspirations. He says that science should be used in order to build such a society and the powers of science should be used by humanistic rulers. He says:

> For the humanist, then, the ideal society is one whose constituent members are all physically, intellectually and morally of the best quality; a

society so organised that no individual shall be unjustly treated or compelled to waste or bury his talents; a society which gives its members the greatest possible amount of individual liberty, but at the same time provides them with the most satisfying incentives to altruistic effort; a society not static but deliberately progressive, consciously tending towards the realization of the highest human aspirations. Science must be made a means for the creation of such a society, but only on certain conditions: that the powers which science offers must be used by rulers who are fundamentally humanist. (BW: 107)

Aldous Huxley says that the present crisis is due to instability in economy, which is because of the commercial attitudinal rule that eventually wants to turn the world into a big supermarket there by devastating the just tastes and wants of the people around the world. He says that mechanisation stands for mass production and mass production leas to preparation of a very wide market with a great number of people with flexible needs and tastes. He says that stability and uniformity are the pre-requisites for any rational plan for improving the quality of civilization. The aim of such destructive economists would be for mass-producers and mass-consumers. Huxley says that this is dangerous and so once stability is achieved in economy, scientific research should not be encouraged because nothing is more dangerous than too much of knowledge.

He says, "So long as scientific research goes on, society stands poised above a potential succession of earthquakes. Any day some new discovery may make all existing equipment obsolete, may revolutionize all existing technique, or else, by changing man's physiological habits, radically alter his whole way of thinking and feeling." (BW: 108)

He says that humanist rulers should not allow the application of some discovery, even though they are for some good purpose, for example the production of synthetic food. He says that one of the branches of science is the field of psychology which is going to be used to distract the attention of people around the world and to persuade the collective attitude of people towards something destructive. He says that such knowledge has already been applied very intelligently on the connection between the people's attitude and the problems of governments. Huxley talks of the possibilities of certain things which sound both remote and as predictions. When he talks of how science is going to influence and the condition of human beings in general, he says that the field of psychology is going to be misused on man as to condition him according to governments in future. He remembers Sigmund Fraud's discovery that the events in the first three months of a new born child decide how the child's personality is going to be as an adult and that the governments in future will invent an idea to implement this sort of mutations in the collective attitude and personality of the population on this earth and decide how should they react to whatever the governments decide and take actions against anything. Aldous says:

> They may, actually, succeed in creating a great world-wide community united by common beliefs and aspirations, common wants, tastes and thoughts. It will be a Holy Roman Empire minus the holiness, a Christendom, but without the Christianity – or if nominally Christian, Christian in a way that neither the primitive convert, nor the mediaeval Catholic, nor the later Protestant would recognise as Christian. It will be the kingdom of industry and the machine. (BW: 111)

This is the reason why Huxley is against scientific propaganda and he says that the idea of a humanist will just be incompatible with a small or large group of people who have the tendency to thraldom, war and bloodshed. He says, "Now personal liberty is, for the humanist, something of the highest value. He believes that, on the whole, it is better to 'go wrong in freedom than to go right in chains' – even if the chains are imponderable, even if they are not felt by the prisoner to be chains." (BW: 111) He says that the field of applied bio-chemistry, pharmacology and drugs can be used in order to change man's character, temperament and intelligence as to be suitable to the governments. He says:

> I will add a few more words by way of summary and epilogue. Science in itself is morally neutral; it becomes good or evil according as it is applied. Ideally, science should be applied by humanists. In this case it would be good. In actual fact, it is more likely to be applied by economists, and so to turn out, if not wholly bad, at any rate a very mixed blessing. It rests with us and our descendants to decide whether we shall use the unprecedented power which science gives us for good or for bad purposes. It is in our hands to choose wisely or unwisely. Alas, that wisdom should be so much harder to come by than knowledge! (BW: 114)

Huxley talks about the evil nature of swindling and corruption in a country. He says that when crime is lucrative, there is an inadequate punishment and the increase in the number of the criminals is rambunctious. When there is a combination of swindling and corruption in a country, it leads to the undue domination of those who are economically rich. Economic progress and democratic government on liberal principles lead to large-scale swindling and criminal corruption of politicians. Huxley says that economic progress, liberal government and corruption practices are unavoidably interconnected.

Huxley says that economic progress is possible only by those who are resourceful and inventive. Such people are interested in creating something that could bring in a change to the society and they are flexible to embrace any change and this group comprises of only a minority in the world. The majority of the people of the world does not welcome change. Change in any form is herculean and excruciating to them and they worship sentiments, but not logic, being fanatical about believing in metaphysical absolutes. The first group of people are driven by the spirit of leading, while the second group is dominated by mere sentiments. Huxley says that the second category of people stand for stability, aggressiveness and the timeliness of an action directed by rash faith in an absolute.

The frailty of this group of people is its inability to adopt to any new change or condition and its attitude towards economic and mental stagnation, unlike the first group of people. Huxley says, "Thus, the strength of a society dominated by men with a pronounced 'persistence of aggregates' likes in its stability and in the violence and the promptitude of the actions dictated by unquestioning faith in an absolute. Its weaknesses are its inability to adapt itself to new conditions and its tendency to economic and mental stagnation." (BW: 143) Huxley glorifies this group of people stating that these men were responsible for the economic growth of the last two centuries, which has necessitated their becoming of the parts of the ruling class. He says that the strength of faith is so intense in the people, who belong to the group of 'persistence of aggregates' and the danger is that men will be rash about enforcing conformity through violence, where there is a strong faith. Huxley says that the noble blood of a martyr is the fertile seed of the Church and the blood of a nonconformist is unavoidable. Huxley says:

> Now, where the 'persistence of aggregates' is strong, faith is strong; and where faith is strong, men have no hesitation in using violence to enforce conformity to their will. The blood of the martyrs is the seed of the Church; the blood of the heretics is its inevitable fruit. Absolutism in government is correlated with absolutism in philosophy and religion; both are the products of faith, of the persistence of aggregates of sentiments. (BW: 144)

Huxley says that there are strength and weakness in both the group, but the undesirable weakness about being manipulated, using the spirit for loyalty and emotional nature is very much with the second group. Huxley says that fascists and communists encourage 'persistence of aggregates' against the mental freedom of the people of this category. Huxley's humane concern is revealed here, when he talks of the two groups of people in the society. He glorifies, but does not condemn the other, because he is sympathetic towards their weakness to be misused for by the selfishness and pride of the powerful people in the world and so he alerts the group.

Huxley points out the fact that man has a well-cherished pride that he is civilized and has developed his intellectual faculties to that extent that there is nothing to be included or developed hereafter, but unfortunately, the modern man is out of the healthy order and discipline. He does not know what is right and wrong and indulges in the capricious process of pleasure-seeking, which ultimately has made him blind on quality, virtues and true strengths in life. Huxley makes a clear-cut distinction between the barbarians and the modern people, quoting the philosopher, Thomas Hobbes, stating that the life of a savages is very untidy and deplorably nasty. Their life involves brutal activities like hunting and they don't have longevity. The civilized people are clean, speak very well and they are blessed with a good and satisfactory life span. Huxley says that the price which the civilized people have given for being not savages is heavy. It is only civilization which has produced powerful and deadly weapons of mass destruction, the deadly cancer, the pitiable slums and newspapers. Huxley writes:

> The English philosopher, Thomas Hobbes, was doubtless right; the life of savages is "nasty, solitary, brutish, and short." But the life of civilized men --- however hygienic, relatively speaking, and long --- is not all beer and skittles. Fate makes no free gifts; it sells, for a price. The price is heavy. Machine guns, cancer, sums, the penny newspaper --- these are a few items of the tribute we pay to fate for the privilege of not being savages. It would be easy to lengthen the list. In this place, however, I shall confine myself to a description of one of the minor horrors of civilisation --- but a minor horror which, if it were not, providentially, escapable, would certainly deserve to be styled a major drawback to civilised life. I refer to what is called polite society. (AHCE: 388)

Huxley says that the leisured society must be avoided, since it has nothing to do with anything really constructive. This society is of two parts and the essence or the by-products of the activities of both the parts are just the same. Huxley says that both the divisions of this society cannot tolerate the easy and simple existence, which is a vacuum for them that they try to fill with useless activities. The means by which these two groups attain this futility is different. The first group of people are simple, children-like, very happy and unspoilt barbarians. They involve in courting, paring, separating, repairing, nest-making, bird-watching and games. The second group of people are into many activities in the name of being readers, intellectuals, and aesthetic people. Huxley says:

> So much for good society of the lower browed variety. What now of the highbrow rich, the aristocratic intellectuals, the leisured patrons of the arts? What of these? They ought, of course, by definition to be superior to the lowbrows. Experience, alas, gives the lie to a priori definitions. I am inclined to think that, on the whole, the highbrows are almost worse than the lows. Those who sin after having seen the light and eaten of the tree of knowledge are more blameworthy than those who sin in pre-Adamite innocence and darkness. (AHCE: 389)

Huxley justifies why the second group has to be punished. He says that the Adam, who has committed a sin after eating the fruit of knowledge is more punishable than the Adam, who committed a sin in all his divine innocence. Being intellectuals is severely misunderstood by the second group, Huxley says that and all that they do, in the name of intellectual activities, is only displaying how much they know about how many things. Huxley talks of the salon spectacles of the respective groups. The first group comes to their salon for public house party and drawing room visits and the second group comes to their salon to meet interesting people and talk. Huxley says that they talk of the latest pictures, scandals, pornographies, eccentricities, the latest books, modes, music, religions, psychologies of love, theories of science and philosophy. Huxley severely attacks these activities and calls them futile. He says that these activities are very agreeable and diverting, but it is a very deeply shocking and unthinkably horrible, if it is taken really seriously.

Huxley is angry on this particular group because he says that art is only another killer of time like playing any game or any romantic flirtation to the people of this group. Religion, for them, is something to be talked about over tea or coffee. They consider religion to be an entertaining subject and not so amusing like scandals. Huxley says that they degrade all important and significant ideas and they have turned all values upside down. They value intellectually talking men and ideas very high, nor for their inbuilt merits, but because of their projected merits which are highly fashionable for them. Huxley is very sorry that literature is just a game of elegance for them and have distanced the true merits of getting associated with the soul of literature. He says:

> In highbrow salons, on the other hand, you must talk --- of the latest pictures, the latest scandals, pornographies, and eccentricities, the latest books, the latest modes; the latest music, the latest religions, the latest psychologies of love, the latest theories of science and philosophy. And it is all, no doubt, very agreeable and diverting; but oh, if you happen to take anything at all seriously, how profoundly shocking and horrible! For to these polished beings, art is only another time killer, like bridge and flirtation; religion is something to be lightly chatted about over the tea and muffins --- an amusing subject, but not, of course, so entertaining as a juicy piece of scandal. All fine and important things are degraded; all values are overturned. Men and ideas are prized in this polite society, not for their intrinsic merit, but because they happen, for one reason or another, to be fashionable. Literature is turned into a sort of elegant game,

in which it is the object of the players to score points of 'style' and 'form' --- as though form and style possessed and real existence apart from substance. (AHCE: 389-390)

Huxley talks of the methods by which the world can be improved and comes out with interesting suggestions to ameliorate the life on this planet. He says that the world that the people are living in is man-made and there are only a few in the world, which cannot be created by man. He begins with nurturing the body and talks of the importance of nutritious food for all and says that man is doing so many things, which are highly destructive to his body and does not take care of it, due to his following of stupid customs and other social impositions. Huxley says, "Take, for example, the all-important matter of diet. A science of nutrition exists, but are its precepts followed? They are not. Half the population is too poor to be able to feed itself properly. (The remedy for this is in the hands of the economic planners.) The other half possesses the means, but neglects the available knowledge and eats either excessively or mistakenly." (BW: 221) It reflects that modern man is either excessive or improper in almost everything that he deals with and the implied meaning is that he is away from even the basic discipline and responsibilities.

Huxley says that the newspaper has a considerable space for the advertisement for laxatives, cold-cures, pain killers and ick-me-ups. It is because of not being careful about taking nutritious food and paying enough attention and care to one's body in general. All these are very harmful drugs and the need for the usages of these drugs originates from the modern man's ignorance about the importance about his body, as a result, the body invites many ailments. Man poisons his body with wrong foods and then needs painkillers to reduce the pain he cannot tolerate. Huxley says that man poisons his body and then in the name of mitigating the pains the poison causes, he further pollutes his body with those painkillers.

Then he complains that life is not worth living and consequently starts blaming the government of his country. He says, "We poison ourselves with the wrong food, then try to mitigate the painful consequences of our folly by poisoning ourselves still further with drugs. After which we wonder why it is that life should seem so little worth living and proceed to blame the Government." (BW: 221) Huxley says that there are factories manufacturing these drugs with efficient machines and with the help of intelligent scientists, but the purpose of these drugs is to temporarily fight the pain and reduce the effect of the other poisons with a less poisonous substance at a cheap rate. Huxley is against pains and inflicting pains on anyone and so he talks about preventing this painful state before they occur so that there would be no necessity for such factories to produce harmful drugs, which depends on man's carefulness towards his body and physical well-bring.

The next idea that Huxley suggests to improve the world is to eradicate the deadly habit of taking intoxicants, stimulants and sedatives. He says that the actual reason behind this particular problem is psychological. Man needs occasional holiday or break to escape the hard realities of life. It is a tragedy that the people of the world spends the ten percent of their total income on intoxicating, stimulating and sedative materials. Huxley says that the habit of taking tea and tobacco also is out of the need to escape the reality or boredom. He says:

> A problem closely allied to that of analgesics, and no less important to us as suffering and enjoying beings, is the problem of intoxicants, stimulants and sedatives. Everywhere and at all times men have felt the need of taking an occasional holiday from the common round of every-day affairs – a holiday from the world and should guess that, at the present time, the inhabitants of our planet spend nearly ten percent of their total income on intoxicants, stimulants and sedatives. Some of these – tea, for example, and are exceedingly powerful drugs. But the purpose served by all of them is the same; people take them in order to escape from the boring or unpleasant reality of their own

characters and the surrounding world. (BW: 225)

Huxley says that man has to adapt to the surroundings and must lead a happy life so that the need for escaping realities and boredom will start diminishing. Life has to be improved in such a way that it becomes very interesting and truly valuable, which will be a real cure for the weakness to think of slipping into an unreal world of dirty and harmful pleasures. Huxley says, "If we can arrange our world in such a way that people's lives will seem to them worth living, there will be a smaller demand for pick-me-up and stupefacients, for booze and dope." (BW: 225) Huxley says that the children must be taught the skills or art of concentrating on something so as to delve deep into anything to explore many things and such intensity of concentration itself is a powerful tool that can be used both for doing a work efficiently and for the personal benefit of constructively diverting one's attention from something boring or disturbing, the practice of which will present the children from following the psychological means to escape anything painful, which is not an art, but a mere distractions that does not enable the children to cure their shortcomings. Huxley says that the advanced areas of science must not be used to nourish the irresponsibility. He says:

> We teach our children none of the techniques of mental concentration and meditation, by means of which it is possible for the individual to escape, by purely psychological means, from the distractions of ordinary life, to forget for a moment an even permanently to transcend the shortcomings of his character. And at the same time we permit irresponsible individuals to use all the resources of applied science in order to tell us lies and to fill our minds with ideas which are either ignoble or idiotic. (BW: 226)

Huxley points out the dreadful effects of watching movies and popular press to escape boredom. He says that seeking these means takes the watchers to a world of fantasy distanced from reality, truth, good sense and human values. Huxley says that these means that take people far away from truth is like the political propaganda used by rich men in a democratic country for their financial benefits and the dictators doing the same with people's mind, creating anarchy. Huxley says that the media of a country has to be honest to publish only what is true about anything, which is the basic need for the true improvement of the world. He strictly says that the popular literature of the world has to be useful to the people like the electric power and transport.

There should be a corporation to monitor the desirability of the content to be given to the people, which includes the comments of the writers on political parties also. News must be bought by the corporation for the monitory benefit of the fetchers so that their dependence on advertisement for their money can be eliminated. The officially appointed editors will be meticulous and careful about ignoring anything worthless and harmful for the public and improper material from getting published. With all these precautious purification of news in general is very much possible with which false propaganda can be curbed. Huxley says that this is the only effective measure to protect the common people from the purposefully enforced vulgarity, which would lay a strong foundation for the birth of the much-awaited improvements of the world.

Huxley says that the people must follow the socio-political norms, which is not possible if they do not have a strong personal morality and a sense of commitment and responsibility. The simple example would be to follow the traffic rules strictly and obey other similar public behaviour. Huxley says that the combination of wanting for something novel but preferring only the old ways of doing it is not only self-contradictive but also highly self-destructive. Huxley comes out with the example of driving a car not on road but on the pedestrians, causing innumerable casualties every year, which is equal to a war. He says that following these ideas shall be fundamentally enough to construct a stable and healthy international society.

Aldous Huxley was not only a man of a very sharp intellect, but also of a clear vision. He sensed that rapid industrialization and massive urbanization are going to change man's lifestyle. He comes out with a prediction that the working hours will be reduced to six hours per day, providing a fertile chance for leisure, in the future. Meditating on his contemporary scenario, Huxley is deeply worried about how the leisurely hours are going to be properly utilized by the people. At present, leisure is a privilege for very few people. But in the coming days, with efficient social organization and sophisticated machinery, more and more people will enjoy the fruits of leisure. He cites three authorities namely, Poincare, G. B. Shaw and H. G. Wells, who have concluded that the human beings of the future world would fill their long leisures 'by contemplating the laws of nature'. Different prophets are also hopeful about the proper utilization of leisurely hours. Huxley says:

> Prophets of the future give fundamentally the same answer to this question, with slight variations according to their different tastes. Henri Poincare, for example, imagined that the human beings of the future would fill their long leisures by "contemplating the laws of Nature." Mr. Bernard Shaw is of much the same opinion. Having creased, by the time they are four years old, to take any interest in such childish things as love, art, and the society of their fellow beings, the Ancients in Back to Methuselah devote their indefinitely prolonged existences to meditating on the mysterious and miraculous beauty of the cosmos, Mr. H.G Wells portrays in Men Like Gods a race of athletic chemists and mathematical physicists who go about naked and unlike Mr. Shaw's austerer Ancients, make free love in a rational manner between the experiments. They also take an interest in the arts and are not above   playing games. (AHCE: 411)

But considering the contemporary social scenario and the attitude of the people, Huxley feels disturbed and acutely sorry for the misuse of leisure. James Boswell in his *The Life of Samuel Johnson*, quotes Samuel Johnson, "All intellectual improvement arises from leisure." (219) Huxley talks about the possible ways of the utilization of leisure by the rich and poor. Most of the rich people's preference, Huxley says, is Monte Carlo and Nice, the places notorious for gambling and prostitutes. Huxley calls these places ironically as "an earthly paradise". He says that there are exceptions of those who seek love and an interesting sort of game with them. Some of the people prefer to be engaged with works of charity, politics, local administration and occasionally with scholarly or scientific studies. But, it is disgustingly disturbing and morally unacceptable to Huxley that the majority of the population is inclined to Monte Carlo. This concept of leisure of the rich people is not at all encouraging or confidence-giving for the orderly, disciplined and qualitative fabrics of the future international society.

Huxley is not confident that the way the poor people are going to utilise their leisure times productively. Since the people do not have lofty associations and meanings with leisure times in general, they tend to choose activities which are mere killers of times, which is going to retain them in the pathetic conditions, which they already are in. He says that the idea of the poor people on leisure is restricted to looking at cinema, films, reading newspapers, cheap literature, listening to radio, gramophone records, and going from place to place. It is quite unthinkable to Huxley, when he thinks of the possibilities for having prolonged leisure times. He predicts that there would be an enormous increase in amorous lifestyle and time killing. Huxley says:

> If tomorrow or couple of generations, hence, it was made possible for all human beings to lead the life of leisure which is now led only by a few, the results, so far as I can see, would be as follows: There would be an enormous increase in the demand for such time-killers and substitutes for thought as newspapers, films, fiction, cheap means of communication, and wireless telephones; to put it in more general terms, there would be an increase in the demand for sport and art. The interest in the fine art

of love-making whole be widely extended. And enormous numbers of people, hitherto immune from these mental and moral diseases, would be afflicted by ennui, depression, and universal dissatisfaction. (AHCE: 414)

Huxley is sure that the majority shall devote their leisure to occupations which are utterly stupid, fruitless and even disgusting. He says that there are philosophers, thinkers, educationalists and social reformers who are angry that leisure times are only for those who have nothing to do with lofty thoughts and productive deeds. People who are very intelligent, knowledgeable and try to make their life more meaningful and rich, prefer no any sort of cheap entertainment. It would be incorrect to assume that Huxley is against the idea of leisure. He refers to Leo Tolstoy, the great Russian writer, who considered leisure as something 'wicked' and 'absurd'. He thought of leisure lovers as conspirators against the welfare of one's race.

Huxley doesn't consider leisure as a curse. He thinks that in a society where there are intelligent and active minds engaged in mental work, leisure would be 'an unmixed blessing'. Since leisure is apparently connected to mental work, some people may pinpoint the loopholes of educational system and Huxley agrees with them. His observation is that plenty of people who have received the best education, employ their leisure as though they had never been educated at all. Therefore, Huxley believes that if education is made really efficient, contemplating the laws of nature would become the leisure of people.

Aldous Huxley dreams of a world free of all the existing problems of both inside and outside man. Huxley does not an extremist like Tolstoy, when it comes to the idea of leisure. He doesn't impose an outright rejection on the idea of leisure to embrace the concept of work. Huxley's writing style is the evidence that he pays enough respect to Tolstoy, when he refutes his idea of leisure. This evidently reveals Huxley as not only as a man of intellect, but also a humanistic thinker loaded with many constructive instructions, ideas and pieces of advice to the people of the world to bring in the most wanted changes in them for the betterment of the world peace and the joy of living. Huxley presents his intense observation, critical opinions and benevolent prescriptions for the entire humanity very convincingly on the canvas of this idea. Huxley's writing style itself, in general, is the indication that he does not want to hurt anyone, since he writes very humorously, when he actually attacks or expresses his moral anger and the tone is so light that any reader can observe that he comes out with sugar-coated expressions for presenting anything bitter and indigestible.

3.2 The ethical views of Aldous Huxley

Huxley talks about how pleasure-giving it is to collect so much about everything and keep in one's mind to stay updated with all the walks of life in the world and the pleasure of being respected by others, and at the same time, he talks of the pains and unnecessary spirit to stay well aware of the contemporary activities of all the fields. He remembers how passionate he was in being up-to-date with the contemporary literature and other fields, just because the societal expectation that educated and intellectual people must be up-to-date with everything. He says, "Yes, the pleasures of being up-to-date are certainly great. But, then, so are the pleasures of not being up-to-date." (AHCE: 373) Huxley makes a confession that he never was happy and comfortable about whatever he read and did with an intention of being up-to-date.

Huxley says that the people who are into this tedious task of being well-informed of many contemporary things and happenings would think poorly of him for his preference and that the reason why he has chosen the state of not being up-to-date is that he prefers to be himself rather than being fashionable. Huxley says that he has stopped caring for the comments and opinions of others on him, which led to this liberated state. He says:

> These people, it is true, still exist, and will certainly think of the more poorly of me for not being up-to-date, and for admitting the fact. The reason why I feel that I can afford to be out-of-

date is this: I have ceased to care two pins what these people --- the intellectually smart, the leaders or follow-my-leaders of metal fashion --- think of me, or indeed of anything else under the sun. To find it more agreeable to be, not fashionable, but myself." (AHCE: 374)

Huxley says that he remembers with the depth of his aloneness how foolish he was in wasting his time to be up-to-date, because he yearned for the appreciation of others in staying fashionable. Huxley says that he remembers reading the book Ulysses, attended many theatres for drams and went to many music concerts, which he deeply regrets because he thinks that he wasted an uncountable valuable hours spent on them. He says:

When, from the depths of my calm solitude, I reflect on the many extraordinarily foolish and time-wasting things I have done for the sake of being up-to-date and earning the approval of the fashionable, I shudder and am amazed that I could ever have been so idiotic. Thus, I remember spending at least seventy-two precious now irremediably perished hours in reading Mr. James Joyce's Ulysses. I remember passing hundreds of evenings at the first nights of the most boring plays (though it is true I was paid for doing so). I remember listening to the whole concerts of music by Mr.Gustav Holst. I remember passing whole afternoons among the landscapes of K.Marchand and his English followers. And for what? To whom is the benefit, as we used to ask in Latin? Merely that I might be able to say that I had read the portentous and boring book, heard the dim music, seen the plays, and thrilled aesthetically before the significance of those painted forms. (AHCE: 374-375)

Huxley says that he is as happy as when he was fashionable now even without that socially supreme status of being up-to-date. He says that he is no more interested in what the intelligentsia of the world has thought about, written or spoken recently and that the distance between himself and the contemporary civilization is the inexhaustible source of serenity, peace and areal happiness in his life. He says, "But now, I find that it really does not matter in that least what the mentally smart think. I find that I am quite happy in out-of-dateness; what is more, I find that I don't miss much. The distance at which I live from contemporary civilization acts, as it were, as a filter." (AHCE: 375)

Huxley talks about the necessity of extricating from the claws of the socially imposed importance of knowing the novelties, which gifts one's leisure and calmness with rich material to meditate on for personal enrichment. Real work starts only after leaving this societal expectation and anxiety that one has to be accepted by those who are truly regarded to be great intellectually. Such a liberation leaves a person at the freedom to think, talk to the people one truly loves and read the books that were in the list to be read, when there is sufficient time. Huxley says that these activities are the principal joys and advantages of not being up-to-date. He says:

> To be free from the socially imposed necessity of knowing about novelties is to endow oneself with leisure and calm. It enables one to work; it leaves one at liberty to think --- a process which, like almost everyone else, I used to detest, preferring to occupy my mind with the various substitutes for thought, from newspapers to the Freudian interpretation of dreams, which modern civilization provides in ever-increasing quantities for the relief of mind-haunted humanity. It leaves one at liberty, I repeat, to think (and once one is used to it, the activity is really quite agreeable); it gives one time and inclination to talk with the few people one likes, about interesting things; and excuses one from having to talk with the causally met many, about the things which one finds boring. It creates the

leisure to read the books one always meant and wanted, but never had the time, to read, owing to the press of new noels, plays, and the like, a knowledge of which is essential, if one is to sustain a conversation is polite and intellectual smart society. These are the principal joy and advantages of not being up-to-date; and very considerable I find them. (AHCE: 375)

Huxley is not happy about the models offered by the world of intellect and so he comes forward courageously as to inform the world that people must know what to do to lead a healthy life, mentally, emotionally and intellectually. They should not take wrong models and expectations from the society that they deem to be superior to them. He announces to the world that original thinking is more important than trying to keep many unwanted information just because the world of fashionable society exposes it to be superior and distinct. Huxley, being a humanist and an intellectual, aims at bringing clarity to the people on the unnecessary weight that they carry pleasurably, without which they shall lead a fee and comfortable life.

Huxley wants to talk to the people of the world about the mentality to taste pleasures in the modern times. He says that the world has seen many dangers to the civilization. The first to be encountered was the militarism of Prussia and then the German military moves and the two famous wars that took place quite unexpectedly for a very long time. Huxley includes the French militarism. He says:

WE HAVE HEARD a great deal, since 1914, about the things which are a menace to civilization. First it was Prussian militarism; then the Germans at large; then the prolongation of the war; then the shortening of the same; then, after a time, the Treaty of Versailles; then French militarism – with, all the while, a running accompaniment of such minor menaces as Prohibition, Lord Northcliffe, Mr.Bryan, Comstockery. (AHCE: 354)

Huxley says that the world civilization was strong enough to withstand the menacing combined attacks of all these enemies admirably well. He says that the dangers that confronts our civilization at present are not the external dangers like men driven by devastating anger, horrible impending war, and the potential possibility of becoming impecunious that wars inflict on the people of the world, leaving them to become uncivilized as to cruelly fight among themselves for mere survival. The most devastative dangers that keep the worthy lives of the people of world under a horrendous state are the dangers that dwell within man. They are the potential threat for the courageous mind of human beings. He says, "No the dangers which confront our civilization are not so much the eternal dangers --- wild men, wars, and the bankruptcy that wars bring after them. The most alarming dangers are those which menace it from within, that threaten the mind rather than the body and estate of contemporary man." (AHCE: 324-355)

Huxley here indirectly teaches the people of the world that it is not the body or the tangible asserts that one amasses which are the most important in life, but the mind, affecting of which, is affecting the vey life of the person concerned. This indirect message is not only philosophical but also spiritual that talks of the most prominent truth about life itself, because modern people are misguided that happiness lies in earning money and leading an incomparably lavish and rich practical life.

Huxley says that pleasure is the most dangerous poison by a process of auto-intoxication that the modern civilization brews within its own bowels. Here Huxley does not talk about all kinds of pleasure, but the intentionally organized pleasure in order to distract the people of the world to execute the command of the top-level government officials and rulers. The organized criminal offence of making people believe that real personal and social pleasures lie only in doing a particular activity, associated with a particular organization and not in any other. The typical example is that the attitude of the people that being a government officer and working very hard for hours together are considered a superior status and a supreme pleasure when compared with being very creative about writing on something interesting to let out one's passion for intellectual freedom, tasting the unique feel of being an author and a critic and feeling a range of freedom that the majority has nothing to do with. He says:

> Of all the various poisons which modern civilization, by a process of auto intoxication, brews quietly up within its own bowels, few, it seems to me, are more deadly (while none appears more harmless) than that curious and appalling thing that is technically known as "pleasure". "Pleasure" (I place the world between inverted commas to show that I mean, not real pleasure, but the organized activities officially known by the same name) "pleasure" --- what nightmare visions the word evokes! Like every man of sense and good feeling, I abominate work. But I would rather put in eight hours a day at a Government office than be condemned to lead a life of "pleasure"; I would even, I believe, prefer to write a million words of journalism a year. (AHCE: 355)

Aldous Huxley says that the man of the past was more logical and courageous than the present man. Their conclusions and decisions through the method of arguments and meditations can be said to be idiotic, but their capacity to be determined about taking a decision or to act in a way as they thought of were stronger than how a modern man makes decisions about something in his life. They believed in their flawless arguments and the cause for which they had to take certain decision, which were well-executed, thanks to their decisive personality. Huxley talks of Wesley, who believed in witchcraft, because he believed in the Bible that talks of witchcraft. So, it is believed that witchcraft is true, based on the statement or belief that the Bible is true. Losing belief in witchcraft is losing faith in the Bible. Huxley sys:

> Our fathers were more logical than we, and more courageous. The conclusions to which their

arguments led them might be manifestly idiotic or immoral; but that did not prevent them, once they were convinced that the premises were sound and the argument flawless, from drawing those conclusions and, if necessary, acting on them. starting from the premises that everything in the Bible is literally true, Wesley was necessarily led to believe in witchcraft. The Bible is true; witchcraft is mentioned in the Bible as existing; therefore, witchcraft exists. The argument is unimpeachable. In the century of Hume and Voltaire, Wesley believed in witches. If you abandon belief in witchcraft, he insisted, you abandon belief in the Bible. He was logical and had the courage of his opinions. (AHCE: 394-395)

Huxley says that he does not agree with the logic or argument of Wesley, but he appreciates the courage to do it and his intellectual honesty. Unlike, the man of the past, the modern man is afraid to take any decision and the reasons, logic and the ideas for the construction of the intentions behind taking a decision do not have any strong impact on his mind and so he is doubtful about the trustworthiness and the possibility of getting success out of following them. Modern man commits the basic mistake of being with so much of compromise, but with too little logical consistency. Huxley's humanistic voice here is on the indecisive nature of the modern man, which is fundamentally self-destructive. He says:

I do not happen to agree with Wesley; but I admire his spirit and his intellectual honesty. There is too much compromise, nowadays and too little logical consistency. We are afraid of drawing the logical conclusions from the premises in which we profess to believe. We do not like to make any very definite or sweeping assertion for fear that by so doing we might be making fools of ourselves. The manifest contradictions which exist between different

sections of our beliefs, between our beliefs and
our actions, we vaguely harmonize, if we try to
harmonize them at all, in some dim Higher
Synthesis, where black is the same as white,
good as evil and nonsense as sense. (AHCE:
395)

Huxley talks against the famous socio-political ideology
or statement that all men are equal in democracy and he says that
this is true only in mystic sense and not in any political or social
sense. Men are all equal in being the children of God and in the
capacity to suffer, love and distinguish good from evil. Men are
equal only in those capacities, but not in their capacity to fight to
govern others or themselves. Huxley says that to believe that all
are equal is the fundamental idiotic mistake of democracy and
people are made believe through such cunning propagations for
the political and economic benefits of rulers, aristocrats and
other powerful people of a democratic country. Huxley says:

Democracy is based on assuming that all men are
equal. Now that assumption is true, but only in a
mystical sense. Men are equal as being all the
children of God – as being all endowed with a
capacity for suffering, loving, and knowing good
and evil. They are not equal in any of those
abilities which make men fit to govern themselves
or others. The mistake of the democrats has been
to suppose that men are equal in every way and
to base practical politics on this gratuitous and
false assumption. (AHCE: 397)

Huxley says that the idea that all are equal in democracy
is not something unimportant and glorifies the true significance
of having such a statement that has a huge impact in the minds of
all citizens of all democratic countries, in spite of having no tangible
evidence to support that statement practically. He says that
equality in democracy, the cradle of the idea of
'humanitarianism', is the concept that deeply modified the
society. Huxley says that the defenders of humanitarianism are
the supporters of the belief that all are equal in democracy. Even
the rich people in a democratic society admit that even the poor

people of the society have the same rights and freedom and serve the poor considerably either directly or indirectly. Huxley's humanitarianism is predominantly exposed here, when he talks of the merits of humanitarianism, which has a very strong connection with the benevolent belief that all are equal in democracy. Even though he talks of the lack of humanitarianism in the world, he does not fail to admit the bright side of the belief. He says:

> It must not be supposed that, simply because the idea of the equality of man is mystical, it is therefore unimportant. On the contrary, it is one of the highest significance. It is an idea which has already profoundly modified future. Humanitarianism is the expression of that idea. We are all humanitarians now, whatever our political opinions and whatever our social position. Even those who are in possession of wealth and power admit that those who possess nothing have certain rights. They are perpetually giving away little bits of their wealth and power to be dispossessed. (AHCE: 397)

Huxley wants to compare the productive impacts of the belief that all are equal in democracy and the destructive consequences of the lack of such an impact under the rule of a tyrant. Unlike the people, who have the freedom and possibilities of getting their basic needs, at least, in a democratic country, in a tyrannical country, people are handicapped by poverty, regrettable conditions and insufficient education that lead them not towards the higher pursuits of life, due to its absence. Huxley says that the paupers and sufferers of a country due to its indifference to equality must be helped by humanitarianism and be enriched so that their life will be improved, giving an unshakable hope for such people to get out the wretched condition for a healthy and comfortable life. Huxley says:

> In tyrannical society, where humanitarian principles are not recognized, nine-tenths of the individuals composing that society are so unfairly handicapped by poverty, bad

conditions, and inadequacy of education that they are not in a position to compete for any of the higher prizes of life. By ameliorating the lot of the dispossessed, humanitarianism removes this handicap, and thus, by multiplying the competitors, tends to create an intenser and therefore biologically more stimulating competition. (AHCE: 398)

Huxley motivates that there must be a sense of competition among the people of a country so that all will strive to become well in life, exhibiting their special capacity and talents so that the country shall have the bright chance of having many able people for the most important governmental activities, which is the actual political justification of humanitarianism. Huxley says that such a spirit for competition eventually increases the number of efficient people for the leadership of a country. He says, "Humanitarianism, then, has a biological function --- to render possible an intenser competition within society. When all men are free to compete and all start equal, the chance of getting able men at the head of affairs is obviously increased. That is the political justification of humanitarianism. Society should be run on humanitarian principles because an increase in the number of competitors increase the chances of efficient leadership." (AHCE: 398) Huxley says that human beings must be changed to bring in humanitarianism to the society and the world ultimately. With the collective change, through a healthy competitive spirit to be highly productive and contributing to the society, the long-awaited glorious societal change can be achieved.

3.3 The educational views of Aldous Huxley

The concept of education of Aldous Huxley is based on the understanding of the inter-connection among knowledge, rationality and human psychology. Huxley says that rational thought is still not possible without knowledge and that human beings know very little about psychology, heredity and the relationship between mind and body. Education is nothing but applied psychology and heredity and applied psychophysiology and says that because of these reasons, rational thinking in the field of education has been distanced. Being knowledgeable about the subject of biological inheritance and the relation between the mind and body is the proper way of meditating on the concept of education, since it is about observational capacity, associating skills in the process of learning and digesting ability to be confident about one's intense knowledge and understanding on a subject. It is not a wonder that Huxley has such a stupendous approach to the concept of education, because he is basically a university professor. Huxley says:

> Rational foresight is impossible without knowledge, and we still know relatively very little bout psychology, or heredity, or the relations of mind and body. By education is simply applied psychology, applied heredity and applied psychophysiology. It follows therefore that rational foresight is still, to a great extent, impossible in the sphere of education. (BW: 133)

Huxley says that every professor has to foresee the child's future development. A teacher or a professor has to observe so as to discover the latent talent of a child to be polished and then only, the activities and assignments related to the learning will not only be effortless but also passionate for the children. He says that a teacher should observe what is a child good at and probably what sort of place the child can occupy in the society in terms of power and efficiency and accordingly training has to be given to the particular child. Huxley says that this is the only strategy to make our educational system very effective. Huxley quotes Mr. J.B.S. Haldane to say that the combined efforts of the experts of the fields of psychology and genetics are necessary so that sorting out of the abilities and personalities of children is possible with which the real training or education is possible. He says:

> Thus, the most important thing that a Professor of Educational Foresight could do is to foresee the child's future development --- what he is likely to do well, what place he can take in the social scheme --- to foresee and to plan his training accordingly. It is only on condition of such foresight that our educational system can

become efficient. Mr. J.B.S. Haldane is of opinion that 'if psychologists are allowed anything like a free hand and co-operate with geneticists' the sorting out of children's abilities and potentialities should become possible 'in the course of the next century.' It is certainly not possible now. (BW: 133)

Huxley says that only a professor should suggest the most efficient system of intellectual and moral training, because there are too many systems in the educational field, but there is no concrete evidence to prove that a particular system is the most effective. So until a professor suggests, no exemplary system can be formulated. Huxley says that the only way to have such a system is to implement the method of formulating the style of giving training according to the necessity and capacity of every child and keep a record of them on the development of their learning capacities and other related abilities. The intellectual achievements, discipline and emotional development are to be watched throughout their lives. Huxley says that without such an intelligent system real intelligence cannot be produced and all that any professor of high efficiency and dedication can do is to be fanciful about the talent of children and be optimistic about their bright future like the parents.

Huxley recommends that a professors of foresight must look for any reference from the past prescriptions in the department of social organisation. The general Education Policy must depend on the attitude of the professors towards education and must be clear whether the future society is going to be communistic, is the government going to be decentralized or not and is the family system to be abolished or preserved. Huxley says that answering these questions are very important and that unless there is a plan for men and women, plans and dreams for children are not at all possible. Huxley says:

Professors of Foresight would be unable to make plans for education without previous reference to the plans of their colleagues in the department of social organization. Is the future society to be communist society or a 'distributive state' of

> small owners? Is government to be a centralised dictatorship or a federation of small local autonomies? Is the family to be preserved, or is it to be, as far as possible, abolished? Upon the answer to these and similar questions of general policy must depend the attitude of our Professors of Foresight towards education. You cannot make plans for children before you have made plans for men and women. (BW: 133)

Huxley comes to talk of the national and international problems, which are connected to the field of education. He says that professors must foresee the danger of war and they must think of reforming the teaching of history with an intention of minimizing the dangerous aspects of nationalist propaganda. Professors are asked to predict the dangers of superstition and the unscientific attitude and approach towards the subject of biology at school level, because it is difficult to have a scientific approach to what is so dear. Huxley also talks of the danger of leisure time and says that it must be used for improving the potentialities of children and that the professors of foresight must prepare the children for their significant leisure times also.

Huxley says that the modern man has become more aware of individuals than the ancient man. People have become conscious about the rights of other people with the rampant nature of humanism, which has very profound effect in the realm of family life. So, the modern man has become highly individualistic in thinking and approaches towards things in general and so he cannot embrace the traditional unquestioned beliefs. The divine associations with family is no more believable to the modern man. 'Scepticism', the offspring of 'individualism', is further strengthened by 'humanitarianism'. Modern people are not only concerned with their rights but also for their children's. They think of the rights of their children and think that they should not be compelled to do anything and they should not be tortured in the name of bringing them into a discipline.

The thought that has become evolutionary in the field of education is that the real purpose of education is to offer the guarantee to every child the feasibility of self-expression.

Parents, being rational about the children's rights, think of their rights and freedom also and so they do not want to bear the weight of their family responsibilities and want to live life for themselves. Parents, in their attempts to reduce their family responsibilities, reduce the size of their family and handover their children to professional experts to make them very talented professionals in the chosen fields. Huxley says:

> But it is not only the attitude of the parents towards their children that has changed; their attitude towards themselves is no longer the same as in the past. Self-consciously individualistic as well as humanitarianism, parents feel that they too have rights. They want to 'live their own lives', 'to express themselves', to have some other than a merely parental *raison d'etre*. In a word, they resent the weight of family responsibilities. Accordingly, they try to mitigate these responsibilities, first by reducing the size of their families and, secondly, by handling over such children as they do produce to professional educators. (BW: 48)

The pleasure and pride of the past family structure and the number of family members are no more in the present century. In the past, for many generations together, a vast family with many a member, lived under one roof. Huxley expresses his exercised state of mind that family, as a structure has become like a single oak tree from a multi-branched banyan tree, because of the increased concern of the modern parents on their children and on themselves also. There are other causes like economic condition and the aspiration to lead a rich and sophisticated life, which is not possible with many children. He says:

> The family has decreased in size. Increasing individuality and self-conscious rendered intolerable the old united family with its three or four generations living under the same roof. From being a banyan the family tree has long since become (at any rate in the West) an oak. Scattered at a distance from the parental stem

the acorns grow up into a separate existence. In the past these separate young trees were prolific; but recently the increase of self-conscious individuality has led, for the reasons   already given, to a reduction in the number of offspring. These psychological causes have been reinforced by economic causes – themselves, very often, of psychological origin. Thus families cannot be big because we must keep up the standard of living. (BW: 48)

Huxley says that the plan of the elders in reducing the size of the family for various reasons are actually against the wish of their children. No child is happy about being a only child of a family. Children have an inbuilt desire to be surrounded with other children and loving people. A big family has many advantages in child-rearing and it is the only prescription for the overall healthy psychological development of children. To be a part of a very big family itself gives the psychological impression that you are an inseparable part of the society, learning and mastering the art of being flexible to others. Children brought up in such a family atmosphere need not undergo any training on how to face the world, when they are out of their schools and colleges, since the very family plays the role of the rest of the world, producing confident, understanding, flexible and daring children. Aldous Huxley says that a only child is a highly crippled child in many ways and that even two children are not a better state, and having four or five members in a family is a very satisfactory state.

The implied comprehension must be that the majority of the families of the modern world is not satisfactory, which has necessitated the role of a professional educator. The professional educator creates an atmosphere, which is equal to that of the family's that makes the children feel as if they are of one family and ultimately they experience a psychological satisfaction. It is very shocking when Huxley says that there are people, who call themselves advanced in the modern world, unknowingly advocate the abolition of family system through suggesting that the professional educator shoulders the responsibilities of taking care of the children from their very infancy state. Huxley says that this view is a potential threat to the noble existence of the time-honoured natural instinct to be gregarious through sentiments and affectionate bonds. A society that is free of any sort of sentimental and affectionate relational bond, is bound to head towards a dangerous and self-devastating selfishness that eventually leads to destruct the rest also. Huxley says:

> Now, from the point of view of the children, small families are not much good. A big family is the world in miniature; to be brought up in a big family is a complete preparation for life. An only child is heavily handicapped. Two children are not very much better off. A family only begins to be really satisfactory when it can count at   least four or five members. From the children's point of view very few modern families are satisfactory. Hence the importance in modern life of the professional educator, who forms an artificial family, within which it is possible for children to find psychological satisfaction. 'Advanced' people propose that the family system should be abolished altogether and that the professional educator, paid by the state, should take control from earliest infancy. Indeed, this view threatens to become the orthodoxy of the modern democratic State. (BW: 48-49)

Huxley says that the insecurity of a state depends on the number of self-conscious individuals. He says that being humanistic is the only cure for this ailment of not caring for others intimately through the negation of their fundamental duties to the family, which shall protest against all sorts of establishments, including the society, government, country and freedom. Huxley says that human standardization is sure to become a political necessity. Huxley comes out with an optimistic note that family as an institution shall never be perished permanently, since it gives immense psychological contentment, but it is not to be denied that presently there is a potential peril, waiting to wipe off the family system from the society.

3.4 The political criticism of Aldous Huxley

Huxley is says that man cannot live without a government and leader. Only insects can be without any governing force from the outside world, since they are driven by a governing instinct, giving them no freedom of action. The people of a superior race also do not actually need any governing body for them to depend on what to do and how to do something and for other disciplines and order, because in any challenging situation, they tend to be virtuous and do anything that is appropriate and rational. Huxley says that people are of two types, the people of the first type look for a chance to place their responsibilities on others and the second type cannot take any lead in their life and so they always look for a leader to instruct them what to do so that they can obey the command and do the task either out of a sense of duty and dignity or at least either to satisfy the requirements of the leader or to get into the goods books of the person. Fortunately, there are other people who are waiting to shoulder the responsibilities of other people. Huxley says that the destiny of those who want others to bear their responsibility and those who want to shoulder others' responsibility are interconnected. Huxley says:

> Man, being what he is, we can see that tit is biologically impossible for him to do without governments and leaders. A society of locusts or lemmings can dispense with leasers, because each individual is internally governed by instincts which allow him no freedom of action; at any given moment, there is only one thing he can do. A race of superior beings, like Milton's angels, for example, could equally dispense with leaders; they could be trusted in any crisis to do the virtuous and the rational thing. Men fall between two stools. Most of us are only too happy to shift the greater part of our responsibilities to other shoulders; we like to be told what to do, which way to go. (AHCE: 364)

Aldous Huxley says that it is only ambition that makes a person a leader and says that it is not enough if a person is driven by ambition because it is the striving to achieve the position of a leader that matters ultimately. All are driven by the lust for power, but not all persons have the intensity of the force to achieve their ambition. Huxley says that the lust for domination and power of an artist leads him not to dominate other men, but to deal with words, colours, bits of stones and the world of his own thoughts. The spirit of domination of a philosopher ends with dominating the entire universe conceptually. A philosopher chops and stretches the dirty facts of experience with a truly procrustean love for tidiness and order so as to fit his system. Huxley sys that everyone is driven by the desire to dominate their neighbours and when the thought is not diminished by any other thought and grows wilder and wilder, the reaching of the position of a leader is possible. He says:

> To begin with, there must be an ambition to become a leader. All of us, I imagine, have a certain lust for power. But the desire varies greatly in the intensity, and the objects over which it is desired to exert power are not always the same. An artist, for example, lusts for domination, not over his fellow men, but over words, over colours, over bits of stone; above all, over his own thoughts. The philosopher, more ambitious, longs to tyrannize over the whole universe. With a truly Procrustean love for neatness and symmetry, he chops and stretches the untidy facts of experience until they fit his favourite system. But philosophers and artists, after all, are rare monsters. The power most people desire is over their neighbours. When that desire is very strong – so strong that it does not shrink before any expense of labour or of thought --- the man who feels it may be said to be ambitious to become a leader. (AHCE: 365)

Huxley says that a true leader has animal magnetism in terms of expressing one's mind. This animal magnetism is a very compatible and friendly charm for the population of the world. The people are enchanted with the formidable magnetism and it truly inspires people and make them become confident, and it commands natural obedience on the part of the listeners and onlookers. What is essential is the combination of animal magnetism with a gift for speaking attractively. It is eloquence that launches this magnetism to a long range, covering a large gathering of people. Huxley says:

> The ambition has now to be satisfied. To do that, it is almost essential that a man should be endowed with a good dose of what the quacks of an earlier age called "animal magnetism". This quality, which seems to be presses itself in varying degrees of intensity. At its most amiable, we call it, charm. At its most formidable, it is that queer power which enables certain people to inspire confidence and, sure of obedience, to command. The would-be-leader should also possess --- the essential complement to this endowment --- a certain gift of the gab. Eloquence enables him to exert his magnetism at long range and over a number of people at the same time. (AHCE: 365)

Huxley says that a successful leader has all sorts of intellectual qualities. The first intellectual quality to be possessed is a prompt and practical intelligence with cunningness. Huxley says that those who have the current prejudices also, have the chance for enjoying permanent success in their life. He says:

> We have now to consider the intellectual qualities of the successful leader. These are, in the first place, a prompt and practical intelligence, and a touch of cunning. Almost equally essential, if success is to be steady and anything like permanent, is a   good dosage of the current prejudices. Certain leaders, it is true, have been relatively free from the prejudices of

the led, and have succeeded in imposing upon them unfamiliar, and therefore unpopular ideas. But their efforts, though often fruitful in the future, have rarely met with an untroubled success during their own lifetime. (AHCE: 366)

Huxley says that it is difficult for any successful leader who has all the expected or prescribed intellectual qualities and practical and prompt intelligence to admit the prejudices of his society, because such a leader cannot be subtle and sceptical. A successful leader with a bundle of contradicting principles or strong ideas cannot thrive for a long time as the most wanted leader, since consistency and being rational is the back bone of being a leader in operation. Huxley says:

Successful leaders are rarely remarkable for their purely intellectual capacities, indeed, it is difficult for a man to be very intelligent and to accept the prejudices of the society in which he lives. They are rarely subtle or sceptical; they do not like the scientific suspense of judgment, preferring always to belief one thing passionately, rather than another, and to make definite decisions even when they have no rational excuse for doing so. (AHCE: 366)

Huxley says that these are the qualities of the leaders of the past and we do not have such leaders in the present world and there is a shortage for leaders more than followers. As a result, we have no other go other than employing those who, according to our practical intelligence and honest observation, do not deserve to be employed at all. It is so painful that the people are still driven by their tradition that teaches them to respect the employed persons and expect that they will keep their instinct to do more harm under control and try to do something constructive to them, and psychologically this particular self-contradictory action and consequences are so stupid as to be at a distance because of its not being fragrant to the mind of the people.

Huxley says that a leader who comes to power to rule an instable society, which has lost its respect for traditional values and order in general, must be both a philosopher and scientist. Such a leader finds the people who depends on the industrial system for their livelihood, deeply rocked by the rottenness from both inside and outside and fids chaos in every field with unbridled rapidity. Huxley here indirectly giving a descriptive account of the present condition of the world and his expectations of the qualities for the leaders to handle all these problems efficiently. He says:

> To rule such a society, a man should be a philosopher and a scientist. He should possess vast knowledge. He should be exquisitely sensitive to every lesson of experience. He should be quick to seize on every new idea, to judge it, and to assimilate the virtue contained in it. He should, in a word, possess all those intellectual qualities which the typical leader of the past --- who is also, alas, the typical leader of the present day --- does not possess." (CE 367)

Huxley says that the condition of the present world is so pathetic that we need the leaders of these qualities to clean and cure the problems to construct the world that was always considered impossible to have by the majority of the sane people both in the past and present. The world was never ruled by a philosopher king and only now the necessity for having such leaders is acutely felt. Huxley says that such a leader cannot be made emerge out of our collective intensive prayer, which is as stupid as not aspiring for such a leader at all. He says:

> It is the highest degree unlikely that the pensive introvert, who cultivates his mind until it becomes capable of philosophic breath and scientific sensitiveness, can also be a man of action, endowed with resolution, practical cunning, animal magnetism, and the necessary pinch of charlatanism. In the whole of recorded history, there is scarcely one example of the philosopher king. Nor, until very recent times, was the need of such a type seriously felt. It is only now, when the world is immensely

complicated, changeful, and unsteady, that he
has become a necessity. But it would be unduly
optimistic to believe that this new kind of leader
will actually make his appearance, however
much we pray for him. (AHCE: 368)

Huxley says that just one leader of this kind is not
enough to make any changes because, if the majority is the
opposite to the ideal type, the most desirable personality cannot
do anything against their collective effort to make him
ineffectual. So cooperation is needed from the leaders of other
countries. A single nation cannot create the possibility of
disarmament, when the neighbouring countries are very
passionate and proud about being threateningly strong in their
military capacity. Huxley says that no nation can be driven by
reason, when the rest is governed by erroneous concepts and
unreasonable misconceptions. He says:

And even if a lonely monster of this kind were
to appear in one country, he could achieve little
or nothing so long as the old type of leader
remained in control of the surrounding states.
One Poincare would be enough to reduce ten
philosopher kings to impotence. A single,
solitary nation cannot possibly afford to embark
on schemes of disarmament while its neighbours
retain their fleets and aeroplanes. Similarly, no
state   could afford to be governed by reason
while the rest of the world was governed by the
good old-fashioned light of unreasoning
prejudice. (AHCE: 368)

Huxley says that the old type of leaders alone will
involve in the destructive activities without minding what shall
happen to the peace of the world, because of their doctrines, but
the new type of leaders shall never take part in any of such
decisions or activities. Huxley is very euphemistic or diplomatic
in giving an indirect expression of what is exactly in his mind,
when he talks about the type of leaders wanted urgently in these
modern times to both prevent irresponsibly dangerous activities

and propaganda, but also not to repeat the indelible shame in the history of mankind. He says:

> We are on the horns of a dilemma. There is every reason to suppose, on the one hand, that leaders of the old school will involve the new and complex and unstable world in fresh and even more appalling calamities. And on the other hand, there seems to be not the slightest probability of a new type of leader being evolved; at any rate, in the immediate and, for us, interesting future. (AHCE: 368)

Huxley says that to be concerned with the distant future is not wise now, when we have an exigency to encounter the immediate future, since there is a peril of going for a full-scale nuclear war. He talks with a style suffused with respects for the leaders, the pain and fear due to his doubt that they may soon be aggressive about their enemies and the hope that the world might overcome the presently existing dangers.

Huxley says that it is not possible for any statesman to be judgemental about the future of something, which is a generalization. He says that it is possible to make any such generalization only with the understanding of the connection between an act and its consequences, the availability of which becomes comfortable for politicians to frame plans and actions. The field of ethics is the record of past deeds and consequences. It can be difficult to foresee the distant future, but it is possible to understand it intelligently with the help of the records of the past. Huxley says that the past record of experience helps mankind in understanding that a full-scale war, an aggressive revolution, an unchained tyranny and prosecution are the sources of destruction. No country can claim to have innocence or ignorance, if it happens to be a part of such poisonous plans and actions. Huxley says:

> It is only by tracing the relations between acts and their consequences that such generalizations can be made. When they have been made, they are available to politicians in framing plans and

action. In this way past records of the relation between acts and consequences enter the field of ethics as relevant factors in a situation of choice. And here it may be pointed out that, though it is impossible to foresee the remoter consequences of any given course of action, it is by no means impossible to foresee, in the light of past historical experience, the sort of consequences that are likely, in a general way, to follow certain sorts of acts. Thus, from the records of past experience, it sees sufficiently clear that the consequences attendant on a course of action involving such things as large-scale war, violent revolution, unrestrained tyranny and persecution are likely to be bad. Consequently,   any politician who embarks on such courses of action cannot plead ignorance as an   excuse. (CEAH: 269)

Huxley says that only static and isolated societies, ruled by an unquestioned tradition, can alone dispense with politics. A large scale political action is unavoidable in an instable, connected and technologically sound society like the modern society. Even if the modern society tries to do away with politics, it unavoidably ends in stultification. Huxley says that political actions must be carried out with the intention of meeting the expected results. Huxley attacks Russia stating that the ownership of the public of the means of production is a great failure, because it has replaced one kind of oppression with another kind. It has replaced money power with the political and bureaucratic power and so Huxley says that before making any political action, it is important to be doubly sure about reaching the target. He says:

Public ownership of the means of production has been put into effect on a large scale only in Russia, where the results of the reform have been, not the elimination of oppression, but the replacement of one kind of oppression by another --- of money power by political and bureaucratic power, of the tyranny of rich men by a tyranny of the police and the party. (CEAH: 276)

Huxley says that humanistic method is the most effective method to improve socio-economic environment and character building training. Conversion and catharsis are also the methods by which these can be achieved, but they are not preferable sine they produce only erratic results, unlike humanistic method which brings the permanent result in the transformation of personality. He says:

> For several thousands of years now men have been experimenting with different methods for improving the quality of human instruments and human material. It has been found that a good deal can be done by such strictly humanistic methods as the improvement of the social and economic environment, and the various techniques of character training. Among men and women of a certain type, startling results can be obtained by means of conversion and catharsis. But though these methods are somewhat more effective than those of the purely humanistic variety, they work only erratically and they do not produce the radical and permanent transformation of personality, which must take place, and take place on a very large scale, if political action is ever to produce the beneficial results expected from it. (CEAH: 276)

Huxley says that a constructive transformation of personality, with the help of a humanistic method, is the soul of the real development of a society. Huxley says that even a society which is humane to some extent, having its own respectable sense of freedom and justice also has the peril of experiencing a great fall and degradation of morality and economic efficiency and richness, which can be prevented only with the act of transforming personalities in the society. Huxley says that nothing productive can be expected from the politicians also, if there is no transformation in the political personalities.

3.5 The anti-war perspectives of Aldous Huxley

Huxley talks of language and the power of language in twisting words truth. Aldous Huxley talks about the psychology behind the animosity of men towards others and how it is maintained. He says that words make a thread on which we attach our experience and that without words or language human beings live spasmodically and intermittently. He says that animal enmity, though so ferocious and wild, is at the mercy of distractions. An animal that shows sign of being angry at another animal, may begin to show the sings of love that actually distracts the alertness of the other animal, unlike human beings. Unlike animals, we are driven by purpose, we can justify and rationalize what happens for us and so we are serious about keeping anything negative and dangerous in our minds.

When a man encounters an enemy, he is very careful about defending himself through unflagging concentration on him as not to let him attack. Even after a long time of either a fight or the avoidance of a possible fight, the word 'enemy' is enough for a man to bring the feelings of rage and hatred to one's mind momentarily and here, in this situation, he is convinced that anger and the spirit of either defending or attacking is the only virtue. Huxley says that the word 'love' also has a magical effect on human's mind. He says that words are not just a medium to express one's thoughts and emotion, they determine the direction of one's thought. Huxley says that ignorance is the best excuse for doing something undesirable and Ignorance is egotism's most effective defence against perfection. Stupidity is the subtlest from of egotism that actually falsifies an experience through words for its own advantage. Our egotism relentlessly fights to preserve itself not only from external enemies but also the better sides of one's personality. He says:

> Ignorance is the best excuse for going on doing what one likes, but ought not, to   do. Our egotisms are incessantly, fighting to preserve themselves, not only from external enemies, but

> also from the assaults of the other and better self with which they are so uncomfortably associated. Ignorance is egotism's most effective defence against that Dr. Jekyll in us who desires perfection; stupidity, its subtlest stratagem. If, as so often happens, we choose to give continuity to our experience by means of words which falsify the facts, this is because the falsification is somehow to our advantage as egotists. (CEAH: 246)

Aldous Huxley says that man's egotism misuses the capacity or power of language to convey something effectively and even to convince himself on something inhuman. The popular ideas on war is the best example with which this operation of egotism can be intensely observed and clearly understood. He says that war is not creditable to the commanders and to the common people who merely tolerate it. The wisdom and sensibility of man know well how horrible and unnecessary is war, but he uses language to falsify these facts and to make the idea of war seem less evil than how it is really. By suppressing and distorting the truth, man protects his sensibilities and preserve his self-esteem. Man knows how unthinkably infernal the nature of war is and so he makes a verbal alternative to that reality to make himself believe that it is not evil and destructive so that he does not react emotionally to war, since it is only the fiction of the concept of war that exists in the cunning and pleasant falsification of the cruelties of war. He says:

> War is enormously discreditable to those who order it to be waged and even to developed sensibilities the facts of war are revolting and horrifying. To falsify these facts, and by so doing to make war seem less evil than it really is, and our own responsibility in tolerating war less heavy, is doubly to or advantage. By suppressing and distorting the truth, we protect our sensibilities and preserve our self-esteem. Now, language is, among other things, a device which men 'use for suppressing and distorting the

truth. Finding the reality of war too unpleasant to contemplate, we create a verbal alternative to that reality, parallel with it, but in quality quite different from it. That which we contemplate thenceforward is not that to which we react emotionally and upon which we pass our moral judgments, is not war as it is in fact, but the fiction of war as it exists in our pleasantly falsifying verbiage. Our stupidity in using inappropriate language turns out, on analysis, to be the most refined cunning. (CEAH: 246)

Huxley says that what is unacceptable, unjust and terrible about the outbreak of war is that it is not the collective decision of a country or the two countries involved, but individuals and unfortunately it is not they who are directly affected, but the innocent and non-participating civilians. Those who are responsible for waging war against a country or countries do not come into spotlight. They are very clever as to express through the finest embellishments of language with rich chosen diction and personifications that war is not for barbarous attack to mercilessly devastate people large in number or make a country crumble under their monstrous strength, but it is something unavoidable for the welfare of their country and it sounds very convincing and acceptable eventually to the pathetic people of the world. Huxley says:

The most shocking fact about war is that its victims and its instruments are individual human beings, and that these individual human beings are condemned by the monstrous conventions of politics to murder or be murdered in quarrels not their own, to inflict upon the innocent and, innocent themselves of any crime against their enemies, to suffer cruelties of every kind.

The language of strategy and politics is designed, so far as it is possible, to conceal this fact, to make it appear as though wars were not fought by individuals drilled to murder one another in cold blood and without provocation, but either by impersonal and therefore wholly non-moral and impassable forces, or else by personified abstractions. (CEAH: 246-47)

The rulers and the top officials in the army of the country have the strategy of personifying the soldiers and commanders, who destroy the buildings or infrastructures of a country and decimate innocent people, as loyal servants, real pillars of fortifications of their country. Huxley says that this personification nurtures the ego of the warriors and they become violently patriotic, thinking that believe that their enemy country must be destroyed because the reason behind the war is with their enemies, when it is actually with their country. He says, "Personification in politics is an error which we make because it is to our advantage as egotists to be able to feel violently proud of our country and of ourselves as belonging to it, and to believe that all the misfortunes, which are due to our own mistakes are really the work of the Foreigner." (CEAH: 247) Huxley's humanism connects the necessity of taking human psychology with uprooting violence.

Huxley says that the real forces behind wars in general are capable of burying the actual reasons for it and declare that an official battle is not between the soldiers of the armies of two countries, but different principles and ideologies and imply attractive euphemisms to talk about the aftermath of a war. Huxley says that this happens against the pricking conscience of soldiers, who are afraid of discussing the terrible things related to war as they are and so to conceal even their own intentions they come to use picturesque metaphors. He says:

> Ignoring the facts, so far as we possibly can, we imply that battles are not fought by soldiers, but by things, principles, allegories, personified activities pitched against one another in single combat. For the same reason, when we have to describe the processes and the results of war, we employ a rich variety of euphemisms. Even the most violently patriotic and militaristic are reluctant to call a spade by its own name. To conceal their intentions even

from themselves, they make use of picturesque metaphors. (CEAH: 248)

Huxley says that the blood-thirsty spirit, clamouring for war, bombards a neighbouring country with powerful explosives and destroy the inhabitants, before it causes such devastations to its own country. The historians and strategists start admiring in their writing that the military officials are so intelligent as to know when and how to strike the countries and soldiers are appreciated to have executed the safeguarding command of their commanders, due to which their country is safe. They talk of the mathematical skills, the masculine decisiveness and brave heart to efficiently execute the attack at the moment of precision. Huxley mocks at them stating that they speak as if they are the civil engineers, talking of the strength of materials and the distribution of stresses. They use abstract phrases like 'man power' and 'fire power' and to put a long experience of sufferings and atrocities of a warfare, they say that it was 'a war of attrition'. Huxley says that a dangerous abstract word, which is a part of all discussions about war is 'force'.

Huxley cites examples in which the word 'force' is very intelligently used to convince the majority to accept the justifications of waging war against a country. He says that those who believe in achieving collective security, imposing military agreements against any aggression, use this word. They say that international peace is not possible unless it is imposed by force and say that the countries that stand for peace for the world must come together in order to use force against any dictatorship, and that they must use force to protect the democratic institutions.

It is an intelligent strategy to perpetuate war through the collective acceptance.   Huxley says that these are the dangerous intentions aesthetically embellished to distract the peace-seeking attention of the majority in the world and says that in war the word 'force' is synonymous with the word 'violence' to the height of the capacity of the fighters. Huxley says that there is a difference between 'force' associated with war and police action. He says that in war 'force' is the use of unlimited violence and treachery against the innocent people, but in the police action, a limited violence and fraud against the guilty. Huxley says:

You cannot have international justice, unless you are prepared to impose it by force." Translated, this becomes: "You cannot have international justice unless you are prepared, with a view to imposing a just settlement, to drop thermite, high explosives and vesicants upon the inhabitants of foreign cities and to have thermite, high explosives and vesicants dropped in return upon the inhabitants of your cities". At the end of this proceeding, justice is to be imposed by the victorious party --- that is, if there is a victorious party. It should be remarked that justice was to have been imposed by the victorious party at the end of the last war. (CEAH: 249)

Huxley says that either we must invent new techniques to settle the existing international and domestic issues associated with the possibility of either continuing the ongoing wars or the possible outbreak of a war in future to be perished by man's cruel weapons of mass destructions. Those who vote for war and not for peace-settlement, in the name of being adventurous and valorous are actually doing something unforgivable and demonic to one's country. It is the Mephistophelean mission of slaughtering the possibility of internal and external peace of man and the world in general. He says:

The alternatives confronting us seem to be plain enough. Either we invent and conscientiously employ a new technique for making revolutions and settling international disputes; or else we cling to the old technique and, using "force" (that is to say, thermite, high explosives and vesicants), destroy ourselves. Those who, for whatever motive, disguise the nature of the second alternative under inappropriate language, render the world a grave disservice. They lead us into one of the temptations we find it hardest to resist --- the temptation to run away from reality, to pretend that facts are not what they are. (CEAH: 251)

Huxley says that man is unimaginably cunning that he uses abstractions, ambiguities, metaphors and similes that take us away from the actual reality of life to protect our minds from reaching clarity. We, intentionally lie a lot to convince us of such falsifications and distortions of truth so that we may have the sophistication and excuse of ignorance. Stupidity and not understanding help us continue to commit and bear the most inhuman crimes. Huxley says that the strategy of the rulers behind personifying a country has to be understood. It is done to achieve a collective psychology of the citizens of the country as if it were a person, having thoughts, feelings and will, through which, the rulers make their power legitimate and permanent. Huxley says that personification is so dangerous that it actually leads to deification, an ardent and blind worshipping of the country and such a government proclaims that its orders are divine and so obedience is the only virtue respected and appreciated. He says:

> By habitually talking of the nation as though it were a person with thoughts, feelings and a will of its own, the rulers of a country legitimate their own powers. Personification leads easily to deification; and where the nation is deified, its government ceases to be a mere convenience, like drains or a telephone system, and partaking in the sacredness of the entity it represents, claims to give orders by divine right and demands the unquestioning obedience due to a god. (CEAH: 253)

This sort of personification deceptively looks to be an act with a noble intention, but it is lunatic and destructively and proud unidentifiably for people who are driven by the concept of patriotism emotionally. This cunning act is futile, barbarous, aggressively greedy and vainglorious and so it knows not anything about justice in general. Huxley says, "The personified entity is a being, not only great and noble, but also insanely proud, vain and touchy; fiercely rapacious; a braggart; bound by no considerations of right and wrong." (CEAH: 254) Huxley says that rulers and leaders have the plan of depersonalizing their opponents, since they do not like morality. These leaders and rulers are into twisting the truth about the opposition parties and create all sorts of abominable abstractions for them. An animalistic antagonism is instilled in their minds through such a diabolically effective propaganda. The leaders and rulers steal the personalities of the people for their selfish political expectations and benefits. Huxley says:

> Rulers of nations and leaders of parties find morality embarrassing. That is why they take such pains to depersonalize their opponents. All propaganda directed against an opposing group has but one aim: to substitute diabolical abstractions for concrete persons. The propagandist's purpose is to make one set of people forget that certain other sets of people are human. By robbing them of their personality, he puts them outside the pale of moral obligation. Mere symbols can have no rights --- particularly when that of which they are symbolical is, by definition, evil. (CEAH: 254-255)

What is absurd and monstrous about war is that men who have no personal quarrel are trained to murder one another in cold blood and by personifying the opposing armies or countries, war is shown as a conflict between individuals. Huxley was deeply disturbed by the ominous effects of the Second World War and began to be busy with activities to contribute towards the death of war through ruminating and suggesting practically feasible ways and means of quelling war permanently. An intense observer and critic of Aldous, Petre Firchow says, "He joined Canon Sheppard's Peace Pledge Union, began to lecture on pacifism, conferred with Gerald Heard on practical ways and means of preventing war, and in 1937 came out with Ends and Means, a closely reasoned, forceful analysis of the motives and futility of war." (23) Huxley's humanism becomes the culmination of his wisdom and intelligence.

Huxley's *Total War and Pacifism*, reflects his prophetic vision on the impending dangers of the future of the world and didactic spirit prescribing human values for the merciless nationalists. The real concern for something has the natural predicting ability on its next course of action and stage. Huxley's mind is so flooded with the inhuman attitude towards the people of the world by aggressive nationalists that he predicts the next evolutionary height of the severity and the manner of war in future.

Huxley talks of the human mind and its evolutionary functions related to the operation of its cruel side and says that the attitude in future will not be based on war dignity and principles, but with full of war crimes. Here winning over and proving one's might is not the concern, but quenching one's inexplicable and uncontrollable thirst for destroying as many people, places and whatever has been meticulously built over many a century on sheer labour that stands as a treasure house of richness in any field. Aldous says that the future war is going to be not with the army of a country. The enemy's major cities and towns and other important places will be devastated, which will not only depopulate the country but also intimidate, leading them to starvation and anarchy. This sort of apocalyptic state they cause will gratify the act of waging a similar kind of war in future than the traditional method of fighting with one's strength. He says:

> But the next European war will not in all probability be fought by armies; nor will blockade be enforced out at sea, but from the air, by the destruction of harbours and docks. No modern strategist is going to risk the safety of his planes and pilots by sending them to attack elaborate pieces of floating ironmongery which, intact, can do him no harm and whose destruction can do him very little good. No, he will order the bombardment of the enemy's towns, not of the hostile fleet. If the towns can be badly damaged and the surviving population reduced to panic,

starvation and anarchy, nothing else matters. The fleet may safely be allowed to steam about and let off its big guns until fuel and ammunition are exhausted. Then it will have to go home – only to fine that there is no home. (BW: 206)

Aldous talks of the intensity of the aspiration for air armaments. He says that the nationalists will aspire and plan to touch the zenith in the construction of their air armaments with the utmost possible weapons, which presently can be nuclear power and that the aggressive planners and fighters will ultimately understand that their aggression will not pay them in any way they desired. Huxley says that the idealists would be shocked by the devastative and cruel side of nationalism because all that they desire is a just increase in the army for national security and the necessary and constructive collaboration with all other national armies against the military power or any country that becomes the threat to the peace of the world in general. He says:

> In regard to air armaments, ardent nationalists and League of Nations idealists agree as to the consummation to be desired. It is this: that there should be such overwhelming air power available that would-be aggressors will see that aggression doesn't pay. They differ only in their views regarding the right means for achieving that desirable consummation. The nationalists want the available air power to be exclusively national. This means that we must adopt a two-power or, if necessary, an n-power standard of air armament. The idealists are shocked by the doctrines and policies of undiluted nationalism. Their demand is for a more modest increase in our bombing fleet, accompanied by collective security – that is to say, by the collaboration of all national bombing fleets against an aggressor nation. (BW: 207)

Aldous says that armament race is actually the intensification of the impossibility of preventing war from emerging into an enemy country's territory and destructing it. It is a stupid and extremely suicidal competitive spirit because such a savage thirst for being a super power in air armaments shall make the army of the country increase it at regular intervals and any such increase will inexorably lead to a corresponding increase in the other countries' air armaments. Aldous says:

> Any increase in our nation air armaments must inevitably lead to a corresponding increase in other people's air armaments. And any increase in the air armaments of the powers allied for the purpose of 'collective security' must inevitably lead to corresponding rearmament on the part of those powers who remain outside the collective system or who, though nominally within it, feel that they are likely to be picked out as aggressors. Armament races are exhausting competitions; the moment one wide feels that it is reaching the breaking point, it will strike. (BW: 207)

Huxley does not support the notion of 'collective security' and says that it is ultimately for grouping of strong nations against a nation, which has committed something aggressive according to the group. He says that mass murder through public shoot out by police in defence of collective security is not accepted, but the physical, economical and psychological consequences of both grouping of nations to attack a nation and police force murdering people for the security of the majority are the same. So the act of attacking a country with a group of nations itself is potentially evil, which is not enough to destroy any evil in general. The only way is to repair the mentality of attacking a country only after the culmination of an act by the particular country, which they call evil and the collective voice of such nations can think of repairing such an evil at its birth itself instead of waiting for the end to happen so that it can be destroyed.

Aldous Huxley says how man is so weak to believe in anything if it is said emphatically many a time. Huxley indirectly says that the mind of human beings is not so strong as to plunge deep into whatever they listen to. Even if man thinks that something is instilled in his mind unchangeably, it is changeable, since man's mind is susceptible to believe in what is repeatedly said with a great emphasis. Huxley, humorously, comes out with the distinction of a cow and a human being in reacting to a stringent order stating that something is not desirable and so it should not be taken. He says that the cow won't follow such an instruction, but human beings are just the opposite to the cow, denying the order that daisy is a dirty flower and so it should not be eaten, failing of which will result in severe punishment. Huxley says that human beings, if told repeatedly that eating pork and lobster is a taboo, they immediately will believe in it and stop talking them with a terrified reverberation of mind.

He says that in certain ways cows are very susceptible and tractable, for example the fear of an individual intimidates the entire herd, but the degree of susceptibility is not intense. The power of speech, vocabulary and other parts of language make the inbuilt frailty of the inclination to accept the suggestions of others. Man comes to believe in anything through a convincing style of speaking on something and he can act in the most irrational and idiotic ways, if properly persuaded. So, what is told three times, sounds extremely compelling like an indefensible enchantment. Huxley says:

> True, in certain respects cows and other gregarious animals are highly susceptible to suggestion. The fear or rage of a single individual easily infects the whole herd. But this suggestibility of gregarious animals, though intense, is limited. Thanks to his invention of speech and letters, the suggestibility of man is absolutely without limits. By suitable suggestion, he can be made to believe or feel anything; he can be persuaded to act in the most manifestly irrational and preposterous ways. For him what is said three times is not only logically true, but actively compelling, like an enchantment. (AHCE: 391)

A refined, rich and gentle, but a strong mocking tone is employed here by Huxley with an intention of making human beings feeling ashamed of their inbuilt weakness to be gullible and irresistibly be fascinated and defeated by the capacity of others to convince on something. Huxley says that this weakness is very effectively manipulated in religion and morality. The cunning techniques of being assertive and unflaggingly repeating something to make people believe in some ideas or constructed principles has been in those spheres for ages. Huxley says that man has started applying this technique in another important realm of political propaganda and advertisement. Huxley's tone of voice is a mixture of pain and anger, when he says that man has to feel proud of employing the technique for political propaganda and advertisement. He says:

> The technique of assertion and unwearying repetition has been employed in these two spheres of human activity from time immemorial. But the merit of having employed it in other spheres than religion and morality belongs to our own and, to a lesser degree, to the preceding generation. To us --- whether British, European, or American --- is due the credit of having invented and perfected the arts of political propaganda and advertisement. We have every right to feel proud of the achievement. (AHCE: 392)

Huxley says that the official propagandist of war time have given us so many descriptions of their methods of spreading an idea, which we can never get our mind off from. Every day and every hour the people of the world are surrounded with propaganda from television and newspapers, he says. Huxley says that Dr. Chalmers Mitchell, in his article on Propaganda, in the supplementary volumes of the *Encyclopedia Britannica* that as a director of propaganda, he had a strong faith in the power of propaganda in controlling public opinion. Huxley says:

> Of political propaganda I do not propose to speak. The official propagandists of wartime

have given us ample descriptions of their methods --- methods which we can see being put into practice all around us, wherever we choose to look. For propaganda is still with us, daily and almost hourly --- propaganda of every political colour, from newspaper we read. Lord Northcliffe, we are told by Dr. Chalmers Mitchell in his article on Propaganda in the supplementary volume of the *Encyclopedia Britannica*, "brought to his (as Director of Propaganda) a limitless faith in the possibility of controlling public opinion. (AHCE: 392)

When it comes to such an effective and mind-changing propaganda, it is not the faith of the people that is the reason for its magical operations, but the thought that it is stupid, if it is not believed. Huxley says that the most convincing proof for the feasibility for the effective administration and controlling of public opinion exists in advertisement, which very effortlessly changes the political opinions of the people and very rarely it so happens that it is possible at the cost of a slight personal sacrifice. Huxley says that the people can be comfortably convinced of the propaganda that Germany feels guilty of its wars and the paradise like Russia without making any mental or intellectual efforts. He says:

> Perhaps the most convincing proof of the "Possibility of controlling public opinion" is to be found in the existence --- the flourishing, exuberant existence --- of advertisement. That people should be induced by propaganda to change their political pinions is not, after all, so very extraordinary. It is only rare, exceptional cases that the change of political opinions involves the slightest perusal sacrifice. We can be convinced, shall we say, of Germany's war-guilt or of the paradisiacal nature of Soviet Russia without having to spend a halfpenny. (AHCE: 392-393)

Huxley says that stating something repeatedly makes sure that the people who hear it change their mind according to what is said and follow thereafter and that the simplest form of making such advertisement takes a mere limitless repetition of the name of a person or object that the advertisement aims at instilling in the minds of the receivers. Huxley talks of the weakness of the people to be brainwashed against something or someone as an introduction to how the political propagandists of both US and USSR brainwash the people of their countries against each other's governmental policies, decisions and even the collective character and attitude of the people.

Huxley talks about the reasons behind either the birth of fascism or the acceptance of this doctrine, the atrocities of fascism and its futility. Huxley talks of the possibilities of an awful war and the humanistic perspective with which the people of the world and the rulers should think of getting back to the state of a promising peace and welfare of the world. So, the most predominating obsession of Aldous Huxley is his tremendous faith in the power of humanism in changing even the most destructive spirit. He says that fascism is not about protecting social status and interests. Huxley says that most of the people of the world has a desire for certainties that actually stands for faith.

Huxley says that uncountable number of modern people think that they are intelligent and well-informed, who believe in the miracles of Jesus Christ, believe in the impeccable personality and capacity of a particular leader and accept him. Huxley says that divinity cannot be intellectualized for the ardent worshippers of a nation, who think that worshipping one's nation is very natural. He says that old tendencies never die and they take new forms for their existence. Fascism does the work of taking a novel form in the field of religious faith or belief. Fascism is like a lightning conductor that powerfully forces the people to throw off their will to believe. Huxley says:

> Most people desire certainties, feel the need of a faith. Modern education makes religious faith difficult, but has done nothing to undermine political faith. Masses of men and women think themselves too intelligent and well-informed to

believe in miracles or the divinity of Jesus, but find not the smallest difficulty in accepting the infallibility of a Leader. The worship of God is an intellectual impossibility for thousands to whom the worship of a divine being, called the Nation, seems the most natural thing in the world. The old tendencies have not been abolished (they never are); they have merely taken new and, on the whole, less desirable channels. Fascism digs these new channels for worship and provides, in its cult of the divine Nation, a kind of lightning-conductor, upon which thousands of reluctant infidels can discharge the accumulation of their will to believe. (BW: 136)

Huxley says that fascism brings a remedy for the inferiority complex. Political and economic situations imposed insufferable insults on millions of people and landed them in despair. The actual rehabilitation for this state of despair is the principle of national or racial superiority. Such a superiority complex gives the people of the race or country the confidence and courage that they are more intelligent and better than even the best, strongest and the most talented in the world, in spite of their failure, misery and general mediocrity. Huxley says that the basic operation of a fascist army is to torture other people. Huxley brings out the alarming nature of fascism and its military purpose to educate the people with the truth about something, which the majority does not seem to care about. Huxley says:

In the second place, fascism provides a remedy for the complex of inferiority. Political and economic circumstances have, since the war, imposed intolerable humiliations on millions of personally blameless men and women, have reduced whole classes and populations to a state of despair. To these, the doctrine of national or racial superiority comes as an instrument of personal rehabilitation; for it assures the down-trodden individual that, in spite of all the specious appearances of failure, misery and general mediocrity, he is really of the salt of the earth and, in some mystical way, wiser and better than even the nicest, the strongest, the most talented of another men. (BW: 136-137)

Huxley brings out how meaningless it is to have a national or racial superiority complex. This statement is an attitude-changing statement, if at all the listener of this type is driven by logic and reason. Huxley talks of the psychological impacts of being in an army, wearing a uniform and the military activities of such people. He says:

Membership of an army provides further satisfactions in the form of exhilarating group emotions (as good, in their way, as the pleasures of drink or of love) and relief from personal responsibility. Nor must we forget the delights of wearing a uniform. A uniform makes a man agreeably conspicuous in a crowd of the un-uniformed and tends to heighten his sex appeal. At the same time, it has some of the charm of a disguise. (BW: 137)

Huxley says that this is the reason why the scientists and technicians of the world must contribute towards the prevention of war and peace establishment. The role of scientists in the greater food production to extirpate poverty from the world is also important, but the major focus must be on the prevention of war. Huxley says, "It is this point that internationally organised scientists and technicians might contribute greatly to the cause of peace by planning a world-wide campaign, not merely for greater food production, but also (and this is the really important point) for regional self-sufficiency in food production." (CEAH: 287) The collective attitude of the people of the world will be flexible to trust, if the prominent scientists confess the dangers of the modern wars and their deep impacts even after so many years.

Huxley is very practical and honest in stating that the construction of a governmental body, which has been the dreams of many political critics and diplomats, may not be expected to be immaculate and effective in the beginning itself. He says that even if World Government is formed, it cannot promise peace for the world, because the lust for power is the cradle of power politics, the culmination of which is the powerful ammunitions and nuclear proliferation. Unless the lust for power is brought under control, no brilliant idea can guarantee security and peace for the entire world. A strong political arrangement is expected to do something to administer the lust for power of man systematically. Huxley says:

> And even if a world government should be set up within a fairly short space of time, this will not necessarily guarantee peace. The Pax Romana was a very civil strife over the question of secession. So long as the lust for power persists as a human trait --- and in persons of a certain kind of physique and temperament this lust is over-falteringly strong --- no political arrangement, however well contrived, can guarantee peace. (CEAH: 290)

Huxley comes out with his recommendations to form a policy for internationally organised science. This policy, Huxley says, will make effective contributions for the maintenance of peace and political freedom and then there must be fruitful discussions on how to solve the problems of food and power. Huxley affectionately orders that all the scientists and technicians of the world must collaborate to make this policy come true, realizing their socio-political responsibilities as scientists and technologists. Huxley says that before undertaking these practices, they must take pledges that they will play the role of scientists, following their basic accountability of contributing to the welfare of the people and the international peace in mind.

Huxley says that the correct term for 'fascism' is 'dictatorship'. He talks of the intrinsic features of the ends and means in general and says that even though the end advocated by the dictatorship looks very appreciable, dictatorship itself is extremely undesirable. Huxley says that good ends does not justify bad means and that the nature of repulsive means changes the very colour of the end and it is ultimately understood that the end does not have something that was originally proposed. He says that good ends are less important, when compared with the good means and that the end achieved will be good, only when the means are good. He says:

> Good ends never justify bad means for the simple reason that, in the process of being used, the bad means change the good ends, so that what in fact is reached is not the goal originally proposed, but some other and worse goal. Good ends, on the whole, are less important than good means. If the means are good, the end reached will also be good. (BW: 203)

Huxley says that military personals and dictators have nothing to do with these great qualities. They neither try to cultivate these qualities in the people nor do they possess. A passive disobedience is all that a dictator expects from his victims, since such a mechanical discipline is instilled in the victims. Huxley says that the entire activity of a self-disciplined artist is a symbolic representation of standing against war and dictatorship. He says,

> War-lords and dictators have no use for such self-discipline. All that they require from their victims is a passive obedience; which they are able to extort because they have previously imposed on them a mechanical discipline form without. There is a very real sense in which the whole activity of the self-disciplined artist is a standing protest against war and dictatorship. It is also a standing protest against pacific liberalism which is merely soft and self-indulgent. (BW: 204)

Huxley is very brilliant in pointing out the qualities needed in order to protest against anything evil and destructive and the character of artists in general. Huxley does a very brilliant job of shedding light on the noble qualities of artists in general, which happens to be the manly qualities needed to protest against anything destructive and justifies that artists are against pacifism and dictatorship. It is a highly productive technique of spreading the spirit of self-analysis in the people of all walks of life as to examine whether they also have all these qualities and if they do have, the seed for protesting against dictatorship will be sowed in the psychology of all the people. Huxley's humanistic endeavours to refine the world for a productive revolution is with this intelligent strategy.

Huxley very firmly states that the most desirable idea for the social reformation is decentralization and self-government everywhere and that non-violence is the method by which the reformation is to be brought about. He strongly states, "So far as the state is concerned, the desirable context for reform is decentralization and self-government all around. The desirable methods for enacting reform are the methods of non-violence." (CEAH: 256) Huxley says that the brilliant methods for self-government for the common people can be discussed only with the understanding on the natural history and psychology of groups.

Huxley attacks the dictators saying that the success of the dictators of the world lies with their capacity to exploit this universal craving of human beings to go beyond the limitations of their personality. They know that the frailty of men is to stay out of themselves emotionally. They were carefully systematic about proving such atmosphere and occasions to make the wish feasible. Huxley says that the crowd around the relic of a saint is actually a substitution to the crowd of a political meeting, a religious procession, military reviews and May Day parades. Huxley's act of associating the 'crowd' with the aforementioned groups is a subtle attack on them, especially the military of any country. It is indirectly said that the soldiers and superior officers of the army have this weakness, which is sufficiently fed by the proud powerful people and dictators around the world. He says that the dictators, while preparing the occasions for the crowd, are careful that the crowd does not have any upward fly as to reach a really superior self and become unattached with such things. Huxley says:

> For the crowd round the relic of the saint they
> have substituted the crow at the political
> meeting; for religious processions, military
> reviews and May Day parades. It is the same
> with Fascist dictators. In all the totalitarian states
> the masses are persuaded, and even compelled,
> to take periodical holidays from themselves in
> the sub-human world of crowd emotion. It is
> significant that while they encourage and
> actually command the descent into sub-
> humanity, the dictators do all they can to prevent
> men from taking the upward road form personal
> limitation, the road that leads toward non-
> attachment to the "things of this world" and
> attachment to that which is super-personal.
> (CEAH: 257)

The dictators are very careful that no one in the crowd should have the upward travel and reach super-personality because a person, who escapes from egotism and reach super-personality, goes beyond his old hero-worshipping and loyal idolatry and becomes indifferent to all establishments of life like divinity, nation, party, class, defined master etc,. This admirable state is attained in solitude and that is why a herd morality is followed by the tyrants to get the crowd into the intoxicated of sub-humanity. Huxley talks of the terrible condition of the majority of the factories in America and says that despotism is ruling the industry and where benevolence is either expected by the employers or given by the authorities, passive obedience is demanded. Huxley, when talking about the atrocities of the tyranny of the authorities in the industry, says what is in the papers and records about the expectations from the workers are entirely different from how they are treated both emotionally and monetarily. He says:

> And if some such scheme is not acted upon, it is
> of small moment to the individual whether the
> industry in which he is working is owned by the
> state, by a co-operative society, by a joint stock
> company or by a private individual. Passive

> obedience, whoever the general in ultimate control may be. Conversely, even if the ultimate control is in the wrong hands, the man who voluntarily accepts rules in the making of which he has had a part, who obeys leaders he himself has chosen, who has helped to decide how much and in what conditions he himself and his companions shall be paid, is to that extent the free and responsible subject of a genuinely democratic government, and enjoys those psychological advantages which only such a form of government can give. (CEAH: 259)

The administrative rules that Huxley is advocating shall not produce any military efficient society, because it is what is already existing. A military efficient society is that which is cursed with a passive obedience and the head of which has the absolute authority to exercise through well-trained hierarchy of administrators. A society composed of men and women habituated to working in self-governing groups is not a perfect war-machine, the members of which have their own will to freely exercise their intellect unlike soldiers who have neither the capacity to think on their own nor will. The soldiers are not to enquire about anything, but to do and die if it is unavoidable.

A decentralized society does not have any room for manipulation unlike the one which is under the control of a dictator. Huxley says that self-governance that exists everywhere and military capacity are quite incompatible. Nations use war as an instrument of policy and so war is deemed to be highly essential and unquestionable. Huxley says that the overpowering and increasing evil of war are inevitably confronted by all in today's world, which necessitates the birth of a novel method of governance that is compatible and highly productive for the entire world that ultimately ensures safety and security. Huxley says:

> In practice this small-scale industrial democracy, this self-government for all, is intrinsically most compatible with business organizations of the last two kinds --- co-operative and mixed. It is

almost equally incompatible with capitalism and state socialism. Capitalism tends to produce a multiplicity of petty dictators, each in command of his own little business kingdom. State socialism tends to produce a single, centralized, totalitarian dictatorship, wielding absolute authority over all its subjects through a hierarchy of bureaucratic agents. (CEAH: 266)

Huxley says with disappointment that when it comes to the context of militarism, all sorts of productive changes to self-governance and decentralization will be distorted and will be used for strengthening the position of a dictatorship or a ruler of anarchy. Huxley says that the excuse to seize the opportunity of absolute power is found intensely, where the international context is militaristic. The aspiring contemplation to misuse a powerful position is always very strong with a dictator, even there is no war. Huxley says that the only way to stop such an even intention is through a proper humanistic education. The mental, emotional and intellectual growth and their nature are constructed by education and so education should be looked at as the most effective cure for almost all personal and social evils.

Huxley says that our society demands only skills associated with fighting and succeeding, and gentleness and refinement do not take us to great heights in today's world, which is quite unfortunate. Paranoiac ambitions are admired as the most important virtue and those who have them are worshipped as though they were God. It is to be noted carefully that the number of books written on Napoleon is more than on anybody else, which is alarming, according to Huxley.

Huxley attacks the collective attitude of the modern society to hero-worship a heroic and successful anti-social personality like a bandit. Russell says that Duces and Fuehrers will stop harming the world, only the people think that they are disgusting as they do with swindlers and pimps. Huxley says that the collective mind set of the people of the world has a power to produce personalities they most dream about an acutely appreciate and says that as long as Caesars and Napoleons are worshipped in the society, many will convert themselves into

Caesars and Napoleons for the simple fact that they want to be liked and appreciated and as a result the world will be miserable with destructive personalities. Huxley says:

> The fact is deeply and alarmingly significant. What must be the day-dreams of people for whom the world's most agile social climber and ablest bandit is the hero they most desire to hear about? Duces and Fuehrers will cease to plague the world only when the majority of its inhabitants regard such adventurers with the same disgust as they now bestow on swindlers and pimps. So long as men worship the Caesars and Napoleons, Caesars and Napoleons will duly rise and make them miserable. The proper attitude toward the "hero" is not Carlyle's, but Bacon's. "He doth like the ape that, the higher he clymbes, the more he shewes his ars." The hero's qualities are brilliant; but so is the mandril's rump. When all concur in the great Lord Chancellor's judgement of Fuehrers, there will be no more Fuehrers to judge.
> Meanwhile we must content ourselves by putting merely legal and administrative obstacles in the way of the ambitious. They are a great deal better than nothing; but they can never be completely effective. (CEAH: 268)

Huxley indirectly accuses that it is only the people of the world who are responsible for all the destructive and evil activities in the world. The implied humanistic message to the people of the world is that the collective attitude and qualities of thinking and preference must undergo a sea-change. The people must correct themselves in terms of their preference to appreciate, long for and encourage villainous personalities without understanding their actual colour with the help of their knowledge with the universal morality for an ideal man, ruler, citizen, leader etc., so that it will not only do wonders in purifying the negative vibration, but also prepares them to stand unitedly against anything that tries to take off their peace and comfort.

Chapter IV

The Humanistic perspectives of Bertrand Russell and Aldous Huxley

4.1 The social reformative concerns of Russell and Huxley

The attitude to refine others and society, for their strength, well-being and peaceful state that offer them a secured, productive and fulfilling life, is out of human nobility and humanitarianism. To weed out both the inbuilt and enforced individual and societal vices and blemishes is basically vital for the dream of building a healthy society. The attitude of the people of the society, mental and emotional health, the societal and political awareness of the people, their educational standard, the personal and socio-political responsibilities of the people etc., must be properly mentored for the construction of such a society. The realm of administration for the society must be with intelligent plans, operations and sustained passion for the development of the society, state and nation.

The plans and decisions that the administrating body takes must be with all good intentions to nurture its people and territorial infrastructure. The social media, social activists, environmentalists, feminists, social reformers and socially responsible writers are the primary forces of concern for the cultural and healthy socio-political atmosphere and activities. They are the whistle blowers and pin-pointers of mistakes and anything undesirable in all the areas of their operations. They come forward to fight whenever there are activities, which are the potential threat to human peace or even life itself.

Humanists focus on the refinement of man as an individual as to become mentally, emotionally and intellectually healthy and strong and so they not only sow the seeds of lofty characteristic qualities and virtues, but also detoxify human mind and intellect in general, since they believe that human society at the macro level will be really qualitative, only if individuals are nourished at the micro level. This is the real seed of social justice. Immanuel Kant in, Kant: Political Writings, says, "The greatest problem for the human species, the solution of which nature compels him to seek, is that of attaining a civil society which can administer justice universally." (39) Bertrand Russell and Aldous Huxley are the best examples for typical humanists of balanced responsibilities, for they not only talk about the national development, bring out the bright and dark sides of the political fabric and moves of their period and suggest vital ideas to prevent the possibilities of the impending wars in the future, but also talk of individual discipline and morality for the unshakable construction of an ideal society.

Huxley presents his intense observation, critical opinions and benevolent prescriptions for the entire humanity very convincingly. Huxley says that a humanist is the one who believes that human nature as a whole should be harmoniously developed and that the sacrifices man makes should be out of his highest interest for the well-being of the entire humanity and not due to anything supernatural. He says, "The humanist is one who believes that our human nature can, and should be, developed harmoniously as a whole – that the sacrifices which man must always make should be made in his own highest interest, and not in the interest of something external to himself – not in the name of any less or any more than human cause." (BW: 107)

According to a humanist, Huxley says, the members of an ideal society are superior in quality physically, intellectually and morally. The society is impeccable in establishing morality in all possible realms that no one will be treated unjustly and no talent goes unrecognised. It becomes the embodiment of personal liberty, garlands altruistic efforts and purposefully dynamic, drifting towards the realization of lofty human aspirations. He says that science should be used in order to build such a society and the powers of science should be used by humanistic rulers. He says:

> For the humanist, then, the ideal society is one whose constituent members are all physically, intellectually and morally of the best quality; a society so organised that no individual shall be unjustly treated or compelled to waste or bury his talents; a society which gives its members

the greatest possible amount of individual
liberty, but at the same time provides them with
the most satisfying incentives to altruistic effort;
a society not static but deliberately progressive,
consciously tending towards the realization of
the highest human aspirations. Science must be
made a means for the creation of such a society,
but only on certain conditions: that the powers
which science offers must be used by rulers
who are fundamentally humanist. (BW: 107)

Reforming the society was the primary obsession of
Aldous Huxley. Helen Watts Estrich, in *The Sewanee Review*,
says, "Huxley saw that the world was out of joint - that the social
and economic systems stood in dire need of reform." (64)
Huxley talks of the condition of the society and the people
before he comes to offer his suggestions to refine them. *The
Quarterly Review of Biology* records, "Aldous Huxley, like a
good physician, attempts to make a diagnosis of the ills of the
world before prescribing a treatment." (366) Huxley
distinguishes between the barbarians and the modern people,
quoting the philosopher, Thomas Hobbes, stating that the life of
savages is very untidy and deplorably nasty. Their life involves
brutal activities like hunting and they don't have longevity. The
civilized people are clean, speak very well and they are blessed
with a good and satisfactory life span. Huxley says that the price,
which the civilized people have given for not being savages, is
heavy. It is only civilization, which has produced powerful and
deadly weapons of mass destruction, the deadly cancer, the
pitiable slums and newspapers. Huxley writes:

> The English philosopher, Thomas Hobbes, was
> doubtless right; the life of savages is "nasty,
> solitary, brutish, and short." But the life of
> civilized men --- however hygienic, relatively
> speaking, and long --- is not all beer and skittles.
> Fate makes no free gifts; it sells, for a price. The
> price is heavy. Machine guns, cancer, sums, the
> penny newspaper --- these are a few items of the

tribute we pay to fate for the privilege of not being savages. (AHCE: 388)

Huxley brings out the problems of his contemporary national and international society. He says that a society has to be laborious and alert about not being vulnerable to anything destructive, especially laziness, a predilection for entertainment and loving leisure time. Huxley says that such a society has nothing to do with anything constructive and prone to be misguided and enslaved very easily by any national and international destructive forces. Huxley says that a leisured society has two parts and the essence or the by-products of the activities of both the parts are just the same. He says that both the divisions of this society cannot tolerate the easy and simple existence, which is a vacuum for them that they try to fill it with useless activities.

The means by which these two groups attain this futility is different. The first group of people are simple, children-like, very happy and unspoilt barbarians. They involve in courting, paring, separating, repairing, nest-making, bird-watching and games. The second group of people are into many activities in the name of being readers, intellectuals, and aesthetic people. Huxley says:

> So much for good society of the lower browed variety. What now of the highbrow rich, the aristocratic intellectuals, the leisured patrons of the arts? What of these? They ought, of course, byd efinition to be superior to the lowbrows. Experience, alas, gives the lie to a priori definitions. I am inclined to think that, on the whole, the highbrows are almost worse than the lows. Those who sin after having seen the light and eaten of the tree of knowledge are more blameworthy than those who sin in pre-Adamite innocence and darkness. (AHCE: 389)

The first group comes to their salon for public house party and drawing room visits and the second group comes to their salon to meet interesting people and talk. Being intellectuals is severely misunderstood by the second group, Huxley says that this group displays its knowledge about many things in the name of being intellectuals. Huxley says that they talk of the latest pictures, scandals, pornographies, eccentricities, the latest books, modes, music, religions, psychologies of love, theories of science and philosophy. Huxley is angry on this group because he says that art is just another killer of time like playing any game or any romantic flirtation to the people of this group.

Religion, for this group, is something to be talked about over tea or coffee. Huxley says that they degrade all significant ideas and they have turned all values upside down. They value bombastic talking and do not understand the true inbuilt merits of great ideas, since they are all impressed with only the presentational fashions and merits. Huxley is very sorry that literature is just a game of elegance for them and that they have distanced the true merits of getting associated with the soul of literature. He says:

> In highbrow salons, on the other hand, you must talk --- of the latest pictures, the latest scandals, pornographies, and eccentricities, the latest books, the latest modes; the latest music, the latest religions, the latest psychologies of love, the latest theories of science and philosophy. And it is all, no doubt, very agreeable and diverting; but oh, if you happen to take anything at all seriously, how profoundly shocking and horrible! For to these polished beings, art is only another time killer, like bridge and flirtation; religion is something to be lightly chatted about over the tea and muffins --- an amusing subject, but not, of course, so entertaining as a juicy piece of scandal. All fine and important things are degraded; all values are overturned. Men and ideas are prized in this polite society, not for their intrinsic merit, but because they happen, for one reason or another, to be fashionable. Literature is turned into a sort of elegant game,

<blockquote>
in which it is the object of the players to score points of "style" and "form" --- as though form and style possessed and real existence apart from substance. (AHCE: 389-390)
</blockquote>

Huxley emphases that leisure time must be productively made use of, if a society is to improve greatly. An individual with no productive activity during an ample free time is bound to be with something negative as the proverb, an idle mind is the devil's work ship, which is applicable with a society also. Bertrand Russell, in his book, *The Conquest of Happiness*, says, "To be able to fill leisure intelligently is the last product of civilization, and at present very few people have reached this level." (208) Psychology says that what one does in free time invariably stands for the core of one's personality.

Huxley talks about the possible ways of the utilization of leisure by the rich and poor. Most of the rich people's preference, Huxley says, is Monte Carlo and Nice, the places notorious for gambling and prostitution. He says that there are exceptions of those who seek love and an interesting sort of game with them. Some of the people prefer to be engaged with works of charity, politics, local administration and occasionally with scholarly or scientific studies. But, it is disgustingly disturbing and morally unacceptable to Huxley that the majority of the population is inclined to Monte Carlo. This concept of leisure of the rich people is not at all encouraging for the disciplined and qualitative fabrics of the future international society.

Huxley is very sure that the poor people are not going to use their leisure productively or meaningfully. Since the people do not have lofty associations and meanings with their lives, they tend to choose activities which are mere killers of times and nothing else, which is going to retain them in the pathetic condition in which they already are. He says that the idea of the poor people on leisure is restricted to looking at cinema, films, reading newspapers, cheap literature, listening to radio, gramophone records, and going from place to place. It is quite unthinkable to Huxley, when he thinks of the possibilities for having prolonged leisure times. He predicts that there would be an enormous increase in amorous lifestyle and time killing, causing mental depression to the people. Huxley says:

> If tomorrow or couple of generations, hence, it was made possible for all human beings to lead the life of leisure which is now led only by a few, the results, so far as I can see, would be as follows: There would be an enormous increase in the demand for such time-killers and substitutes for thought as newspapers, films, fiction, cheap means of communication, and wireless telephones; to put it in more general terms, there would be an increase in the demand for sport and art. The interest in the fine art of love-making whole be widely extended. And enormous numbers of people, hitherto immune from these mental and moral diseases, would be afflicted by ennui, depression, and universal dissatisfaction. (AHCE: 414)

Russell has similar views on the attitude of the society. He talks about the pathetic condition of the world due to the mental, emotional and intellectual decay, which the majority of the modern population is least bothered about. Russell says that a rich man in the ancient time was expected to quote Latin poets to judge Italian Renaissance pictures and appreciate classical music, and so a man of the period had a considerable knowledge about the literature of his country and France, which they remembered even in their eighties. In the modern times, such expectations are only with professors and professors belonging to the various departments know only about their branch of knowledge.

Russell says that the modern professors know just what is least important in literature and that ignorance has become the hallmark of social eminence. He says that modern world does not find any leisure because their sense of pleasure has become very tiresome as their work, resulting in the increase of cleverness and decrease of wisdom, because modern man does not find time to meditate on a thought so intensely as to have distilled wisdom out of it. He says:

> The result is that while cleverness has increased, wisdom has decreased because no one has the time for the slow thoughts out of which wisdom, drop by drop, is distilled. A problem such as the prevention of war, the urgency of which is obvious to everyone, is dismissed with a shrug of the shoulders in the hope that circumstances will solve it without the aid of human thought. But circumstance, unaided, are not likely to be so kind. (MO: 35)

Russell says that the increase in cleverness and wisdom is the reason why the majority of the people of the world are indifferent to the greatest thought like the prevention of war, the most urgent idea to be executed, which only serious and careful human efforts will solve. Russell aims at bringing in a sea-change in the minds of the people of the world to be sensible about their personal, social and political responsibilities and get ready to solve the most important contemporary issues, especially the prevention of war that the whole world is afraid of.

Russell and Huxley know that only individual reformation will lead to socio-political reformation and revolution. Russell says that the frailty of the modern people to seek admiration from other people in the society is to be cured for a healthy living, since this attitude is a severe distraction from the burning socio-political issues of the period.

Robert E. Goodwin and Hans Dieter Klinge in their book, *Political Theory: An Overview by Iris Marion Young*, says, "Social life is fraught with vicious power competition, conflict, deprivation, and violence, which always threaten to destroy political space." (49) Russell wants the people of the world not to seek their comfort and peace outside of themselves. He says that though many people are under the impression that they are living only to the contentment of their conscience and do not pay attention to the opinion of others, the majority of the people of the world seeks to impress others.

Russell says that only a few do not care for the opinion of others, and they are the real heroes. He says that it is really important to observe whose admiration people desire to attain. An average man aspires to get the respect of his colleagues, wife, children and subordinates. He is very particular that his business associates must think that he is so special and capable that they must have an eternal respect and admiration for him, but he never minds to know how well his wife and children love him and tries to persuade himself that during a crisis his children would come to him to seek his advice. He says:

> The average man desires the respect of his colleagues, of his wife and children (if possible), and of his underlings. He hopes that his business associates do not consider him a simple fellow whom anybody could take in. He takes pains not to realize how well his wife knows him. He tries to persuade himself that in a crisis his children would turn to him for advice. The average married woman tries to impress other married women. She tries to persuade them that her husband is richer than theirs and her children more successful. If she is well-to-to, she tries to display better taste than her neighbours in the management and decoration of her house. As they are playing the same game, this requires great skills and much thought. (MO: 50)

Russell says that the desire to impress a wide range of people comes from the spirit for an achievement that is glorified eternally. Russell comes out with some examples of great men who were driven by the spirit of impressing the world. Anatole France's Pontius Pilate convinced himself that the posterity will understand him and get him justice after his death, when he incurred the ranker of the Emperor. Julius Caesar had Alexander the Great as his rival in his mind, in spite of the glorious victories he had. The eminent men of the past lived with an intention of living forever in the minds of the people of the world even after their death.

Russell says that such a desire to be immortalized in the pages of history of the world has been decreased thanks to the newspapers of the present days. So, today's world knows that the possible admiration from the readers of history is less than the contemporary fame that one could possibly attain. Russell indirectly expresses his discontentment and amazement, when he says that the fame of a film star, at the height of his career, in the present day, exceeds even Alexander the Great and Julius Caesar's. He says:

> The fame of a film star at the present ay far exceeds that of Alexander or Caesar at the height of his career. Probably more people know the name of Einstein now than have known the name of Archimedes in all the centuries from his day to our own. The effect of all this is that admiration is sought in more ephemeral forms than those formerly desired. Men's work becomes less statuesque and there is more effort to make it appeal to all and sundry. (MO: 51)

Russell says that the present possibility of getting instant fame throughout the world is immense and that is the reason why the number of people who know Einstein is more when compared with those who know of Archimedes in all the centuries from his days and says that the admiration of the modern world is ephemeral than how it was in the past. The desire for posthumous fame lingers in almost all very prominent men along with the fear of having something bad in their biography and so they are afraid of their biographers and as a result, in the life of eminent people hypocrisy has replaced spontaneity. Bertrand Russell states that admiration is not offered to what is truly admirable and those who are admired do not deserve it.

The peace of a society depends on the peace of the family and so Russell cogitates on the marital issues of the modern times. Russell says that marriage is expected to make anyone become complete and fulfilled, but unfortunately it is attributed to unhappiness. He says that the actual reason lies partly both with economics and social customs. He says that the conventional idea that husband and wife should spend their leisure time together is not an intelligent idea, as it is suitable for a couple of similar tastes. He continues to say that his taxi driver's wife does not have any taste for intellectual lectures and does not like him also to enjoy any such lectures without her company. Russell says that many husbands and wives are ready to sacrifice their pleasures on the jealousy of the pleasures of their partners and calls it dangerous to object and prevent other people's pleasure out of jealousy than to be selfish about pursuing one's own. He says that if a husband and wife are to be compatible and happy, there must be some sort of social separateness. Russell says:

> The convention that husbands and wives should spend their leisure hours together is a bad one. No doubt my taxi driver's wife does not care for lectures and also does not like him to go to them without her. Many husbands and many wives will forgo their own pleasures out of jealousy of their pleasures that they imagine that their partners as desiring. It is much more harmful to object to other people's pleasures than it is to be a trifle selfish in pursuing one's own, and a certain amount of social separateness of husband and wife is necessary if they are not to become dull and incapable of finding anything to say to each other. (MO: 36)

The second reason, economic difficulty, is more serious, he says and that an unmarried man, unlike a married man, is free to be lavish about his money for his leisure time and amusement, including searching for a wife. He says that well-educated and intellectual married men will find that their freedom and leisure time for intellectual pursuits have vanished and educated and intellectual women are bound to feel the loss of freedom and time to explore the world of intellect more intensely than men do, if they remain childless and as a result both have some feeling against the institution of marriage. Russell says that this problem cannot be cured unless the state undertakes the entire expense on children. Russell says that this condition can be effectively changed with the adoption of an intelligent attitude towards child-rearing. He says that when compared with affection, science and other skills and even intelligence are of no use and nothing can replace affection. Science and the acquired skills should supplement affection, if not, it will produce unexpected dangerous results.

Huxley says that the modern people have become conscious about the rights of other people with the rampant nature of humanism, which has very profound effect in the realm of family life. So, the modern man has become highly individualistic in thinking and approaching things in general and so he cannot embrace the traditional beliefs. The divine associations with family are no more believable to the modern man. 'Scepticism', the offspring of 'individualism' is further strengthened by 'humanitarianism'. Modern people not only feel for their rights but also for their children. They think of the rights of their children and think that they should not be compelled to do anything and they should not be tortured in the name of bringing them into a discipline. Parents, being rational about the children's rights, think of their rights and freedom also to enjoy their life and so they do not want to bear the weight of their family responsibilities. Such an attitude results in reducing the size of their family and handover their children to professional experts to make them very talented professionals in the chosen fields. Huxley says:

> But it is not only the attitude of the parents towards their children that has changed; their attitude towards themselves is no longer the same as in the past. Self-consciously individualistic as well as humanitarianism, parents feel that they too have rights. They want to 'live their own lives', 'to express themselves', to have some other than a merely parental *raison d'etre*. In a word, they resent the weight of family responsibilities. Accordingly, they try to mitigate these responsibilities, first by reducing the size of their families and, secondly, by handling over such children as they do produce to professional educators. (BW: 48)

Psychology talks of the connection between a child being in a large group of people and its healthy physical and psychological growth. James C. Davies in his famous book, *Human Nature in Politics the dynamics of political behaviour* says, "If an individual does not develop, within the family, the sense of belonging, dignity, and indeed individuality, which are necessary for him to become a relatively autonomous and unique person, he is more likely to end up a complete social isolate than a participant in anything." (35) The pleasure and the pride of the past family structure and the number of family members are no more in the present century. In the past for many generations together, a vast family with many a member, lived under one roof. Huxley expresses his exercised state of mind that family as a structure has become like a single oak tree from a multi-branched banyan tree. There are other causes like economic condition and the aspiration to lead a rich and sophisticated life, which is not possible with many children. He says:

> The family has decreased in size. Increasing individuality and self-conscious rendered intolerable the old united family with its three or four generations living under the same roof. From being a banyan the family tree has long since become (at any rate in the West) an oak. Scattered at a distance from the parental stem the acorns grow up into a separate existence. In the past these separate young trees were prolific; but recently the increase of self-conscious individuality has led, for the reasons already given, to a reduction in the number of offspring. These psychological causes have been reinforced by economic causes – themselves, very often, of psychological origin. Thus, families cannot be big because we must keep up the standard of living. (BW: 48)

No child is happy about being a single child of a family. Children have an inbuilt desire to be surrounded with other children and loving people. A big family has many advantages in child-rearing and it is the only prescription for the overall healthy psychological development of children. To be a part of a very big family gives the psychological impression that they are inseparable parts of the society, learning and mastering the art of being flexible to others. Children brought up in such a family atmosphere, need not undergo any training on how to face the world, when they are out of their schools and colleges, since the very family plays the role of the rest of the world, producing confident, understanding, flexible and daring children. Aldous Huxley says that being the only child in a family is a highly crippled state in many ways and that having even two children is not a better state, but having four or five members is a very satisfactory state.

The implied comprehension must be that the majority of the families of the modern world is not satisfactory, which has necessitated the role of a professional educator. The professional educator creates an atmosphere, which is equal to that of the family's that makes the children feel as if they are of one family and ultimately they experience a psychological satisfaction. It is very shocking when Huxley says that there are people who call themselves advanced in the modern world, who advocates the abolition of family system, suggesting that the professional educator shoulders the responsibilities of taking care of the children from their very infancy state. Huxley says that this view is a potential threat to the noble existence of the time-honoured natural instinct to be gregarious through sentiments and affectionate bonds. A society that is free of any sort of sentimental and affectionate relational bond is bound to head towards a dangerous and self-killing selfishness that eventually leads to kill the rest also. Huxley says:

> Now, from the point of view of the children, small families are not much good. A big family is the world in miniature; to be brought up in a big family is a complete preparation for life. An only child is heavily handicapped. Two children are not very much better off. A family only begins to be really satisfactory when it can count at least four or five members. From the children's point of view very few modern families are satisfactory. Hence the importance in modern life of the professional educator, who

forms an artificial family, within which it is possible for children to find psychological satisfaction. 'Advanced' people propose that the family system should be abolished altogether and that the professional educator, paid by the state, should take control from earliest infancy. Indeed, this view threatens to become the orthodoxy of the modern democratic State. (BW: 48-49)

Huxley says that the insecurity of a state depends on the number of self-centred individuals and that being humanistic is the only cure for this ailment of not caring for others intimately through the negation of their fundamental duties to the family, which shall protest against all sorts of establishments, including the society, government, country and freedom. Huxley says that human standardisation is sure to become a political necessity. He says optimistically that family as an institution shall never perish permanently, since it gives immense psychological contentment, but it is not to be denied that presently there is a potential peril, waiting to wipe off the family system from the society. Russell talks of the importance of being affectionate rather than being very intelligent and knowledgeable, when he talks of the importance of child-rearing.

Russell declares to the world that an ignorant person blessed with a rich affection is better for an infant than a very intelligent and knowledgeable person with no heart, but if a well-informed person is fond of children is the much better about having children. Russell impliedly says that a man with an enriched heart is more desirable than a man with an enriched brain. He says, "The ignorant person with affection is perhaps better for an infant than a well-informed person who has no heart; but a well-informed person who is fond of children is much better than either." (MO: 37) Russell says that it is insane to think and conclude that female intelligence is inferior to masculine intelligence. Even if women had been left to the freedom of being themselves, would not have invented machines. If they had been asked to contribute effectively for human civilization, they would not have forgotten to preserve human values, shinning mechanical ingenuity totally. He says:

> It would be foolish to draw the inference that female intelligence is inferior to that of the male. Men have set a standard of intelligence and have instinctively set it to suit themselves; they have created a mechanical civilization which largely ignores human values. Women left to themselves would, I believe, never have invented machines. But if they had been able freely to contribute to the sum total of civilization, they would not have forgotten to preserve what is valuable in human life and would not have been led astray, as men have been, by a blind worship of mechanical ingenuity. (MO: 76)

Bertrand Russell talks of the deceptive appearance of the American Society that it gives importance to women's emancipation and that women have achieved equality, but they are not true. He says that the ideal of America is equality from the beginning of the history of the declaration of American Independence. Even though America brags about its ideal of equality, it has used its ideal only in some compatible political directions and not in the society. Social equality is the basic necessity that every citizen of a country needs in order to experience the fundamental freedom and joy of life. This American ideal has not been experienced by the people, especially Negro men and women. Still they are considered inferior to the white race and the black Americans undergo insults and oppressions in the society, even though, the political ideology of the country strongly condemns.

Russell says that women have political equality with men, but not economic equality, which is very important for women in the modern world to be independent and feel confident about their constructive side. The wife of a rich man will have enough money to spend, but the women of other classes depend on their earning husbands for money. The women, according to the law, have their rights to share the income of their husbands, but still it is unfortunate that the true emancipation, economic independency, of women has not been attained. Russell says:

> Although equality was, from the moment of the Declaration of Independence, proclaimed as a principle, it was only applied in such directions as were politically convenient. For a long time, nobody thought of it as including Negroes or women. Even now, although women have political equality with men, they do not, as a rule, have, economic equality, which is in many ways more important. Among the rich, a wife normally has money of her own, but in other classes she depends upon her husband's earnings. The law gives her a right to a share of his income, and to alimony when she gets tired of him or he of her; but it does not give her the economic power that belongs to the person who earns money. (MO: 269)

Huxley talks of two groups of people in the society. He says that economic progress is due to resourceful and inventive people. Such people are interested in creating something that could change the society and they are flexible to embrace any change and this group comprises of only a minority in the world. The majority of the people of the world does not welcome change. Change in any form is Herculean and excruciating to them and they worship sentiments, but not logic, being fanatical about believing in metaphysical absolutes. The first group of people are driven by the spirit of leading, while the second group is dominated by mere sentiments. Huxley says that the birth of the second category of people is stability and aggressiveness, the timeliness of an action directed by rash faith in an absolute.

The frailty of the second group of people is its inability to adopt to any new change or condition and its attitude towards economic and mental stagnation, unlike the first group of people. Huxley says, "Thus, the strength of a society dominated by men with a pronounced 'persistence of aggregates' likes in its stability and in the violence and the promptitude of the actions dictated by unquestioning faith in an absolute. Its weaknesses are its inability to adapt itself to new conditions and its tendency to economic and mental stagnation." (BW: 143) Huxley insists on adaptability because it is the most wanted to sustainability and growth.

Huxley glorifies the first group of people stating that these men were responsible for the economic growth of the last two centuries, which has necessitated their becoming of the parts of the ruling class. He says that the strength of faith is so intense in this group of people and the danger is that men will be rash about enforcing conformity through violence, where there is a strong faith. Huxley says that there are strength and weakness in both the groups, but the weakness about being manipulated due to the spirit for loyalty and emotional nature is very much with the second group.

Huxley proposes the methods by which the world can be improved and comes out with interesting suggestions to ameliorate the life on this planet. He begins with nurturing the body and talks of the importance of nutritious food for all and says that man is into many destructive activities and habits to his body, due to following stupid social impositions. Huxley says that what is a chronometer to a savage is his own body to a modern man and that man is stupid in spite of his intelligence. Huxley says:

> Take, for example, the all-important matter of diet. A science of nutrition exists, but are its precepts followed? They are not. Half the population is too poor to be able to feed itself properly. (The remedy for this is in the hands of the economic planners.) The other half possesses the means, but neglects the available knowledge and eats either excessively or mistakenly." (BW: 221)

Huxley says that there are advertisements on newspapers for laxatives, cold-cures, pain killers and ick-me-ups, which are all harmful drugs, because of the people's carelessness about their health and the invited ailments. Man poisons his body with wrong foods and then needs painkillers and in the name of mitigating the pains, he further pollutes his body with those painkillers. Then he complains that life is not worth living and consequently starts blaming the government of his country. He says, "We poison ourselves with the wrong food, then try to mitigate the painful consequences of our folly by poisoning ourselves still further with drugs. After which we wonder why it is that life should seem so little worth living and proceed to blame the Government." (BW: 221) The personal responsibilities of the people to safeguard themselves and the country is emphasised here.

The next idea that Huxley suggests to improve the world is to eradicate the deadly habit of taking intoxicants, stimulants and sedatives, which are out of psychological problems. Man needs occasional holiday or break to escape the hard realities of life. It is a tragedy that the people of the world spends the ten percentage of their total income on intoxicating, stimulating and sedative materials. Huxley says that the habit of taking tea and tobacco is also out of the need to escape the reality or boredom. He says:

> A problem closely allied to that of analgesics, and no less important to us as suffering and enjoying beings, is the problem of intoxicants, stimulants and sedatives. Everywhere and at all times men have felt the need of taking an occasional holiday from the common round of every-day affairs – a holiday from the world and should guess that, at the present time, the inhabitants of our planet spend nearly ten percent of their total income on intoxicants, stimulants and sedatives. Some of these – tea, for example, and are exceedingly powerful drugs. But the purpose served by all of them is the same; people take them in order to escape from the boring or unpleasant reality of their own characters and the surrounding world. (BW: 225)

Huxley says that man has to adapt to the surroundings and must lead a happy life so that the need for escaping realities and boredom will start diminishing. Life has to be improved in such a way that it becomes very interesting and truly valuable, which will be a real cure for the weakness to think of slipping into an unreal world of dirty and harmful pleasures. Huxley says, "If we can arrange our world in such a way that people's lives will seem to them worth living, there will be a smaller demand for pick-me-up and stupefacients, for booze and dope." (BW: 225) The psychological understanding that the curing of it is a matter of making life more interesting is brilliant with the humanistic care to improve the people.

Huxley points out the dreadful effects of watching movies and popular press to escape boredom, which takes the watchers to a world of fantasy distanced from reality, truth, good sense and human values. There should be a corporation to monitor the desirability of the content to be given to the people, which includes the comments of the writers on political parties also. News must be brought by the corporation for the monitory benefit of the fetchers so that their dependence on advertisement for their money can be eliminated. Huxley says that the children must be trained on the art of concentrating to escape boredom and the taste for creative doings must be cultivated. People must have a strong personal morality and a sense of commitment and responsibility to follow the socio-political norms.

Russell is against wasting food material and the crop productions wasted for many purposes. He says that the present condition of the world is really pathetic and it is suffering from two kinds of misfortunes. The first problem is that there are people who genuinely think that the world has to be peaceful and all the people of the world should be comfortable and happy, but cannot purchase any good to offer those who suffer and the second misfortune is that there are people who have what those who suffer terribly are in need of, but do not sell. Russell says that the second type of people want to make a huge profit out of their surplus goods. Russell says that the surplus of coffee in Brazil is used as a fuel on the railways and it is burnt in large funeral pyres in the lonely valleys of the county. There is a gut of rubber due to the fact that the workers of the country cannot help taking rubber from the trees. He says:

The world at the present day is suffering from two misfortunes: there are people who desire good which they cannot purchase, and there are people who have goods which they cannot sell. Those who have goods which they cannot sell are adopting various ingenious means of disposing of their surplus. IT would be demoralizing to wage earners to pay wages for work not done; therefore they continue to produce the good that they cannot sell but adopt various means of destroying them after they have been produced. Brazil, which suffers from a surplus of coffee, has taken to using it as fuel on the railways and to burning it on large funeral pyres in lonely valleys. There is a glut of rubber, which is unfortunately made worse by the fact that the natives cannot be restrained from tapping the rubber trees. Fortunately rubber trees are subject to a pest, which has hitherto been combated but which is now about to be encouraged. (MO: 54)

Bertrand Russell's humanism is very transparent through the exhibition of his worry that many downtrodden, unemployed and forsaken population of this world are into starvation and the concern that they must be given enough food. He says that the rotting food in the West America and Canada could be given to those people of starvation around the industrial regions so that the world would be really richer, which can be achieved at the cost of the inhuman profits of the individual capitalist. This is possible only by an organized public endeavour and the humanistic motive of which will be unstoppably undeniable. Russell recommends:

There is food rotting in the West of the United States and Canada; there are unemployed populations starving in all he industrial regions throughout the world. If the food were brought to the starving populations, and they were set to wok such as would satisfy the wants of Western farmers, the world would be the richer even I no individual capitalist made a profit. The motive of individual profit has apparently broken down, and only organized public effort will restore the economic life of the world. (MO: 55)

Aldous Huxley says that the present crisis is due to instability in economy, which is because of the commercial attitude that wants to turn the world into a big super market. He says that mass production, due to mechanisation, leads to the birth of wide markets with a great number of people with flexible needs and tastes with the help of destructive economists. Huxley says that this is dangerous and so, once stability is achieved in economy, scientific research should not be encouraged because nothing is more dangerous than too much of knowledge.

4.2 The ethical views of Russell and Huxley

Ethics have significant role to play in the perpetuation of a peaceful society by serving various purposes. Albert Schweitzer says, "Ethics is the activity of man directed to secure the inner perfection of his own personality." (30) Bertrand Russell and Aldous Huxley both as responsible writers and intense humanists have the ethical task of disciplining and capacitating individuals in the society so that they can be ready to encounter any sort of personal and socio-political problems in their lives. Russell talks of optimism as an idea and the wrong belief associated with it. He says that optimism is ethical and so it should not be used with anything ethically wrong. Russell seeks reason or intellect to look at the concept of optimism and does not attach any sort of sentiments with it. Russell says that optimism has to be practically believable and it should not be out of any rash belief or imagination. To be optimistic about something must sound feasible and gettable, if not, it causes irritation. He cites the example of a doctor, who is optimistic about curing, with the prescription of an effective medicine for the ailment and says that a friend who has mere words of cheering a person with some disease is quite an annoyance. He says:

The fact is that optimism is pleasant so long as ti is credible, but when it is not, it is intensely irritating. Especially irritating is the optimism about our own troubles which is displayed by those who do not have to share them. Optimism about other people's troubles is a very risky business unless it goes with quite concrete proposals as to how to make the troubles disappear or grow less. A medical man has a right to be optimistic about your illness if he can prescribe a treatment which will cure it, but a friend who merely says, 'Oh I expect you will soon feel better', is exasperating.' (MO: 70)

Russell says that people who have talked so optimistically about the past two years, which has shown the world all possible negative spectacles, are like the cheerful friend, who has no moral freedom or right to make any such expression, and not like the medical man, who is a contributor basically and so he hopes his patient to get well soon. A mere cheerfulness has nothing to do with improving the poor condition of those who are starving, Russell says, since he prefers reason to emotion. He says:

Most of the people who have talked optimistically thought the last two years about the bad times have been in the position of the cheerful friend rather than of the medical adviser, and I doubt whether their cheerfulness has added much to the happiness of those who were starving.

In every kind of trouble what is wanted is not emotional cheerfulness but constructive thinking. This fact is gradually being borne in upon the world by the world-wide depression, and in this I perceive the only basis for optimism that our present troubles afford. These troubles can be cured by constructive thinking, not by ballyhoo. (MO: 70)

Russell says that it is only constructive thinking that will safeguard people at their worst times and not being emotional or expecting moral and emotional support. This particular piece of advice stands to be the panacea for all the socio-political problems that Russell and Huxley deal with. This is the judicious combination of didactism and humanism.

Huxley talks against the famous socio-political ideology or statement that all men are equal in democracy and he says that this is true only in mystic sense and not in any political or social sense. Men are all equal in being the children of God and in the capacity to suffer, love and distinguish the good from evil. Men are equal only in those capacities, but not in their capacity to fight to govern others or themselves. Huxley says that to believe that all are equal is the fundamental idiotic mistake of democracy and people are made believe through such cunning propagations for the political and economic benefits of the rulers, aristocrats and other powerful people of a democratic country. Huxley says:

> Democracy is based on assuming that all men are equal. Now that assumption is true, but only in a mystical sense. Men are equal as being all the children of God – as being all endowed with a capacity for suffering, loving, and knowing good and evil. They are not equal in any of those abilities which make men fit to govern themselves or others. The mistake of the democrats has been to suppose that men are equal in every way and to base practical politics on this gratuitous and false assumption. (AHCE: 397)

Huxley says that the idea that all are equal in democracy is not something unimportant just because it is true that it has only mystical value now. Huxley glorifies the true significance of having such a statement that has a huge impact in the minds of all citizens of all democratic countries, in spite of having no tangible evidence to support that statement practically. He says that equality in democracy, the cradle of the idea of 'humanitarianism', is the concept that deeply modified the society. Huxley says that the defenders of humanitarianism are the supporters of the belief that all are equal in democracy. Even the rich people in a democratic society admit that even the poor people of the society have the same rights and freedom and serve the poor considerably either directly or indirectly. Huxley's humanitarianism is predominantly exposed, when he talks of the merits of humanitarianism, which has a very strong connection with the benevolent belief that all are equal in democracy. He says:

> It must not be supposed that, simply because the idea of the equality of man is mystical, it is therefore unimportant. On the contrary, it is one of the highest significance. It is an idea which has already profoundly modified future. Humanitarianism is the expression of that idea. We are all humanitarians now, whatever our political opinions and whatever our social position. Even those who are in possession of wealth and power admit that those who possess nothing have certain rights. They are perpetually giving away little bits of their wealth and power to be dispossessed. (AHCE: 397)

Huxley says that unlike the people, who have the freedom and possibilities of getting their basic needs, at least, in a democratic country, in a tyrannical country, the people are handicapped by poverty, regrettable conditions and insufficient education that lead them not towards the higher pursuits of life. Huxley says that the paupers and sufferers of a country due to its indifference to equality must be helped by humanitarianism and enriched so that their life will be improved, giving an unshakable hope for such people to get out the wretched condition for a healthy and comfortable life. Huxley says:

> In tyrannical society, where humanitarian principles are not recognized, nine-tenths of the individuals composing that society are so unfairly handicapped by poverty, bad conditions, and inadequacy of education that they are not in a position to compete for any of the higher prizes of life. By ameliorating the lot of the dispossessed, humanitarianism removes this

> handicap, and thus, by multiplying the competitors, tends to create an intenser and therefore biologically more stimulating competition. (AHCE: 398)

Huxley motivates that there must be a sense of competition among the people of such a country so that all will strive to become well in life, exhibiting their special capacity and talents so that the country shall have the bright chance of having many able people for the most important governmental activities, which is the actual political justification of humanitarianism. Huxley says that such a spirit for competition eventually increases the number of efficient people for the leadership of a country. He says:

> Humanitarianism, then, has a biological function --- to render possible an intenser competition within society. When all men are free to compete and all start equal, the chance of getting able men at the head of affairs is obviously increased. That is the political justification of humanitarianism. Society should be run on humanitarian principles because an increase in the number of competitors increase the chances of efficient leadership. (AHCE: 398)

Bertrand Russell is against killing human beings in any way, including a person killing himself, suicide. He strongly condemns suicidal tendency and calls it irresponsibility towards life and incapability to withstand the inbuilt challenges of life. Russell attacks the encouragement and justifications that people with suicidal tendency give themselves. He expresses his deep humanistic concern that no one should suffer in this world and find life intolerably painful to that extent that the person wants to leave this world. His natural sympathy and mercy towards human ordeals and sufferings disturbed him so deeply that he himself made such confessions on many private and public platforms.

A true humanist not only has an interest in the prosperous life of all human beings, but also has the capacity and concern to listen to the just reasons of the people who has a lot of grievances and complains against life in general. Russell talks about how true are the reasons of the people who try to commit suicide. William Edelglass, in his articile, Levinas on Suffering and Compassion, says, "In suffering, the overwhelming weight of existence entangles and suffocates the existent; the self is burdened and attempts an impossible escape." (45) Russell, in spite of his empathy, comes out with the roaring announcement that suicidal attitude is not only a personal stupidity but also a social negative tendency.

Russell says that attempted suicide is equal to attempted murder in England and America and anyone who tries to commit it on the reason that his or her life is insufferably painful, is imprisoned with the intention of making them love life. Russell says that it is irrational to consider the attempt to kill oneself is a crime and no punishment will prevent such an attempt. The understanding that to kill yourself is like killing others seems idiotic to Russell. He gives the example of throwing one's wristwatch into the sea and says that there is difference between throwing someone's watch and one's own watch into the sea and on any ground and to consider them on equal light is not intelligent and logical. He says:

> To say that it is as bad to kill yourself as to kill someone else seems to me absurd. If I take someone else's watch and throw it into the sea, I'm a criminal, but if I throw my own watch into the sea, I am at worst foolish, and if the watch is worthless, I may even be quite sensible. What applies to my watch applies also to my life. When I take another man's life I am taking what does not belong to me, but the question of taking my own life is clearly one that concerns me more than it does anyone else. (MO: 67)

Russell believes that through producing clear logical evidences to justify the just reasons behind an action, the doer of the action will understand the logic, which will eventually make him capable of thinking on his own in a logical way on the other side of his deeds, if it is negative and self-destructive. Russell says that the subject of suicide is to be considered not on its merits but in relation to human sacredness. He says that it is illegal to take the phrase 'human sacredness' very seriously because it is a hypocrisy and states that as long as war remains a part of the government, it is a mere hypocrisy to use 'human sacredness' against the poor, downtrodden and helpless people, whose miseries prompt them to commit the inhuman and pathetic act, which means that as long as war, a symbol of mass destruction of mankind, is deemed to be absolutely necessary, the thought that life is divine and holy is a great joke, because both are contradictory. The destructor knows not the sacredness of that which is destroyed by him. This truth is a very sharp edge of the blade of humanism that Huxley holds against the blood-thirsty war lovers.

Huxley says that world civilization was strong enough to withstand the menacing combined attacks of all these enemies admirably well. He says that the dangers that confront our civilization at present are not the external dangers like men driven by devastating anger, horrible impending war, and the potential possibility of becoming impecunious that wars inflict on the people of the world, leaving them to become uncivilized as to cruelly fight among themselves for mere survival. The most devastative dangers that keep the worthy lives of the people of world under a horrendous state are the dangers that dwell within man. They are the potential threat for the courageous mind of human beings. He says, "No the dangers which confront our civilization are not so much the eternal dangers --- wild men, wars, and the bankruptcy that wars bring after them. The most alarming dangers are those which menace it from within, that threaten the mind rather than the body and estate of contemporary man." (AHCE: 324-355) It reflects the boon of mankind to be hopeful about life, in spite of any sort of natural or man-made dangerous happenings.

Huxley, here, indirectly teaches the people of the world that it is not the body or the tangible asserts that one amasses, which is the most important in life, but the mind, affecting of which is effecting the life itself of the person concerned. This indirect message is not only philosophical but also spiritual that talks of the most prominent truth about life, because modern people are misguided that happiness lies in earning money and leading an incomparably lavish and rich practical life.

Huxley talks about the wrongly associated activities to the idea of pleasure.The organized criminal offence of making people believe that real personal and social pleasures lie only in doing a particular activity, associated with a particular organization and not in any other. The typical example is that the attitude of the people that being a government officer and working very hard for hours together are considered a superior status and supreme pleasure when compared with being very creative about writing on something interesting to let out one's passion for intellectual freedom, tasting the unique feel of being an author and a critic, and feeling a range of freedom that the majority has nothing to do with. He says:

> Of all the various poisons which modern civilization, by a process of auto-intoxication, brews quietly up within its own bowels, few, it seems to me, are more deadly (while none appears more harmless) than that curious and appalling thing that is technically known as "pleasure". "Pleasure" (I place the world between inverted commas to show that I mean, not real pleasure, but the organized activities officially   known by the same name) "pleasure" --- what nightmare visions the word evokes!   Like every man of sense and good feeling, I abominate work. But I would rather put in eight hours a day at a Government office than be condemned to lead a life of "pleasure"; I would even, I believe, prefer to write a million words of journalism a year. (AHCE: 355)

Russell talks of different kinds of readers and their purposes behind their act of reading and his humanistic concern that everyone must read to extirpate their ignorance and prejudices to be clear and knowledgeable. He wants to promote a serious type of reading that makes people with strong intellect and original thinking. Russell says that the majority of people does not read as the popular belief. The majority in the world just read picture papers and among them the majority never goes to books as such for real reading. The readers who know the real taste of intense reading of all kinds and of all branches together make a small number, says Bertrand Russell.

Russell says that only these people read with the intention of acquiring knowledge and information and that only young people belong to this group. This group reads in order to fly away from all their mental conceits and prejudices and are really mature. Russell says that it is unfortunate that a great number of readers reads to have support neither for their knowledge nor for opinions, but for the sheer pleasure of escaping into the world of imagination, escaping this hard reality of life. He says:

> The majority of mankind red nothing at all; of the remainder, the majority red only the picture papers. Of those who read something more than picture papers, the majority never gets as far as books. All the readers of books – grave and gay, profound and superficial, scientific, literary or lurid – all put together are a very small fraction of the population. Nevertheless, they differ among themselves in all sorts of ways. There are those who read in order to acquire information; they are generally very young. These are those who read in order to acquire confirmation of their prejudices; these people are what is called mature. But the great bulk of readers are seeking neither knowledge nor support for their own opinions, but an escape from reality into the world of imagination. (MO: 65)

This act of escaping from reality to dwell in the world of imagination takes all kinds of forms. Novelettes and films offer the crudest form of slipping into a utopian world for unreal and vicarious pleasures. They are living an unreal world, where an obscure young man or woman achieves splendid success or experience a rich and joyful married life and this happens at a greater level with those who slip into the past history and imagine the abundance and glory of the past ages. The next stage is with the subject of astronomy, wherein the aspects of the world of colourful imagination can be found.

Russell says that the stars in the book, Jeans and Eddington are very fortunate to lead a quiet and undisturbed life. They are not troubled by the problems of the people in the actual world like a tax collector, the illness of their children and business depression. Unlike the real life, the life of the characters in the utopian world sooth the readers like the imagination with the stars or nebula. People not only need soothing experience but also excitement. Russell confesses that it is only excitement that prompted his desire for reading.

He says that psychoanalysis says that the inclination to escape from reality is bad, which Russell partly disagrees. He says that if imagination makes a person neglect his or her responsibilities, it is destructive and so deplorable, but if it nourishes a person to become constructive, it is highly preferable and appreciable. He says, "The desire to escape from reality becomes a bad thing when it produces delusions or cause a man to neglect his business." (MO: 66) Russell cites some examples. A poor man harassed by his creditors can find a relief, imagining that he is the President of the Bank of France, which is utterly stupid and the person can be punished for escaping reality. A young woman who forgets herself being into the romantic tale of King Cophetua and neglecting her duty, finally loses her job. But there are other forms of forgetting the real world and fleeing into the world of imagination, which are very much desirable.

Russell actually talk of creativity and the role of the power of imagination in making a person be gifted with a creative bent of mind. Mozart, one of the greatest music composers of the history of profound classical music with the highest standard, escaped reality to reach the pleasure dome of creative imagination not to be affected by the worries of his debts, which gifted him with the rarest of music talent and genius. Had Mozart taken the words of the psychoanalysts, he would have been very careful about his balance sheet, but the world would have lost his ever inspiring symphony. Russell says:

> But there are other forms of escape from reality which are wholly desirable. Mozart used to compose music in order to forget his duns and his debts by escaping into a world of phantasy. If he had followed the advice of eminent psychoanalysts, he would instead have drawn up a careful balance sheet of receipts and expenditures and set to work to devise economies by which the two could be made to balance. If he had done this, he would have lost his income, and we should have lost his music. Escape from reality, as this instance shows, is not undesirable when it is into a world of imagination recognized as such and used as a means of making reality itself more tolerable. (MO: 66)

Russell says that to escape this reality for the world of imagination to get something very precious with which the hard realities of life can be tolerated and accepted is not deplorable, because such an effort with the world of fancy brings a great boon to the world to soothe 'the fret and fever' of life. Russell says that the most useful inventions would have been possible without this sort of attempt and so he encourages this sort of reading that ultimately makes readers create something valuable, which they return to the reality with.

Huxley talks about how pleasure-giving it is to be educated with everything to stay updated with all the walks of life in the world and the pleasure of being respected by others, and at the same time, he talks of the pains and unnecessary spirit to stay well aware of the contemporary activities of all the fields. He remembers how passionate he was in being up-to-date with the contemporary literature and other fields, just because of the societal expectation that educated and intellectual people must be up-to-date with everything. He says, "Yes, the pleasures of being up-to-date are certainly great. But, then, so are the pleasures of not being up-to-date." (AHCE: 373) Huxley makes a confession that he was never happy and comfortable about whatever he read and did with an intention of being up-to-date.

Huxley says that the reason why he has chosen the state of not being up-to-date is that he prefers to be himself rather than being fashionable. Huxley says that he has stopped caring for the comments and opinions of others, which led to this liberated state. He says:

> These people, it is true, still exist, and will certainly think of the more poorly of me for not being up-to-date, and for admitting the fact. The reason why I feel that I can afford to be out-of-date is this: I have ceased to care two pins what these people --- the intellectually smart, the leaders or follow-my-leaders of metal fashion --- think of me, or indeed of anything else under the sun. I find it more agreeable to be, not fashionable, but myself. (AHCE: 374)

Huxley says that he remembers how foolish he was in wasting his time to be up-to-date, because he yearned for the appreciation of others in staying fashionable. Huxley remembers reading the book Ulysses, attended many theatres for dramas and went to many music concerts, which he deeply regrets because he thinks that he wasted an uncountable valuable hours spent on them. He says:

> When, from the depths of my calm solitude, I reflect on the many extraordinarily foolish and time-wasting things I have done for the sake of being up-to-date and earning the approval of the fashionable, I shudder and am amazed that I could ever have been so idiotic. Thus, I remember spending at least seventy-two precious now irremediably perished hours in reading Mr. James Joyce's Ulysses. I remember passing hundreds of evenings at the first nights of the most boring plays (though it is true I was paid for doing so). I remember listening to the whole concerts of music by Mr.Gustav Holst. I

remember passing whole afternoons among the landscapes of K.Marchand and his English followers. And for what? To whom is the benefit, as we used to ask in Latin? Merely that I might be able to say that I had read the portentous and boring book, heard the dim music, seen the plays, and thrilled aesthetically before the significance of those painted forms. (AHCE: 374-375)

Huxley says that he is as happy as how he was fashionable even without that socially supreme status of being up-to-date. He says that he is no more interested in what the intelligentsia of the world has thought about, written on or spoken on recently and that the distance between himself and the contemporary civilization is the inexhaustible source of serenity, peace and areal happiness in his life. He says, "But now, I find that it relays does not matter in that least what the mentally smart think. I find that I am quite happy in out-of-dateness; what is more, I find that I don't miss much. The distance at which I live from contemporary civilization acts, as it were, as a filter." (AHCE: 375) Huxley says that liberating oneself from the societal expectation and anxiety is significant for the freedom to think, talk to the people and loved ones and read the favourite books to the heart. Huxley calls these doing these is the principal joy and advantage of not being up-to-date. He says:

It leaves one at liberty, I repeat, to think (and once one is used to it, the activity is really quite agreeable); it gives one time and inclination to talk with the few people one likes, about interesting things; and excuses one from having to talk with the causally met many, about the things which one finds boring. It creates the leisure to read the books one always meant and wanted, but never had the time, to read, owing to the press of new noels, plays, and the like, a knowledge of which is essential, if one is to sustain a conversation is polite and intellectual smart society. These are the principal joy and advantages of not being up-to-date; and very considerable I find them. (AHCE: 375)

Huxley wants to inform the world that people must know what to do to lead a mentally, emotionally and intellectually healthy life. They should not take wrong models and expectations from the society that they deem to be superior to them. He announces to the world that original thinking is more important than trying to keep many unwanted information just because the world of fashionable society exposes it to be superior and distinct. Huxley, being a humanist and an intellectual, aims at bringing clarity to the people on the unnecessary weight that they carry pleasurably, without which they shall lead a fee and comfortable life.

4.3 The educational views of Russell and Huxley

Russell and Huxley have expressed the condition of the system of education in their period and given their suggestions to refine and strengthen this most important field with a view to shape the international society. All the views of both these humanistic writers on the condition of the educational system and their suggestions and recommendations are applicable even in the modern times. Russell and Huxley bring out the regrettable impacts of the system of education in their period on the people of the world. This shows that people are what they are thanks to the impact of the education imparted to them. Both Russell and Huxley are not happy with the collective attitude of the people of the world about many disciplines and responsible reactions and actions to be taken against many personal, social and international political scenarios.

Russell's idea of education primarily focuses on training children. It recommends interesting methods of teaching so as to inspire children and not train them on the art of imitating the teachers, since being a mere imitator makes them mere slaves, executing the commands of their superiors. Huxley believes that it is only education through which people can attain true freedom. Rudolf B. Schmerl, in *Chicago Review*, says, "Huxley mentions education and decentralization as methods to be used for the retention of freedom. Education is to emphasize individual responsibility to counteract the growing tendency to submerge the individual in a more easily manipulated group" (41) It indicates that the true meaning of freedom from ignorance can be attained only through education.

Russell says that the Kindergarten and Montessori systems of education were invented by those who were ignorant about both advanced styles of instructing children and the ultimate fruits of education. He says that the powerful role of education is to shape the character of children and their opinions. Russell talks of the frailty of children of being impressionable to the beliefs of their parents and teachers and says that the acquisition of their belief is unconscious with children that stays with them permanently.

Russell says that education is for promoting original thinking and decision making, which must be out of the wishful operation of intelligence in a particular situation and not about being efficient about mechanical doings. Huxley also is of the same opinion that education must make children become the best in almost all the situations and realms that they are bound to be a part of. Huxley, in his essay, "Education on the Non-verbal Level", says, "A good education may be defined as one which helps the boys and girls subjected to it to make the best of all the worlds in which, as human beings, they are compelled, willy-nilly, to live." (280-281) Bertrand Russell says that education should not teach children how to choose a political party to be a member of it, but enables them to choose intelligently between parties. He says:

> Education would not aim at making them belong to this part or that, but at enabling them to choose intelligently between the parties: it would aim at making them able to think, not at making them think what their teachers think. Education as a political weapon could not exist if we respected the rights of children. If we respected the rights of children, we should educate them so as to give them the knowledge and the mental habits required for forming

independent opinions; but education as political institution endeavours to form habits and to circumscribe knowledge in such a way as to make one set of opinions inevitable. (BWBR: 380)

Russell says that an ideal system of education must cultivate the art of critical and creative thinking and it must not produce students, who think like their teachers. Martin Luther King Jr, in the book, *The Papers of Martin Luther King, Jr*, says, "The function of education is to teach one to think intensively and to think critically. Intelligence plus character - that is the goal of true education." (124) He says that education policy must be out of true respect for the fundamental rights of children and must aim at capacitating children with the natural inclination for constructing independent opinions so that education as a political weapon shall become ineffective.

Swami Vivekananda says that every human being is potentially divine and education is the tool with which the inbuilt perfection in everyone is brought out. He says, in the *Complete Works of Swami Vivekananda*, "Education is the manifestation of perfection already in man." (358) it is the height of cruelty that students are never given a chance for this realization and so real human resource is not properly utilized. The formulators of educational policies must know what is a good life, what is the potentialities of human beings and the interconnection between understanding the fruits of life and the goals to be achieved in the field of education.

These perspectives of Bertrand Russell on education resembles the educational views of Aldous Huxley. Huxley says that the actual concept of education is applied psychology and heredity and applied psycho-physiology and so the modern world must meditate on these subjects to establish an ideal system of education. He says that the majority of human beings knows not anything about psychology, heredity and the interconnection between mind and body and so rational thinking does not find its place in the field of education. Huxley says that the real fruits of education are observational capacity, associating skills and digesting ability to be clear and confident about one's understanding on a subject. He says:

> Rational foresight is impossible without knowledge, and we still know relatively very little bout psychology, or heredity, or the relations of mind and body. By education is simply applied psychology, applied heredity and applied psycho-physiology. It follows therefore that rational foresight is still, to a great extent, impossible in the sphere of education. (BW: 133)

Russell talks about the present pathetic condition of the educational system due to the institutional influence and compulsion for their own benefit, devastating the latent light of the future pillars of the world, children. Modern educational system focuses on the capacity of students to achieve material wealth and lucrative positions, which ultimately makes them very ordinary. Russell says that the more a person is educated, the less is the impulse and original thinking to be decisive and creative in life and they live with the mechanical aptitude taught in schools and colleges.

Russell talks about the pathetic condition of teachers also due to which education in its original sense is not available in the modern world. He says that the teachers do not have freedom to be the guardians and mentors of the children at their own sought after time and desire. Authority in education is understandably unavoidable, but Russell says that it must not go to the extent of damaging liberty. The plight of teachers due to the work-load that they straddle with must be understood and teachers struggle with their large classes, fixed and stagnant curriculum and overwork and so, they can only produce students with mediocrity, without any reverence for the child. He says that such a reverence is possible only with affection that they are tender, weak and that the teachers are strong and wise. The teachers will have an indifference and contempt for the children for their inferior status of being beginners, if they don't have this compassion. He says:

In education, with its codes of rules emanating from a Government office, its large classes and fixed curriculum and overworked teachers, its determination to produce a dead level of glib mediocrity, the lack of reverence for the child is all but universal. Reverence requires imagination in respect of those who have least actual achievement or power. The child is weak and superficially foolish, the teacher is strong, and in an everyday sense wiser than the child. The teacher without reverence, or the bureaucrat without reverence, easily despises the child for these outward inferiorities. (BWBR: 380-381)

He says that children are sacred, tough to define, vast, unadulterated purity, very precious and the growing principle of life. A teacher with real reverence for the children feels accountable with humility that exhibits something noble. Such an accountable person knows that they are superficially weak, dependent and helpless, and becomes really trustworthy to the children. He will have imaginations about the growth and strength of the children and their accomplishments and powerful positions in future, in terms of excavating their strength and potency. He will have such dreams about the children and will be longing to help them win the battles of their aspirations. He will do it not for satisfying any institutional expectations or authority but to help the children explore their potentiality and operate at its height, experiencing the fulfilment of self-actualizing and reaching inspiring heights in their life. Russell says that only such a concerned teacher will be an omnipotent and heroic teacher to his authority, without allowing it to invade the principles of the liberty of educating children. He says:

The man who has reverence will not think it is his duty to 'mould' the young. He feels in all that lives, but especially in human beings, and most of all in children, something sacred, indefinable, unlimited, something individual and strangely precious, the growing principle of life, and an embodied fragment of the dumb striving

187

of the world. In the presence of a child he feels
an unaccountable humility --- a humility not
easily defensible on a rational ground, and yet
somehow nearer to wisdom than the easy self-
confidence of many parents and teachers. The
outward helplessness of the child and the appeal
of dependence make him conscious of the
responsibility of a trust. His imagination shows
him what the child may become, for good or
evil, how its impulses many be developed or
thwarted, how its hopes must be dimmed and the
life in it grow less living, how its trust will be
bruised and its quick desires replaced by
brooding. will (BWBR: 381)

The prescriptions of Russell for the responsibilities of
teachers are comparable with Huxley's. Huxley says that even a
single teacher in a school or college, who is enthusiastic about
teaching the children, can become a strong contributor for the
children. He, in his essay, "Teaching and the Realities of Life",
says:

But even when exposed to only one good
teacher in every ten or twelve, the best of them
do remarkably well. But what of those children
who lack the wit and the will to educate
themselves in the teeth of all obstacles? For
them the mediocrity of most of the artists in
teaching is a very serious matter. A good teacher
can inspire them to learn to the limits of their
native capacity. Under poor teachers, they will
learn next to nothing. (67)

Huxley says that every professor must have a vision
about the future of children and that teachers must discover the
latent talents of children so that they can be polished and
nurtured and they would become experts in their respective
talents. Accordingly, activities and assignments must be given to
the students, which they would embrace passionately and
wholeheartedly. Huxley says that only professors must suggest
the most efficient and effective system of intellectual and moral

training, since there are too many systems without any valid proof on which is the best method. He says that the only way to have an effective system of training is to give training to children according to their capacity and necessity and suggests that there must be a record on the learning capacities and other related abilities.

The intellectual range, activities and achievements, and emotional developments must be watched throughout their lives. Huxley says that only such an effectively watchful, critical and measuring system can produce real intelligence and originality, which would be the best supporting and encouraging method of shaping the minds and intellects of the students. Huxley says that all professors of high efficiency and dedication must be optimistic about the talents and bright future of the students like their parents. Huxley impliedly says that ideal professors must play the role of the parents also as to have a responsible association with the students both intellectually and emotionally.

Russell emphasizes on education for all and says that the world needs very knowledgeable and talented doctors, advocates and engineers and wants the students community, when they want to go for higher education, to be meticulous about understanding their preference for a branch of study and its compatibility with their personality and aspirations as directed by their internal voice to climb the greatest possible heights in the walk of life. He says, "All children must continue to be taught how to read and write, and some must continue to acquire the knowledge needed for such professions as medicine or law or engineering. The higher education required for the sciences and the arts is necessary for those to whom it is suited." (BWBR: 382) Russell says that the subject of history is the most controversial, since it is taught in all countries to exaggerate their bright side to give an impression to their citizens that their country is the best in all possible ways, hence superior to the rest.

Huxley says that professors must have the capacity to predict the dangers of war and must think of refining the teaching of the subject of history so as to minimize the evil aspects of national propaganda. He says, "Some things, however, our Professors could do at once and without reference to anyone. Foreseeing the dangers of war, they could reform the teaching of history, so as to minimize the element of nationalist propaganda." (BW: 133) Huxley says that it is the fundamental responsibility of the professors to explain the dangers of superstition and unscientific attitude towards the subject of biology at schools so that biology as a subject will become so dear to the students by which they can understand how precious life is. Huxley goes to the core of humanism through these suggestions to the field of education, since he knows that the problem is in the seed and not the grown up problems. If the young minds are properly made healthy and ethical, the world will soon be alright. It is only those who are truly worried about the chaotic nature of human beings and the world can think very seriously as to give solutions that could cure those problems permanently.

Today's system of education must believe that good manners are more important than a sharp and productive intellect or artistic creation and vital energy which are the real sources of the progress of the world. The preclusion of free enquiry is unavoidable as long as the purpose of education is to produce only belief and not thought, which is done to compel the young people to be opinionated on matters that are to be doubted. Russell says that education must bolster the instinct and desire for truth and not for creating conviction that a particular creed is the truth. Russell says that inactive children with mere beliefs become prejudiced, cynical, intellectually hopeless and they become hyper-critical about everything to make all look foolish, being unable to be operated by any creative impulse, thereby destructing it in others.

He says that a strong rational attitude is the only virtue to escape from this misleading forces. He says, " In those whose minds are not very active the result is the omnipotence of prejudice; whole the few whose thought cannot be wholly killed become cynical, intellectually hopeless, destructively critical, able to make all that is living seem foolish, unable themselves to supply the creative impulses which they destroy in others." (BWBR: 384) The spirit for fighting comes from belief, suppressing freedom of thought. Freedom of thought produces and intensifies mental vigour, which is important for not only fighting for the right but also for a good life.

Education is conceptualized as a drill to achieve unanimity through slavishness and is chiefly advocated that it is the path to victory and prosperity. There are many important practical affairs that require the power of human intellect and intelligence and not inactivity or docility. Russell says that education that produces gullibility in children brings them to the stages of mental decay very quickly and that at least, a minimum of indispensable development can be achieved only through a spirit for free enquiry. He says, "Education in credulity leads by quick stages to mental decay; it is only by keeping alive the spirit of free inquiry that the indispensable minimum of progress can be achieved." (BWBR: 384) To be credulous is to be preposterous and so, it leads to the decay of one's mental capacity, the cure of which is with sharpening the intellect through its unbridled operation.

Russell says that certain mental habits like obedience and discipline, being ruthless for worldly success, the acceptance of the teachers' wisdom are instilled in the minds of students by the teachers and the educational system, which are against life itself. Independence and impulse are more important than obedience and discipline and the ethics of education is justice. Contempt should be replaced with reverence and the capacity to understand the ideas and opinions of others. It should stop forcing children to embrace credulity and encourage them to doubt constructively. The kind of education which is wanted presently must cultivate the love for mental adventure and being bold in thoughts. Getting satisfaction out of reaching a status and feeling superior about having subordinates are the immediate evil effects of an undesirable system of education, which promotes only acquiring material power and richness. He says:

> Certain mental habits are commonly instilled by those who are engaged in educating: obedience and discipline, ruthlessness in the struggle for worldly success. Contempt towards opposing groups, and an unquestioning credulity, a

passive acceptance of the teacher's wisdom. All these habits are against life. Instead of obedience and discipline, we ought to aim at preserving independence and impulse. Instead of ruthlessness, education should try to develop justice in thought. Instead of contempt, it ought to instil reverence, and the attempt at understanding; towards the opinions of others it ought to produce, not necessarily acquiescence, but only such opposition as is combined with imaginative apprehension and a clear realization of the grounds for opposition. Instead of credulity, the object should be to stimulate constructive doubt, the love of mental adventure, the sense of worlds to conquer by enterprise and boldness in thought. (BWBR: 384)

Obedience, according to Russell, is yielding one's will to an outside direction and it is the counterpart of authority and that blind obedience to authority hampers the natural growth and function of the intellect of the children. Russell talks of the plight of teachers also by their authority. He says that the authority thinks that the teachers can work like bank clerks for hours, which will produce intense lassitude and lack of interest out of irritation of nerves and shall eventually be mechanical in their speaking and activities with the children. Teachers should be given enough freedom to have natural love for teaching.

Russell talks of how teachers should be and function with children, while teaching them. He says that a class, having children small in number is highly preferable, which is compatible with not only pleasurable teaching but also the feasibility to have an eclectic teaching methods. Russell says that teachers should not think of dealing with as many ideas as possible in a day. They should think of teaching a subject and the extent to which it can be taught should be under consideration according to the mental needs of the students in the class. This leads to a friendly relationship between teachers and students instead of hostility, which actually extirpate the misunderstanding that education does take away their pleasurable time and joy. He says:

> A teacher out to have only as much teaching as can be done, on most days, with actual pleasure in the work, and with an awareness of the pupil's mental needs. The result would be a relation of friendliness instead of hostility between teacher and   pupil, a realization on the part of most pupils that education serves to develop their own lives and is not merely an outside imposition, interfering with play and demanding many hours of sitting still. (BWBR: 385)

Russell is against the bombastic displaying of the successes, since it waters the negative competitive spirit. Instead of nurturing the competitive spirit, the latent inclination for knowledge in young children has to be nourished. The talents of children in being competitive and learning ideas and information by heart are very disinterestedly supervised and examined by the teachers for the purpose of awarding diplomas and degrees. Russell condemns this system stating that it is, for the abler students, nothing but a long tiresome task of giving and receiving examination tips and textbook facts because there is no time for the indulgence in intellectual predilections. The most intelligent students are ultimately disgusted with their learning, which they try to forget to get into a life of useful actions and these children also get into the trap of running for money, which seriously affects their spontaneous desires in life. He says:

> For the abler boys there is no time for thought, no time for the indulgence of intellectual taste, from the moment of first going to school until the moment of leaving the university. From first to last there is nothing but one long drudgery of examination tips and textbook facts. The most intelligent, at the end, are disgusted with learning, longing only to forget it and to escape into a life of action. Yet there, as before, the economic machine holds them

<blockquote>
prisoners and all their spontaneous desires are bruised and thwarted. (BWBR: 387)
</blockquote>

Russell says that the examination system makes the children think of knowledge from an utilitarian point of view that it is a road to money-making and not the truth that it is a gateway to wisdom. The examination system affects those who have a strong intellectual interest and so they feel the pressure of being compelled to prepare for mere examinations. Russell says that almost all children consider education as a means to attain the status of being superior to others. This system is corrupted and putrefied with ruthlessness and social inequality.

Russell says that accepting the wisdom of a teacher passively does not take independent thought and looks deceptively rational because of the belief that the teacher knows whatever he teaches more than his pupils. He says that students of passive acceptance cannot become leaders and they will be in search of leaders, instead of taking the position of a leader, since they have been accustomed to being only followers. He says that there cannot be any room for independence of thoughts, even though promoting this is a part of an educational system. So the students must be given the freedom of thinking and articulating their opinion freely through conducting various activities that necessitate critical thinking and being expressive, connecting with others. He says:

<blockquote>
Passive acceptance of the teacher's wisdom is easy to most boys and girls. It involves no effort of independent thought, and seems rational because the teacher knows more than his pupils; it is moreover the way to win the favour of the teacher unless he is a very exceptional man. Yet the habit of passive acceptance is a disastrous one in later life. It causes men to seek a leader, and to accept as a leader whoever is established in that position. (BEBR: 388)
</blockquote>

Russell aims at refining human mind and psychology through creative thinking to become rational beings with the right kind of education. Hope is the creative principle of human activities, he says. It is only the spirit of safeguarding anything good that has made man great and modern education is not inspired by hope and so does not achieve great results, since careful desire to preserve the past than the hope of creating future is the dominating force of the administrators of the field of teaching. He says that the purpose of education is not to be teemed with dead facts, but to create. It should be out of inspiration and not like the wish to restore the old and shimmering beauty of something valuable after it has vanished. He is optimistic and has a vision that in the future, the world of constructive thoughts will dominate and become the ruler of the world and says that those who are taught with the aim of creating such personalities shall be with the true essence of life. They will be suffused with hope and joy and become great contributors to the unshakable faith in the glory that human endeavours can create in this world.

4.4 The political criticism of Russell and Huxley

Bertrand Russell talks about the role of a nation in shaping individuals and individuals' efforts to bring laurels to their country by bringing their latent talent out to that extent that they become exemplary personalities in their respective fields. Russell says that the greatness of a country lies in producing powerful individuals. He says that a nation that stands majestically among other countries of the world has its superior impact on its citizens also. The citizens are very proud and confident that they belong to a soil that is highly respected in the international community, which acts as a stimulus to the individual's talents, pursuits and achievements. He cites examples of the birth of great individuals in many fields of a few countries whenever they succeeded in wars. He says:

> There can be no doubt that national success is a stimulus to individual achievement. When the Athenians had beaten the Persians, they built the Parthenon and produced Aeschylus. When the English had defeated the Spaniards, they produced Shakespeare. The victories of Louis

XIV were associated with the great age of French literature. Instances of this sort of thing could be multiplied indefinitely. (MO: 52)

Russell talks of the individual productivity also, which has no connection with the success and greatness of a nation. He says that Bach, Mozart and Beethoven became musical genius which has nothing do with the greatness of their countries. Spinoza belongs to an oppressed race and the country he belongs to was about to be defeated, when he raised to greatness. Russell says that the architecture of a country and its achievements in building majestic and colossal buildings do have an influence on the pride of its citizens and so it is said that the great men in various fields and their achievements are the pride of their nation.

Russell makes a brave statement, "It is a curious fact that the more democratic a country becomes, the less respect it has for its rulers." (MO: 44) Russell says that the indifference of the citizens of a country to democracy depends on the intensity of its democratic nature. He says that aristocratic people and foreign conquerors are actually to be hated but unfortunately they are not despised. Nations, which select men who have gained universal admiration and love to govern them, expect them to be the best and wisest so that they can deal with the delicate and responsible act of managing other people's affair. Bertrand Russell reflects the bitter facts about being in politics and the typical identity or characteristic qualities of a politician in the modern world. He says that in most of the democratic countries of the world, even to call a person a politician is to associate many unpatriotic emotions. It is implied that the word 'politician' has become synonymous with being a criminal.

Russell says that a good person, who is popular in his area or community, would never think of getting electoral votes and even if he endeavours, he would be a miserable failure and that those who win vote are not of admirable kind. Russell says that this problematic paradox was not foreseen by the pioneers of democracy, because it was not the case with their time. Great men come to power to rule a country, when the country meets democracy for the first time and it becomes stultified, when this form of government is well-established. He says:

In most democratic countries to call a man a politicians is to say something derisive about him. The men who enjoy the good opinion of the community, with few exceptions, do not seek to win its votes and would be unsuccessful if they did, while the men who win votes are apt to be professionals of a not wholly admirable kind. (I am not thinking of those who obtain the highest offices) This is a paradox which was not foreseen by the pioneers of democracy. Indeed, it was not true in their day. When democracy is new it usually brings great men to the fore but it loses this merit as it becomes well established. Why is this? (MO: 44)

Russell says that Archangel, as an independent candidate, will not be selected in the election, in competition with Satan and Beelzebub. He asks, "Why is it that, if Satan and Beelzebub were nominated as the official candidates and the Archangel Gabriel stood as an independent, the Archangel would have no chance of being elected? For that is the fact, strange as it may seem." (MO: 44) Here Russell is critical about the collective inferior attitude and indifference of the people towards individual, societal and political governance. The people are of the opinion that independent candidates can never win because they are just new-comers, which is also a reason why individual candidates do not get enough votes to win and reach power.

Russell says that the majority of the people in this world votes to a particular candidate without making any reasonable inquiry into the character, ability and merits of the person, because they are used to vote to the person, which is shockingly mechanical and irresponsible. They vote for the person mechanically because they have seen their fathers voting for the person and the fathers did it because, their fathers did it in the same fashion. Russell indirectly scorns that people do not know how precious it is the right to vote. They know not anything about any governing structure and all that they know is their family and leading an ordinary life full of ignorance about any man-made productive structure for the well-being of the people. He says, "The ultimate reason, I believe, is nothing more recondite than habit. Most men without inquiring into the merits of the particular candidate, vote as they always have voted, and always have voted as their fathers have always voted. This applies to reformers just as much as to conservatives." (MO: 45) Russell says that it is very difficult to break this abdominal habit and until it happens, good people will have no place in politics. Russell says that this state, which is dominated by the force of habit from a very long distance of ancestral attitude has to be mitigated at least, though not uprooted and that people should understand that the sort of criticism that we have on politicians in democracy is actually a criticism on ourselves, because we ultimately have the politicians we deserve to be ruled. Russell says:

> No one can free himself from the force of habit, and if he could, he would be reduced to such a condition of doubt that he would achieve nothing. Yet so long as habit holds sway, good men will have little chance in politics.
>
> Is there, then, no solution? Yes, but it is a matter of degree; we must be dominated by habit to some extent but we might be less so than we are. And that lessening might make all the difference. Meanwhile, let us remember that in a democracy criticism of our politicians is criticism of ourselves – we have the politicians we deserve. (MO: 45)

Russell advocates the necessity of understanding how important it is to know about politics and administration in general and exercise the basic right of being a citizen of a country by having knowledge about the historical, social and political condition of the land. He also says how important carefulness and responsibility are in choosing our leaders to rule us. Russell says that people must know everything about the political system and those who compete with themselves in ruling them so that they can decide, based on their capacity and personal character and personality, the administration of their country.

Huxley says that man cannot live without a government and leader. Only insects can be without any governing force from the outside world, since they are driven by a governing instinct, giving them no freedom of action. The people of a superior race also do not actually need any governing body for them to depend on what to do and how to do something and for other disciplines and order, because in any challenging situation, they tend to be virtuous and do anything that is appropriate and rational. Huxley says that men are of two types, the first type looks for a chance to place their responsibilities on others and the second type cannot take any lead in their life and so they look for a leader to instruct them what to do so that they can obey the command and do the task, either out of a sense of duty and dignity or at least either to satisfy the requirements of the leader or at least to impress the person. Huxley says that the destiny of those who want others to bear their responsibility and those who want to shoulder others' responsibility are interconnected. Huxley says:

> Man, being what he is, we can see that tit is biologically impossible for him to do without governments and leaders. A society of locusts or lemmings can dispense with leasers, because each individual is internally governed by instincts which allow him no freedom of action; at any given moment, there is only one thing he can do. A race of superior beings, like Milton's angels, for example, could equally dispense with leaders; they could be trusted in any crisis to do the virtuous and the rational thing. Men fall between two stools. Most of us are only too happy to shift the greater part of our responsibilities to other shoulders; we like to be told what to do, which way to go. (AHCE: 364)

It is not enough, if a person is driven by ambition, since all are driven by the lust for power, but not all persons have the intensity of the force to achieve their ambition. Huxley says that the lust for domination and power of an artist leads him not to dominate other men, but to deal with words, colours, bits of stones and the world of his own thoughts. The spirit of domination of a philosopher ends with dominating the entire universe conceptually. A philosopher chops and stretches the dirty facts of experience with a truly procrustean love for tidiness and order so as to fit his system. Huxley says that everyone is driven by the desire to dominate their neighbours and when the thought is not diminished by any other thoughts and grows wilder and wilder, the reaching of the position of a leader is possible. He says:

> To begin with, there must be an ambition to become a leader. All of us, I imagine, have a certain lust for power. But the desire varies greatly in the intensity, and the objects over which it is desired to exert power are not always the same. An artist, for example, lusts for domination, not over his fellow men, but over words, over colours, over bits of stone; above all, over his own thoughts. The philosopher, more ambitious, longs to tyrannize over the whole universe. With a truly Procrustean love for neatness and symmetry, he chops and stretches the untidy facts of experience until they fit his favourite system. But philosophers and artists, after all, are rare monsters. The power   most people desire is over their neighbours. When that desire is very strong – so   strong   that   it does not shrink before any expense of labour or of thought --- the man who feels it may be said to be ambitious to become a leader. (AHCE: 365)

There is a strong urge to follow by the majority of the people of the world that there is a languishing waiting for ideal leaders. The followers may not possess the typical strong qualities of a leader, but they can identify a person with the qualities that they expect or demand in him. It is absolutely great to be a leader with all sorts of desired qualities, but the followers, who play the role of critics and who makes the emergence of such a leader a great sensation, are also significant in the socio-political scenario. Bertrand Russell in his book, *Power: A New Analysis*, says:

> The Power impulse has two forms: explicit, in leaders; implicit, in their followers. When men willingly follow a leader, they do so with a view to the acquisition of power by the group which he commands, and they feel that his triumphs are theirs. Most men do not feel in themselves the competence required for leading their group to victory, and therefore seek out a captain who appears to possess the courage and sagacity necessary for the achievement of supremacy. (15)

Huxley says that a true leader has animal magnetism in terms of expressing one's mind. This animal magnetism is a very compatible and friendly charm for the population of the world. The people are enchanted with the formidable magnetism, which truly inspires people and make them become confident, and it commands natural obedience on the part of the listeners and onlookers. What is essential is the combination of animal magnetism with a gift for speaking attractively. It is eloquence that launches this magnetism to a long range, covering a large gathering of people. Huxley says:

> The ambition has now to be satisfied. To do that, it is almost essential that a man should be endowed with a good dose of what the quacks of an earlier age called "animal magnetism". This quality, which seems to be presses itself in varying degrees of intensity. At its most amiable, we call it, charm. At its most formidable, it is that queer power which enables certain people to inspire confidence and, sure of obedience, to command. The would-be-leader should also possess --- the essential complement to this endowment --- a certain gift of the gab. Eloquence enables him to exert his magnetism at long range and over a number of people at the same time. (AHCE: 365)

Huxley says that a successful leader has all sorts of intellectual qualities. The first intellectual quality to be possessed is a prompt and practical intelligence with cunningness. Huxley says that those who have the current prejudices have the chance for enjoying permanent success in their life. He says:

> We have now to consider the intellectual qualities of the successful leader. These are, in the first place, a prompt and practical intelligence, and a touch of cunning. Almost equally essential, if success is to be steady and anything like permanent, is a good dosage of the current prejudices. Certain leaders, it is true, have been relatively free from the prejudices of the led, and have succeeded in imposing upon them unfamiliar, and therefore unpopular ideas. But their efforts, though often fruitful in the future, have rarely met with an untroubled success during their own lifetime. (AHCE: 366)

Huxley says that it is difficult for any successful leader, who has all the expected or prescribed intellectual qualities and practical and prompt intelligence, to admit the prejudices of his society, because such a leader cannot be subtle and sceptical. A successful leader with a bundle of contradicting principles or strong ideas cannot thrive for a long time as the most wanted leader, since consistency and being rational is the back bone of being a leader in operation. Huxley says:

> Successful leaders are rarely remarkable for their purely intellectual capacities, indeed, it is difficult for a man to be very intelligent and to accept the prejudices of the society in which he lives. They are rarely subtle or sceptical; they do not like the scientific suspense of judgment, preferring always to belief one thing passionately, rather than another, and to make definite decisions even when they have no rational excuse for doing so. (AHCE: 366)

Huxley says that these are the qualities of the leaders of the past and we do not have such leaders in the present world and there is a shortage for leaders more than for followers. As a result, we have no other go other than employing those who, according to our practical intelligence and honest observation, do not deserve to be employed at all. It is so painful that the people are still driven by their tradition that teaches them to respect the employed persons and expect that they will keep their instinct to do more harm under control and try to do something constructive to them.

Huxley says that a leader, who comes to power to rule an instable society, which has lost its respect for traditional values and order in general, must be both a philosopher and scientist. Such a leader finds the people, who depends on the industrial system for their livelihood, deeply rocked by the rottenness from both inside and outside and fids chaos in every field with unbridled rapidity. Huxley here indirectly giving a descriptive account of the present condition of the world and his expectations of the qualities for the leaders to handle all these problems efficiently. He says:

> To rule such a society, a man should be a philosopher and a scientist. He should possess vast knowledge. He should be exquisitely sensitive to every lesson of experience. He should be quick to seize on every new idea, to judge it, and to assimilate the virtue contained in it. He should, in a word, possess all those intellectual qualities which the typical leader of the past --- who is also, alas, the typical leader of the present day --- does not possess" (CE 367)

Huxley says that just one leader of this kind is not enough to make any changes because if the majority is the opposite to the ideal type, even the most desirable personality cannot do anything against their collective effort to make him ineffectual. So cooperation is needed from the leaders of other countries. A single nation cannot create the possibility of disarmament, when the neighbouring countries are very passionate and proud about being threateningly strong in their military capacity. Huxley says that no nation can be driven by reason, when the rest is governed by erroneous concepts and unreasonable misconceptions. He says:

> And even if a lonely monster of this kind were to appear in one country, he could achieve little or nothing so long as the old type of leader remained in control of the surrounding states. One Poincare would be enough to reduce ten philosopher kings to impotence. A single, solitary nation cannot possibly afford to embark on schemes of disarmament while its neighbours retain their fleets and aeroplanes. Similarly, no state could afford to be governed by reason while the rest of the world was governed by the good old-fashioned light of unreasoning prejudice. (AHCE: 368)

Huxley says that the old type of leaders alone will involve in the destructive activities without minding what shall happen to the peace of the world, because of their doctrines, but the new type of leaders shall never take part in any of such decisions or activities. Huxley is very euphemistic or diplomatic in giving an indirect expression of what is exactly in his mind, when he talks about the type of leaders wanted urgently in this modern times to both prevent the dangerous activities and propaganda, but also not to repeat the indelible shame in the history of mankind. He says:

> We are on the horns of a dilemma. There is every reason to suppose, on the one hand, that leaders of the old school will involve the new and complex and unstable world in fresh and even more appalling calamities. And on the other hand, there seems to be not the slightest probability of a new type of leader being evolved; at any rate, in the immediate and, for us, interesting future. (AHCE: 368)

Huxley says that to be concerned about the distant future is not wise now, since there is an impending peril of going for a full-scale nuclear war. Huxley's words are suffused with respects for the leaders, pain and fear due to his doubt whether they will soon be aggressive about their enemies and the hope that the world might overcome the presently existing dangers.

4.5 The anti-war perspectives of Russell and Huxley

Russell and Huxley were among the men greatly disturbed with the insecure state of the world after the World Wars. They started spending much of their life time only in propagating humanism and solid ideas to prevent human brains from strategizing a full scale nuclear war, which would result in the total annihilation of lives on the globe. They desired to extirpate war from the world and the glorious state of mutual love and care to be rampant, promising the joy of eternal security and prosperity to human beings. Bertrand Russell and Aldous Huxley, being startled witnesses of the two World Wars and their unspeakable cruelties and irrecoverable devastations thrown to the world, are vehement attackers of the very idea of being pugnacious to dominate and make a nation or the world subservient to one or a group of nations. They reproach fight in any form and war in particular that stamps on people mercilessly and so they hold up the flag of humanism to spread compassion and love across the world. Russell confesses in his autobiography:

> The period from 1910 to 1914 was a time of transition. My life before 1910 was as sharply separated as Faust's life before and after he met Mephistopheles. I underwent a process of rejuvenation, inaugurated by Ottoline Morrell and continued by the War. It may seem curious that the War should rejuvenate anybody, but in fact, it shook me out of my prejudices and made me think afresh on a number of fundamental questions. (225)

Stephen Spender, an eminent poet, in *Aldous Huxley, A Memorial Volume,* talks of Huxley's individuality and distinction as a writer and humanist. He says that Huxley was terrified with the unimaginable devastations of the World Wars and their deadly consequences as described in Joseph Conrad's *The Heart of Darkness*. He weapons of mass destruction, the uncontrollable development of science and its misuse were the haunting thoughts. He says:

> I don't mean by terrified that he was frightened for himself, but that he had the vision   of what Conrad described as the heart of darkness, the never-ceasing consciousness of what men are doing to themselves with their weapons of destruction and their means of scientific improvement, and of the still more terrifying things that they are likely to do in the future. But he always believed that by resolute use of reason and imagination catastrophe could be avoided. (20)

Russell says that his adult life has been in utter gloom and shaken at the terror prevailing all over the world due to the World Wars and that the world has seen the start of the decomposition of human values and civilization, since the eruption of the first world war. He says, "The world since 1914 has been one in which civilized ways of life and humane feelings have steadily decayed; and there is, as yet, little sign of a contrary tendency." (FF: 223) He says that war has been the basic instinct of primitive man, but man has travelled a long way through many levels of his cultural evolution and become civilized and intelligent, but still the drive for fight and blood-shed, through which he wants to feel superior and powerful, is inextinguishably with him.

Barbaric culture had a civilization, which was superior to the morality of the modern civilization. There was no demonic thirst in the barbaric society for blood shed on the entire globe just to prove one's might to the world or feel superior. The modern world is a slave to the developed ego to dominate others and to be destructively mighty. Nationalism does not spread love and brotherhood, since it teaches love for one's county. Psychologically nationalism is the antithesis of universal brotherhood. Jiddu Krishnamurti in his book, On Relationship, says:

> The nationalist is a curse because through his very nationalistic, patriotic spirt, he is creating a wall of isolation. He is also identified with his country that he builds a wall against another. And what happens when you build a wall against something? That something is constantly beating against your wall. When you resist something, the very resistance indicates that you are in conflict with the other. So nationalism, which is a process of isolation, which is the outcome of the search for power, cannot bring about peace in the world. The man who is a nationalist and talks of brotherhood is telling a like. He is living in a state of contradiction. (13)

Russell says that there was an advent of powerful machines and a huge production in America and Britain, which the other countries wanted to follow and as a result a considerable part of human capacity of advanced nations was spent to produce machines to destroy the other advanced nations. Russell says that so long as the attitude to perish the competitors persists, every brilliant improvement in the field of science is fatal to the very existence of human beings. Russell says, "The older competitive doctrines which have come down to us from the times of tribal warfare are no longer true. Two powerful groups can always prosper more by co-operation than they can by competition." (FF:135) It indicates that the strategies of the ancient times are not compatible with the modern necessity. Inter-dependency is more preferable to an animalistic competitive spirit for mutual growth.

In the modern world, two powerful countries try to prove to be superior to each other through armaments. Russell says that the rash and belligerent act of increasing military strength and lethal weapons has pushed the present world to the limits of insecurity, restlessness and hopelessness, and the only reason for this unfortunate state is the tension between the East and the

West. Russell says that the existing enmity between East and West is capable of bringing down the catastrophic possibility of ending in nuclear war that would reduce both to ashes. He unleashes a didactic command that America and Russia must stop their fight for power superiority and stay in agreement not to be nightmares to the rest of the world.

The bitterness for each other is so deep-rooted for many generations with haunting thoughts about each other's wickedness that even a slight flexibility from any side would be surrendering to absolute evil. The irrational authorities of these countries distract the people from the truth. Erich Fromm says, "The source of irrational authority, on the other hand, is always power over people. This power can be physical or mental, it can be realistic or only relative in terms of the anxiety and helplessness of the person submitting to this authority." (6) The recollection of destructive activities, news spread and speeches against each other are the major damaging factors of the tenuous possibility of falling into a bond of affability.

Aldous Huxley as a humanist was much concerned with the destructive side of scientific advancement. He was very much annoyed by how science makes life miserable, when it is used for military power. June Deery, in the book, *Aldous Huxley and the Mysticism of Science*, says, "As a young man, it seemed to him painfully ironic that, as one of humanity's greatest achievements, science was rel1dering life meaningless." (146) Hopelessness and meaninglessness are inter-related and when a well-educated and optimistic personality like Aldous Huxley says that the idea of meaninglessness was the impact of the Wars, the intensity has to be understood.

Huxley very strongly records his anti-war views in his book, *An Encyclopedia of Pacifism*. He records that war is the product of men with cruel intentions and the modern war is capable of killing people large in number. He says, "War was always wrong, and war-makers have always been men of criminal intentions; science has now provided the war- makers with the power of putting their intentions into destructive action on a scale which was undreamt of even a quarter of a century ago." (49) Huxley says that the official propagandists of war time have given so many descriptions of their methods of spreading an idea. Every day, the people of the world are surrounded with propaganda from television and newspapers, he says, as a result the images about war, their country and the enemy country are thrust upon them.

The frailty of the people is misused and the people are confused and start to believe in the falsehood, shunning what is true. Jiddu Krishnamurti in his book, *To Be Human*, says, "We have become image worshippers, not worshippers of truth, not worshippers of righteous life, but worshippers of images, the national image with its flag…" (28) Huxley indicates that Dr. Chalmers Mitchell, in his article on Propaganda, in the supplementary volumes of the *Encyclopedia Britannica* says that as a director of propaganda, he had a strong faith in the power of propaganda in controlling public opinion. Huxley says:

> Of political propaganda I do not propose to speak. The official propagandist of wartime have given us ample descriptions of their methods --- methods which we can see being put into practice all around us, wherever we choose to look. For propaganda is still with us, daily and almost hourly --- propaganda of every political color, from newspaper we read. Lord Northcliffe, we are told by Dr. Chalmers Mitchell in his article on Propaganda in the supplementary volume of the *Encyclopedia Britannica*, "brought to his (as Director of Propaganda) a limitless faith in the possibility of controlling public opinion. (AHCE: 392)

A refined, rich, gentle, but strong mocking tone is employed by Huxley with an intention of making human beings feel ashamed of their inbuilt weakness for being gullible and irresistibly be fascinated and defeated by the capacity of others to convince on so as to accept it. Noam Chomsky says that in a totalitarian society, whatever is given as an official news by the state is trusted by the citizens. He says, "In a totalitarian society, the mechanisms of indoctrination are simple and transparent. The state determines official truth. The technocratic and policy-oriented intellectuals parrot official doctrine, which is easily identified." (86) The operation of reason and free enquiry is with the death of gullibility.

Huxley says that this weakness is very effectively manipulated in religion and morality. The cunning techniques of being assertive and unflaggingly repeating something or to make people believe in some ideas or constructed principles have been in those spheres for ages. Huxley says that man has started applying this technique in another important realm of political propaganda and advertisement. Huxley's tone of voice is a mixture of pain and anger, when he says that man has to feel proud of employing the technique for political propaganda and advertisement. He says:

> The technique of assertion and unwearying repetition has been employed in these two spheres of human activity from time immemorial. But the merit of having employed it in other spheres than religion and morality belongs to our own and, to a lesser degree, to the preceding generation. To us --- whether British, European, or American --- is due the credit of having invented and perfected the arts of political propaganda and advertisement. We have every right to feel proud of the achievement. (AHCE: 392)

This clearly indicates that the predominating fear, hatred and suspicion from each side do not necessitate the possibility of amicable smiles. The hatred is due to the clash between the Western freedom and the communist menace. Russell gallantly declares that the governments of both US and USSR are criminals. He says, "I do not mean either East or West is impeccable. On the contrary, I think the governments of both are deeply criminal." (FF: 218) The advocacy of humanism is so brave that it does not spare on anybody cruel however powerful and dangerous they are. The fight is between two different attitudes – freedom and communism, which is resolvable only by humanism.

Huxley says that what is unacceptable, unjust and terrible about the outbreak of war is that it is not the collective decision of a country or the two countries involved, but the powerful governing individuals and unfortunately they are not affected, but the innocent and non-participating civilians. Michael Mandelbaum says, "The mechanism of prevention was straightforward: The people would refuse to vote themselves into war. The reason for this also is straightforward: while the rulers reaped the gains from warfare, it was the people who invariably paid the price." (24) The people, who are responsible for waging war against a country or countries, do not come into spotlight. They are very clever as to express through the finest embellishments of language with richly chosen diction and personifications that war is not for barbarous attack to mercilessly devastate people large in number or make a country crumble under their monstrous strength, but it is something unavoidable for the welfare of their country and it sounds very convincing and acceptable eventually to the pathetic people of the world. Huxley says:

> The most shocking fact about war is that its victims and its instruments are individual human beings, and that these individual human beings are condemned by the monstrous conventions of politics to murder or be murdered in quarrels not their own, to inflict upon the innocent and, innocent themselves of any crime against their enemies, to suffer cruelties of every kind.
>
> The language of strategy and politics is designed, so far as it is possible, to conceal this fact, to make it appear as though wars were not fought by individuals drilled to murder one another in cold blood and without provocation, but either by impersonal and therefore wholly non-moral and impassable forces, or else by personified abstractions. (CEAH: 246-47)

Aldous Huxley says that man's egotism misuses the power of language to convey something effectively and even convince on something inhuman. Huxley indicates that it is done by commercial and political organizations to instil ideas to make them tractable to their words and commands. Huxley, in his *Brave New World*, says:

> Meanwhile impersonal forces over which we have almost no control seem to be pushing us all in the direction of the Brave New Worldian nightmare; and this impersonal pushing is being consciously accelerated by representatives of commercial and political organizations who have developed a number of new techniques for manipulating, in the interests of some minority, the thoughts and feelings of the masses. (7)

The popular ideas on war is the best example with which this operation of egotism can be intensely observed and clearly understood. Huxley says that war is not creditable even to the commanders and soldiers, since they are also psychologically manipulated to demolish buildings and places and slaughter human beings, and pathetically the common people are forced to accept, tolerate and sacrifice their lovely lives to the animalistic instincts of those who truly operate all the army generals, commanders and soldiers.

The wisdom and sensibility of man knows well how horrible and unnecessary war is, but he uses language to falsify these facts and to make the idea of war seem less evil than how it is really. By suppressing and distorting the truth, man protects his sensibilities and preserve his self-esteem. Man knows how unthinkably demonic the nature of war is and so he makes a verbal alternative to that reality to make him believe that it is not evil and destructive. He does not react emotionally to war, since it is only the fiction of the concept of war that exists in the cunning and pleasant falsification of the cruelties of war. He says:

> War is enormously discreditable to those who order it to be waged and even to developed sensibilities the facts of war are revolting and horrifying. To falsify these facts, and by so

> doing to make war seem less evil than it really
> is, and our own responsibility in tolerating war
> less heavy, is doubly to or advantage. By
> suppressing and distorting the truth, we protect
> our sensibilities and preserve our self-esteem.
> Now, language is, among other things, a device
> which men 'use for suppressing and distorting
> the truth. (CEAH: 246)

The rulers and the top officials in the army of the country have the strategy of personifying the soldiers and other commanders, who handle the destructive weapons to destroy buildings or infrastructures of a country and decimate innocent people as the divine saviors, loyal servants of their countries and the real pillars of the fortifications of their country. Huxley says that this personifications nurture the ego of those who involve themselves in war and they become violent about being patriotic and strongly believe that they are fighting and killing their enemy country because the reason behind the war is with their enemies, when it is actually with their country.

Huxley says that the real forces behind wars in general are capable of burying the actual reasons for it and declare that an official battle is not between the soldiers of the armies of two countries, but different principles and ideologies and imply attractive euphemisms to talk the aftermath of a war. Huxley says that this happens against the pricking conscience of soldiers, who are afraid of discussing the terrible things related to war as they are and so to conceal even their own intentions they come to use picturesque metaphors. He says:

> Ignoring the facts, so far as we possibly can, we
> imply that battles are not fought by soldiers, but
> by things, principles, allegories, personified
> activities pitched against one another in single
> combat. For the same reason, when we have to
> describe the processes and   the results of
> war, we employ a rich variety of euphemisms.
> Even the most violently patriotic and militaristic
> are reluctant to call a spade by its own name. To
> conceal their intentions even from themselves,

they make use of picturesque. metaphors
(CEAH: 248)

Huxley does not believe that violence is constructive. Talcott Parsons, in an article in, *American Journal of Society*, records, "Mr. Huxley makes a great deal of what he alleges to be the ineffectiveness of violence as a means of achieving ends. It is true that violence, like other modes of coercion, tends to breed more violence, and that its efficacy is strictly limited." (832) Huxley says that the blood-thirsty spirit, clamouring for war, bombards a neighbouring country with powerful explosives and destroys the inhabitants, before it causes such devastations to its own country. The historians and strategists start admiring in their writing that the military officials are so intelligent as to know when and how to strike the countries and soldiers are appreciated to have executed the safeguarding command of their commanders, due to which their country is safe.

The admirers talk of the mathematical skills and the masculine decisiveness and brave heart to efficiently execute the attack at the moment of precision. Huxley mocks at them stating that they speak as if they are the civil engineers talking of the strength of materials and the distribution of stresses. They use abstract phrases like 'man power' and 'fire power' and to put a long experience of sufferings and atrocities of a warfare, they say that it was 'a war of attrition'. Huxley says that a dangerous abstract word, which is a part of all discussions about war is 'force'.

George Santayana talks about Russell's determination to fight against irrational rule, the egoistic nature of powerful people, the sufferings of the world and other socio-political evils in any form. He says, "This I am sure Lord Russell would be the first to deplore, being as he is the most perceptive and liberty-loving of men. Yet a certain partisan zeal has reverted his attention on evil to be abated, and his passion on preventing suffering, extirpating error, and abolishing privilege." (116) This indicates Russell's just and humanistic strictness about what he was fighting for.

Russell says that no country in the world was the strong opposition of the possibilities for another war. He says that the Disarmament Conference was of no use because it was about renewing some old fruitless agreements, which no country will follow as soon as a war breaks out. There was neither intelligence nor an emotional care that the people of the countries concerned should be safe and comfortable. The people of the conference seemed to have thrown of their intelligence and decided not to present anything that could possibly lessen the possibility of a war. He says:

> All this is well known, and yet, incredible as it may seem, the governments show a rooted opposition to all serious attempts to prevent war. The Disarmament Conference, after long deliberation, decided merely to renew certain futile agreements which, as everyone admits, will be broken on the day that war breaks out. The assembled governments decided to flout the intelligence of the civilized world and to make it clear that they would do nothing whatever to make war less likely or less horrible. (MO: 113-114)

Huxley says that it is really pathetic that there are many people, who believe that war is essential and it is fundamentally correct and that is why many nations, in spite of knowing the degree of the possible destruction of a modern war, react to any peace talk as to make it lead to a war. Aldous says it in an article, under the title, 'The Double Crisis'. He says:

> The idea that war between nations is right, proper and inevitable, remains a kind of axiom and, as it were, a necessity of thought. The appalling experiences of the last 30 years have taught collective humanity precisely nothing. The nations of the world continue to think and feel and act in the same old ways-the ways that are positively guaranteed to lead to catastrophe. (201)

Russell describes how the eminent people of powerful countries could not do anything constructive towards the prevention of any destructive act. He says that Einstein, with his friends, with an intention of establishing peace, went to Geneva Conference to find out some hope to do something about it, but the conference did not reach any productive agreement. Then they wanted to have a congress to discuss what should intelligent people do to save Europe from being self-destructive, but the Swiss Government did not accept to conduct a meeting at Switzerland, in the pretext of stating that it ought to be done by communists. The French Government was also did not co-operate with the noble intentions and even the British Prime Minister did not even reply. He says:

> Einstein, who is universally recognized as the greatest man of our age, went to Geneva during the conference to find out whether there was hope of anything being done. The conference having proved futile, Einstein and various other friends of peace, many of them eminent and highly respectable, attempted to hold a congress that should consider what intelligent people could do to save Europe from suicide. The Swiss Government refused them permission to meet in Switzerland, on the pretext that friends of peace must be Communists. The French Government proved equally unfriendly. The British Prime Minister, personally appealed to, did not even reply; apparently he is now ashamed of his honourable record in the Great War. (MO: 114)

Huxley says that fascism brings a remedy for the inferiority complex. Political and economic situations imposed insufferable insults on millions of people and landed them in despair. The actual rehabilitation for this state of despair is the principle of national or racial superiority. Such a superiority complex gives the people of the race or country the insurmountable confidence and courage that they are more intelligent and better than even the best, strongest and the most talented in the world, in spite of their failure, misery and general mediocrity. Huxley says that the basic operation of a fascist army is to torture other people. Huxley brings out the alarming nature of fascism and its military purpose to educate the people with the truth about something, which the majority does not seem to care about. Huxley says:

> In the second place, fascism provides a remedy for the complex of inferiority. Political and economic circumstances have, since the war, imposed intolerable humiliations on millions of personally blameless men and women, have reduced whole classes and populations to a state of despair. To these, the doctrine of national or racial superiority comes as an instrument of personal rehabilitation; for it assures the down-trodden individual that, in spite of all the specious appearances of failure, misery and general mediocrity, he is really of the salt of the earth and, in some mystical way, wiser and better than even the rest, the strongest, the most talented of another men. (BW: 136-137)

Russell says that men, who possess dominating power, are stupid enough to think that the devastation of mankind is better than submitting themselves to someone inferior or equally powerful. Russell says that such people are intoxicated with the pleasure of fanaticism and are blind to the fast approaching human excellence to be tasted. A.J. Ayer says, "While he has an extensive knowledge of history, of which he makes effective use, Russell's approach to social questions is more moral than historical." (177) Russell says that the problem to be quelled does not exist in the outside world, but with the mind of man. Men should realize that they are not only drifting towards the internal command of their animal instincts but also that their actions are suicidal. Russell says:

> What I do say is that the way of the trouble is psychological and consists in making men realize, on both sides of the Iron Curtain, that neither side can hope to win any good thing until

there is mutual rapprochement. And, in bringing about such a lessening of tension, I can think of nothing more effective than the realization of the happiness that the whole human race might enjoy if only it would allow itself to do so. (FF: 135)

Huxley reflects his prophetic vision on the impending dangers of the future of the world and didactic spirit, prescribing human values for the merciless nationalists. The real concern for something has the natural predicting ability on its next course of action and stage. Huxley's mind is so flooded with the inhuman attitude towards the people of the world by aggressive nationalists that he predicts the next evolutionary height of the severity and the manner of war in future. Sanford E. Marovitz, in his book, *Aldous Huxley and the Nuclear Age: "Ape and Essence"* in Context, says:

> But Huxley had already rejected this eventuality as plausible when he wrote a year earlier in Science, Liberty and Peace that he believes man in a position of power is more tempted to use it for self-aggrandizement than to conform with political agreements meant to restrain him. Consequently, he asserts that atomic energy is and will be for the foreseeable future "politically and humanly speaking, in the highest degree undesirable. (116-117)

Huxley talks of the human mind and its evolutionary functions related to the operation of its cruel side and says that the attitude in future will not be based on war dignity and principles, but with full of war crimes. Here winning over and proving one's might is not the concern, but quenching one's inexplicable and uncontrollable thirst for destroying as many people, places and whatever has been meticulously built over many a century on sheer labour that stands as a treasure house of richness in any field. Aldous says that people talk of strengthening military power and ammunitions to destroy the army of another country, but future war is going to be on not the army of a country or countries but the enemy's major cities and towns and other important places, which will not only depopulate the country but also intimidate, leading them to starvation and anarchy. This sort of apocalyptic state that they cause will gratify the act of waging a similar kind of war in future than the traditional method of fighting with one's strength. He says:

> But the next European war will not in all probability be fought by armies; nor will blockade be enforced out at sea, but from the air, by the destruction of harbours and docks. No modern strategist is going to risk the safety of his planes and pilots by sending them to attack elaborate pieces of floating ironmongery which, intact, can do him no harm and whose destruction can do him very little good. No, he will order the bombardment of the enemy's towns, not of the hostile fleet. If the towns can be badly damaged and the surviving population reduced to panic, starvation and anarchy, nothing else matters. The fleet may safely be allowed to steam about and let off its big guns until fuel and ammunition are exhausted. Then it will have to go home – only to fine that there is no. home (BW: 206)

Huxley is of the opinion that the thirst for being powerful will not be quenched by even series of victories, but will be aggravated it. Glenn Smith, in his book, *The Phi Delta Kappan*, says, "Huxley saw much earlier than most? at the very beginning of World War II? that an Allied victory on the battlefield would ensure, not the triumph of peace and democratic living, but accelerated militarism." (509) Aldous says that armament race is actually the intensification of the impossibility of preventing war from encroaching an enemy country's territory and destructing it. It is a stupid and extremely suicidal competitive spirit because such a savage thirst for being a super power in air armaments shall make the army of the country increase it at regular intervals and any such increase will inexorably lead to a corresponding increase in the other countries' air armaments. Aldous says:

Any increase in our nation air armaments must inevitably lead to a corresponding increase in other people's air armaments. And any increase in the air armaments of the powers allied for the purpose of 'collective security' must inevitably lead to corresponding rearmament on the part of those powers who remain outside the collective system or who, though nominally within it, feel that they are likely to be picked out as aggressors. Armament races are exhausting competitions; the moment one wide feels that it is reaching the breaking point, it will strike. (BW: 207)

The major development and improvement of powerful weapons of mass destruction was during the World War I and the deadly weapons used in World War II were the improved weapons used in World War I, except the atomic bomb. The Encyclopaedia of Humanities and Social Sciences says, "Technology goes to war. More major military technological innovations occurred during WWI than any other war in history. With the single important exception of the atomic bomb, all of the important means of warfare of WWII were merely improvements or modifications of weapons in use in 1918." (479) Russell talks about the terrible effects that could possibly be experienced by the people, if another war breaks out. He says that the powerful ammunitions with which the war could be fought with to burn the world into ashes.

Russell says that aeroplanes and poison gas have strengthened the evil intentions of bringing the world to a single point of painful cry and become nothing. British Humanists Association, in an article entitled, *A Humanist's Discussion of War*, records, "Some humanists, such as the famous philosopher Bertrand Russell, have campaigned against weapons of mass destruction and been conscientious objectors and pacifists." (1) Russell says that if there is a war between England and France, within a few seconds of its outbreak, all the people of the cities of London and Paris will be dead and within another few days, all the industries of the cities will be pulverized, the railways would be destroyed and the terrified population would fight with each other for food and kill each other, and the left over people will be without any culture. Russell says:

> If there should be a war (say) between England and France, it is to be expected that, within a few hours of its outbreak, practically all the inhabitants of London and Paris would be dead. Within a few days, all the main centers of industry would be destroyed and most of the railways would be paralyzed. The population, maddened with terror, would fight with each other for stores of food, and those who were most successful would retire into lonely places, where they would shoot all who approached them. Probably within a week, the population of both countries would be halved, and the institutions which are the vehicles of their culture would be destroyed forever. (MO: 113)

Bertrand Russell says that the solution for this problem of ever increasing tension is not to be found it war, but in reconciliation, leading to a graduation diminution of mutual hatred and fear. The commencement of this arm-race was due to the foolish belief that it is only an increase in armaments that provides and ensures their safety and security, for which both Russia and America spend so much of their wealth and money on their military capabilities, which otherwise could well be utilized for the proper development of the infrastructure and the rich well-being of their people, there by being exemplary in how to develop one's country out of a true nationalistic spirit to the rest of the world.

Russell advocates toleration as the backbone of constructing a trustworthy agreement to defend world security and peace. "The evil lies in the dogmatic temper, not in the particular character of the dogma. Since modern weapons leave us with no choice except all to live together or all to die together, the preservation of human species demands a greater degree of mutual tolerance than has ever before been necessary." (FF: 275) Russell says that there should be freedom for thinking and expressing opinion throughout the world so that people shall fight for peace and universal security for human life. He says, "Liberty of thought and speculation, without which there can be no mental or moral progress, is continually hampered where there is an atmosphere of fear." (FF: 136) Russell says that man should think honestly to make the existing indignation and fear less virulent with the sharp intellect developed over the period of time. He says:

> If however, the reign of fear can somehow be made to cease on both sides of the Iron Curtain – or, if not to cease, at any rate to grow less virulent – intelligence and skill, which have never before been as great as they are at the present moment, and which are, in fact, the very cause of our present dangers, may be ruined into fruitful channels, and our grandchildren may look back to our time as the last moment of the dark ages from which, as from a long tunnel, mankind will have emerged into the sunshine and happiness of mutual harmony. (FF: 136)

Russell is utterly fearless in stating openly that the main reason for not attaining any reconciliation so far to stop this futile fight, is the low-level rationality of both the US and USSR. They don't rationalize the dangerous condition and the selfishness involved between themselves for superiority and that the rest of the world is and shall be affected. If there is an announcement that one of them has increased its armaments to a certain level, the other side also cannot help increasing its power to be at least capable of protecting it. Andew G. Bone in his book, *Détente or Destruction, 1955-57*, says, "Most generally, peaceful progress in international relations was constantly imperilled by the "mutual suspicions" of the rival blocs. This harmful legacy of mistrust impeded détente while accentuating the ever-present risk of nuclear war. Russell had a keen appreciation of the most volatile elements of international politics in the mid-1950s." (20) Russell says that neither side thinks of going for a reconciliation because both think that a declaration for a peaceful reconciliation will give an impression that they are afraid of the other. He says:

> One of the things that make this situation so apparently hopeless is that it has on both sides a certain low-level rationality. Each side believes that the other will attack if it has a good hope of victory. Each side is therefore persuaded that its armaments must be strong enough to deter the other side from attack. When either side increases its armaments, the other side's fears are increased, and therefore the other side's armaments are still further increased. Neither side dares to start the conciliatory movement or to emphasize the evils to all mankind that would result from war, for if it does so, the other side, it is thought, will take such action as a proof of fear and will therefore be encouraged in bellicosity. (HSEP: 223-224)

The only way to settle this issue is that the governments of the countries of Neutral Power must think of talking to both the countries, which can neither be taken for cowardice nor will it be suspected for hostility. Russell says that the public opinion has much influence on anything, but it has nothing to do with talking to the Russian Government and that is why other countries with a very friendly attitude and spirit must approach these two super-powers to help them talk it out and come to a pact that actually increases the respect for each other's supremacy and humane intelligence. He says:

> The first step, I think, be taken by neutral Powers. They have two advantages: one of these is that they cannot be accused of cowardice, the other, which is even more important, is that they can speak to Governments without being suspected of hostility. In Western countries, public opinion is still a force. But to have any influence upon Russia, it is necessary to be able to persuade the Russian Government --- and only Governments can hope to do this with any effect. (HSEP: 224)

Russell strongly thinks that India a land of spiritually and non-violence and it stands for pacifism as the core of its doctrine and so, he wants the Indian government to appoint a commission that consists of eminent Indian politicians, economists, scientists and military personals, the purpose of which is to curb the possible devastation that a full scale war could bring not only to the superpowers, but also the neutrals. He says that India should make such a detailed and meticulous report and present it to all the governments of other powerful countries, inviting them to freely be critical of the prediction and Russell is so sure about any disagreement from any country on such a presentation. He says:

> I should like to see the Government of India appoint a Commission, consisting solely of Indians, who should be eminent politicians, economists, scientists or military men, the purpose of the Commission being to investigate in a wholly neutral spirit the evils to be expected if the cold war became hot, evils not by any means confined to the belligerents but affliction neutrals also, though probably in a lesser degree. I should wish the Government of India to present this report to be Governments of all the Great Powers, and to invite them to express either agreement or disagreement with its forecasts. I think that, if the work of the Commission were adequately performed, disagreement would be very difficult. (HSEP: 224)

Russell says that such a peace treaty is not possible in the near future unless an authoritative neutral investigation demonstration with no bias comes to unite both the superpowers. If so, it will be trustworthy and genuine, in spite of the fact that it is going to be tested with many questions out of selfishness, fear and pride. Russell says, "I do not know whether, in the immediate future, it would be possible to bring about this belief on both sides, but I think it would become much easier to bring about if it were backed by an authoritative neutral investigation demonstrating without bias how little either side could hope to gain by aggression." (HSEP: 224-225) Russell says that when the two countries become one in understanding that what is presented by the neutrals is true and war is not the solution for their problems, negotiations would be possible soon and the existing tension will rapidly diminish, which will redeem the traditional courtesies in diplomatic intercourse.

Russell says that the presentation must lead to the decision-making of a Congress on what solutions to be made to achieve stability rather than committing the mistake of giving a diplomatic victory to one of them or both. Russell says that the state of mind necessary for the two sides to come to a realization and then to an agreement is to be brought about by the neutrals. He says:

> If once it were agreed and acknowledged on both sides that war is not the solution, negotiations would soon become possible and the tension would rapidly grow less. The first step would be to diminish the asperities of official propaganda and restore traditional courtesies in diplomatic intercourse. The next step would be a Congress to consider all the points in dispute, and to seek such solutions as should give stability rather than such as involved diplomatic victory for this side or that. If each side were genuinely actuated by the wish to diminish the risk of war, such mutual concessions would no longer be so difficult as they are at present. And I think that in bringing about the necessary state of mind on both sides, neutral powers can play a beneficent and decisive part. (HSEP: 225)

Russell says that the first resolution should be internationalizing of the administration and supervising of atomic energy. Russell says that it was America, which was ready to get into a peace treaty in the beginning, but the suspicion of Russia broke the possibility and even now the suspicion remains unsuspended or not even diminished, after which American suspicion became intense on Russia. Russell says that the reversal of this situation is possible now because both the countries have the most dangerous atom and hydrogen bombs. He says:

> Of these, the first to be tackled would probably have to be the internationalizing of the control of atomic energy. America made a wholly praiseworthy endeavour in this direction at the end of the last war, but Russian suspicions made the endeavour abortive. Since that time Russian suspicions have not grown less, and American suspicions have hardened. We must hope for a reversal of this process, and I think that a reversal has become more possible since both sides have possessed atom and hydrogen bombs. (HSEP: 225-226)

Russell says that the role of scientists in quelling war plays a major role. Men of science should not think that their responsible role in the society is not just to offer knowledge and create efficient machines but should be operated by the basic moral responsibility of making life safe and comfortable to the people. The ultimate responsibility of scientists is to contribute effectively towards the security and peace of the world. So they should not invent anything that would become a potential peril to human existence at any time. They should know the value of life and its beauty and should bear great respect for them more than anything else. Scientists should be humanistic in their perception of the world and people and should operate compatibly. He says:

> It is impossible in the modern world for a man of science to say with any honesty, 'My business is to provide knowledge, and what use is made of the knowledge is not my responsibility'. The knowledge that a man of science provides may fall into the hands of men or institutions devoted to utterly unworthy objects. I do not suggest that a man of science, or even a large body of men of science, can altogether prevent this, but they can diminish the magnitude of the evil. (FF: 230-231)

Russell says that scientists, who play a vital role in building a national power, should be productive and not destructive with their creative intelligence. They ought to spread the value of using certain branches of science for the well-being of the people such as increasing food production to wipe off poverty and poor lifestyle in their respective countries rather than just producing weapons to nourish barbarous instincts. They should proclaim that it is an utter waste to spend so much money, which is out of human toil of their brothers and sisters, to spend on activities to turn lives and marvellous constructions to ashes, but to spend on productive plans to make their citizens' life fertile and satisfactory. This is possible only with mushrooming love for oneself, people, country and the world of which a country is a dependent part. The significance of interdependency which has made nations and people come together and learn the truth that unity rules peace and prosperity. Russell suggests:

> There is another direction in which men of science can attempt to provide leadership. They can suggest and urge in many ways the value of those branches of science of which the important practical uses are beneficial and not harmful. Consider what might be done if the money at present spent on armaments were spent on increasing and distributing the food supply of the world and diminishing the population pressure. In a few decades, poverty and malnutrition, which now afflict more than half the population of the globe, could be ended. But at present almost all the governments of great states consider that it is better to spend money on killing foreigners than on keeping their own subjects alive. (FF: 231)

Russell says that real freedom and peace is possible only when all nations and the people of the world realize their responsibilities to live connected through mutual respect and love for all. John M. Owen, in the book, *International Security*, under the title, 'How Liberalism Produces Democratic Peace', says, "Two things are needed for freedom. First, persons or nations must be themselves enlightened, aware of their interests and how they should be secured. Second, people should like under enlightened political institutions, which allow their true interests to shape politics." (94) Russell says strongly that unless there is a strong collective force from the people all over the world against the weapons of mass destruction, a nuclear war is unstoppable. He says that an invincible opposition from the people is the strongest force against which no weapon can operate.

The world should realize that the military and political men of the strong nations, who are the minority, decide to wage war due to which the majority of people, who are innocent, are victimized. So it is fundamentally the citizens of every nation, who are to honestly ruminate and take action against safeguarding their life and the posterity. Russell says, "Although many of the people who take this extreme view profess to be democrats, they nevertheless consider that a small percentage of fanatics have a right to inflict the death penalty upon all the rest of mankind." (FF: 216) Russell says that modern democracy and the methods of popularizing something are not ethical but deeply affect public opinion. He says that it is the moral responsibility of the media to present the actual information about the cruelty and the possible range of devastation of the war, using weapons of mass destruction and should make a silent revolution through the people of the world against nuclear war. He says:

> The consequence is that what ought to be known widely, throughout the general public, will not be known unless great efforts are made by disinterested persons to see that the information reaches the minds and hearts of vast numbers of people. I do not think this work can be successfully accomplished except by the help of men of science. They, along, can speak with the authority that is necessary to combat the misleading statements of those scientists who have permitted themselves to become merchants of death. If disinterested scientists do not speak out, the others will succeed

in conveying a distorted impression, not only to
the public but also to the politicians. (FF: 230)

Huxley attacks the collective attitude of the modern society to hero-worship a heroic and successful antisocial personality like a bandit. Russell says that Duces and Fuehrers will stop harming the world, only the people think that they are disgusting as they do with swindlers and pimps. Huxley says that the collective mind set of the people of the world has a power to produce personalities they most dream about and acutely appreciate and says that as long as Caesars and Napoleons are worshipped in the society, many will convert themselves into Caesars and Napoleon because they want to be liked and appreciated and as a result, the world will be miserable with destructive personalities. Huxley says:

> In our societies men are paranoically ambitious, because paranoiac ambition is admired as a virtue and successful climbers are adored as though they were god. More books have been written about Napoleon than about any other human being. The fact is deeply and alarmingly significant. What must be the day-dreams of people for whom the world's most agile social climber and ablest bandit is the hero they most desire to hear about? Duces and Fuehrers will cease to plague the world only when the majority of its inhabitants regard such adventurers with the same disgust as they now bestow on swindlers and pimps. So long as men worship the Caesars and Napoleons, Caesars and Napoleons will duly rise and make them miserable. The proper attitude toward the "hero" is not Carlyle's, but Bacon.' (CEAH: 268)

Huxley indirectly accuses that it is only the people of the world who are responsible for all the destructive and evil activities in the world. The implied humanistic message to the people of the world is that the collective attitude and qualities of thinking and preference must undergo a sea-change. The intensity of the standard of the morality of the people is not enough, due to which they become weak to be dominated and manipulated. Carles Pigden in his book, *Russell on Ethics*, says:

> Naked power occurs when the subjects do not subscribe to the morality handed down by the rulers. This can happen for two reasons: either (1) because the subjects subscribe to a different morality (as when the rulers are foreign conquerors or the subjects are heretics); or (2) because the subjects – perhaps under the influence of something like 'the subjectivity of values' – cease to have strong moral beliefs. (205)

The people must correct themselves in terms of their preference to appreciate, long for and encourage villainous personalities without understanding their actual colour with the help of their knowledge with the universal morality for an ideal man, ruler, citizen, leader etc,. so that it will not only do wonders in purifying the negative vibration, but also prepares them to stand unitedly against anything that tries to take off their peace and comfort. Niccolas Murray, in his book, *Aldous Huxley, An English Intellectual*, says:

> However perfect the social machinery nothing can be achieved without reforming the individual: 'No human society can become conspicuously better than it is now, unless it contains a fair proportion of individuals who know that their humanity isn't the last word and who consciously attempt to transcend it.' These are the ideas which Huxley and Heard were starting to explore around this time through various alternative communities in southern California. (334)

Russell is so confident about the implementation of a peace treaty against all the weapons of mass destruction and waging war against any country. He says that the real blissful state before 1914 cannot be achieved very soon, but if the world realizes its impending emergence, such a revival of hope is reachable and the presently existing terrible state is exterminable. He says:

> It is obvious that the first necessity is the creation of a system in which attack by either side will be no longer a pressing danger. But this is only the first step. Asia and Africa will remain to be dealt with and the aim must be to find ways of admitting them to equality without anarchy. I do not suggest that this is easy, but it will become gradually possible when both East and West have ceased to be a menace to new freedom. For it will then be possible, in spite of propaganda to the contrary, to persuade Asia and Africa that we have both the power and the will to benefit them. (FF: 237)

Russell does not create a suspicion that he does not know the serious and painstaking efforts involved in the ideas he suggests, but creates confidence through recollecting a worth-remembering productive achievement of the past. An amiable handshake was possible through relentless efforts to bring a half-century of enmity between Russia and Britain. He says, "All the disputes that caused a half-century of enmity between Russia and Britain were solved by a month or two of negotiation, and from then until 1917 any criticism of the Czarist Government was frowned upon." (FF: 214) This news of the past is very promising that a similar effective pact possible even now.

It reflects that Russell and Huxley are very optimistic about creating the awareness about the peril of losing the peace of the wold to the blood-thirsty spirit of the heads of some powerful countries in the world. Power is never indestructible and is possessed by a single person or a group for a very long period of time for destructive purposes, because power is interpersonal and when there is no a compatible reaction for the continuation for the possession of power from the majority of the people, it is bound to diminish and become nothing very soon. The book, *Political Behaviour Reader in Theory and Research* says:

Power is an interpersonal situation; those who hold power are empowered. They depend on and continue only so long as there is a continuing stream of empowering responses. Even a casual inspection of human relations will convince any competent observer that power is not a brick that can be lugged from place to place, but a process that vanishes when the supporting responses cease. (91)

The truth that power is interpersonal itself is the surest indication that it is vulnerable and can be incapacitated with the non-cooperation of the people and so it shines with a great optimism that all that is necessary is the endeavour to seek legitimate solutions with the support of the majority of those who truly care for the world peace. Franklin Roosevelt, in *Public Papers of the Presidents of the United States*, says, "If civilization is to survive, we must cultivate the science of human relationships - the ability of all peoples, of all kinds, to live together, in the same world at peace." (615) The modern world's prescription is not war for war, but peaceful reconciliations through using the well-developed intelligence and wisdom.

4.6 The Ideas of Russell and Huxley on World Government

World Government stands for the idea of having a single government for all nations of the world. Many political critics are of the opinion that World Government is a natural progression. The advocators of World Government display distinct reasons why it is an ideal or necessary form of government, even though it was doubted by many. The advocators of World Government, like Imanuel Kant, say that it is the solution for the most important threat called war. The development of weapons of mass destruction can be under control. The global poverty and financial instability, lack of care and facilities for infectious diseases and pandemics, environmental degradation and climate change are also the reasons for the considerations for the formation of such a

Universal Governance. They are confident that it will create the much-awaited unity among all the nations of the world.

The idea of forming a World Government is the culmination of the humanistic cogitations of Russell and Huxley for the establishment of peace and security to all the nations of the world. The reason or need for any form of government arises from the concept of an impeccable administration by an ideal leadership for security and administrative effectiveness. The necessity for the invention of a new form of government is determined by the socio-political situation of a country like voting for a change of leader in the democratic election. The frightfully paining sight of the devastations caused by the World Wars, especially the nuclear attack on Hiroshima and Nagasaki, and the unnecessary and unintelligent decisions that led to the wars were the reasons behind the serious thoughts of many political thinkers, particularly Bertrand Russell, on the formation of World Government as soon as possible.

Russell says that there are three most important reasons why World Government must be built. He says that the world is very sure that there is an intense possibility for the extinction of human race from the phase of this earth, if World War III occurs. The consequence of the war shall make the left out people from all the countries of world go back to barbarism, if at all some people survive the war. All advanced progress in knowledge shall be destroyed and leading life as slaves shall be the immediate consequences of the possible third World War. Russell says that another world war shall occur and at the end either the US or the USSR shall win and unavoidably the whole world shall have to desire for a single government to be formed under the victorious country, which can be done even before such a war.

Russell says that either the US or USSR shall be rule the world, in case of another war. If so, there will not be any successful rebellion in the world thereafter. There will be occasional assassinations, but a great level of peace can be guaranteed with the collective armed forces of the most dangerous weapons under a single government. All the countries in the world shall experience prosperity and they will be out of any fear for tyranny or war thereafter. The rulers and military personals with the spirit for fighting will become refined due to their strong conviction that no war or blood-thirsty fight is possible. Therefore Russell says that a World Empire has to be built either under the US or the USSR than to perpetuate the terrible state of being prone to war and victimization.

Russell suggests three important ideas for a stable world. He says that all the important armaments must be under the governance of a single powerful body, which shall preclude the possibilities of the emergence of any great war. He says that plans must be prepared to make the poor parts of the world prosperous like the western part of the world and that the world population, which is rampant, must be controlled. Russell says that the fears that rule us every day shall vanish, if all these problems are solved and thereafter the world shall witness the flourishing of literature than the growth of science. Russell, by the world 'literature', the mirth and joy of life shall be prosperous, since 'literature is the mirror of life'. He goes on to say that the kingdom of peace and prosperity that man has lost due to mutual suspicion and hatred can be restored by his intelligence now.

Huxley is also a strong advocate of World Government. He knows that the cradle of any crime is the mind of a human being and so the mind of such people must be refined, in spite of any sort of fortification to prevent the emergence of war in any form. He says that even if World Government is formed, it cannot promise peace for the world, because the lust for power is the cradle of power politics, the culmination of which is the powerful ammunitions and nuclear proliferation. Unless the lust for power is brought under a control, no brilliant idea can guarantee security and peace for the entire world. A strong political arrangement is expected to do something to intimidate or administer the lust for power of man systematically.

Huxley comes out with his recommendation to form a policy for internationally organised science. Huxley says that this policy will make effective contributions for the maintenance of peace and political freedom. There must be fruitful discussions on how to solve the problems of food and power. Huxley affectionately orders that all the scientists and technicians of the world must collaborate to make this policy come true, realizing their socio-political responsibilities. He says that before undertaking these practices, they must take pledges that they will play the role of scientists, keeping in mind their basic accountability of contributing to the welfare of the people and the international peace. Huxley says that humanistic method is the most effective method to improve socio-economic environment and character building training, which brings the permanent result in the transformation of personality.

The peace-seekers, humanists, socio-political critics and the reformers have the unshakable confidence in man's humane side that has been responsible for the intelligent design and construction of the international society and its functioning. It is only the fanatic minority that languishes and plans for war, but the majority of the people of the world are for peaceful and humanistic life. The intelligence of man, in spite of being destructive at times, has made discoveries and inventions that have solved so many human problems, cured the pains, sufferings and diseases of mankind, which gives the promise that man shall loose hope in the idea of war and blood sooner or later, uprooting the fear about war and paving way for a deep-rooting peace for the entire world.

Chapter V

Twentieth Century is the darkest period of the pages of human history, marked with wars that brought about the unseen devastations that intimidated the entire human existence, racial and gender oppressions, political upheavals that created the possibilities for another unthinkably cruel war, a strong sense of insecurity throughout the world, spiritual vacuum, moral degradation and most importantly the spirit of melancholy to the sense of personal, ethical and socio-political responsibilities and creations in life in general. The thirst for true freedom from the claws of the most powerful nations to the people of the world has still been unquenched. The socio-political picture of the twentieth century is blatantly and regrettably unsatisfactory. Human society of this century could not find its expected mental, emotional, moral and intellectual evolutionary growth, since they have been severely hampered by these disastrous aspects of this century.

Russell says that the twentieth century has witnessed a lots of social discontentment caused by economic antagonism between the privileged and the labouring class. Racial and religious hostilities and oppression of women are very serious social problems during this century, which are still found in our present society. People were not totally free from the clutches of superstitions and dogmas that mutilated human minds and turned morally weak. In the name of scientific civilization, a large number of people are trying to pursue materialistic desires attaching less importance to the human values, which are the very fundamental norms for achieving true happiness in life. According to Bertrand Russell an ideal society is that which is free from all these problems. Howard Woodhouse, in his article, *The Concept of Growth in Bertrand Russell's Educational Thought* in *The Journal of Educational, Thought*, says:

> Russell recognizes that the external conditions which enhance healthy emotional and intellectual growth are more complex as well as emphasizing the need for subtlety and sensitivity

in drawing out the individual's potential. Russell also stresses the need for freedom from oppression. In circumstances of fear, of overt force, of arbitrary discipline or of the stultifying labour so prevalent in the modern world the individual is not likely to realize his potential. (12)

Huxley says that a humanist is the one who believes that human nature as a whole should be harmoniously developed and that the sacrifices man makes should be out of his highest interest for the well-being of the entire humanity and not due to anything supernatural. Albert Einstein, in the book, *Ideas and opinion*, says, "A man's ethical behaviour should be based effectually on sympathy, education, and social ties and needs; no religious basis is necessary. Man would indeed be in a poor way if he had to be restrained by fear of punishment and hope of reward after death." (39) According to a humanist, Huxley says, the members of an ideal society are superior in quality physically, intellectually and morally. The society is impeccable in establishing morality in all possible realms that no one will be treated unjustly and no talent goes unrecognised. It becomes the embodiment of personal liberty, garlands altruistic efforts and purposefully dynamic, drifting towards the realization of lofty human aspirations. He says that science should be used in order to build such a society and the powers of science should be used by humanistic rulers.

Huxley talks of two groups of people in the society. The first group is creative, resourceful and inventive and the second group is stable, aggressive and believes in the metaphysical absolutes. The first group is flexible to change and fit enough to be leaders unlike the second group, which finds any change difficult and so they are the followers. Huxley says that the primary socio-psychological barrier to vital development in life is laziness. He says that the collective spirit of a society must be being laborious, shinning the predilection for entertainments and leisure time.

Huxley says that such a society cannot be constructive and is prone to be misguided and enslaved easily by any national and international destructive forces. Huxley says that a leisured society has two parts. The first group of people are simple, children-like, very happy, gregarious and unspoilt barbarians, involving themselves in entertainments most of the times. The second group of people are into many activities in the name of being readers, intellectuals, and aesthetic people, but never serious about any subject. Huxley says that they degrade all significant ideas and they have turned all values upside down.

Huxley says that the rich people, in their leisure, prefer to go to the places notorious for gambling and prostitutes and the poor people do not have lofty associations and meanings with their lives. They tend to choose activities which are mere killers of times and nothing else. He says that the idea of the poor people on leisure is restricted to looking at cinema, films, reading newspapers, cheap literature, listening to radio, gramophone records, and going from place to place. He predicts that there would be an enormous increase in amorous lifestyle and time killing, causing mental depression to the people, in the future. This paternal worry itself is the moral decree that the habit of utilizing leisure time must be cultivated and mushroomed everywhere.

Russell has similar views on the attitude of the society. He talks about the pathetic condition of the world due to the mental, emotional and intellectual decay, which the majority of the modern population is least bothered about. Russell says that a rich man in the ancient time was expected to be very refined in his taste for literature and music, but in the modern times, such expectations are only with professors and professors. Russell says that the modern professors know just what is least important in literature and that ignorance has become the hallmark of social eminence. He says that the sense of pleasure of the modern people has become very tiresome as their work, resulting in the increase of cleverness and decrease of wisdom.

Russell and Huxley know that only individual reformation will lead to socio-political reformation and revolution. Russell says that the frailty of the modern people to seek admiration from other people in the society is to be cured for a healthy living, since this attitude was a severe distraction from the burning socio-political issues of the period. He wants the people of the world not to seek their comfort and peace outside of themselves. Russell says that the desire to impress a wide range of people comes from the spirit for an achievement that is glorified eternally. Russell comes out with some examples of great men who were driven by the spirit of impressing the world. Julius Caesar had Alexander the Great as his rival in his mind, in spite of the glorious victories he had. The eminent men of the past lived with an intention of living forever in the minds of the people of the world even after their death. He says that such a desire to be immortalized in the pages of history of the world has been decreased thanks to the newspapers of the present days.

Huxley says that modern parents know about the freedom of their children and have a sense of importance to themselves also, due to which, there is no traditional love and affection at home. In the past for many generations together, a vast family with many a member, lived under one roof, the pleasure and the pride of which is not in the present world. This state, in the long run, shall result in the destruction of the family system in the society. He says optimistically that family as an institution shall never perish permanently, since it gives immense psychological contentment, but it is not to be denied that presently there is a potential peril, waiting to wipe off the family system from the society.

Huxley talks of child-rearing and the threat to the existence of the institution of family. No child is happy about being the single child of a family. Children have an inbuilt desire to be surrounded with other children and many loving people, which plays a vital role in the physical, emotional, psychological and intellectual growth, because in such an atmosphere they live with the cross-section of the society. It is very shocking when Huxley says that there are people who call themselves advanced in the modern world, who advocates the abolition of family system, suggesting that the professional educator shoulders the responsibilities of taking care of the children from their very infancy state. Huxley says that this view is a potential threat to the noble existence of the time-honoured natural instinct to be gregarious through sentiments and affectionate bonds. A society that is bereft of any sort of sentimental and affectionate relational bond is bound to be self-destructive.

Bertrand Russell's humanism does not exclude his advocacy for equality and women's liberation. He talks of the deceptive appearance of the American Society that it gives importance to women's emancipation and that women have achieved equality, but they are not true. Russell says that women have political equality with men, but not economic equality, which is very important for women in the modern world to be independent and feel confident about their constructive side.

To spread an awareness about nutritious food to stay healthy is the primary idea of Huxley to improve the world. The next idea is to eradicate the deadly habit of taking intoxicants, stimulants and sedatives, which are taken often out of felling boredom. Taking tea and watching movies are also for escaping the boring realities of life. Huxley says that to be distanced from the realities of life is hate life itself and that life has to be improved in such a way that it becomes very interesting and truly valuable, which will be a real cure for the weakness to think of slipping into an unreal world of dirty and harmful pleasures. Huxley says that the children must be trained on the art of concentrating to escape boredom and the taste for creative doings must be cultivated.

Russell is against wasting food material, throughout the world, due to over production of crops and says that the food materials wasted must be collected and given to the starving downtrodden, unemployed and forsaken population of this world. This is possible only by an organized public endeavour and the humanistic motive of which will be encouraged. Russell's humanistic intentions reach the psychological issues like pessimism and suicidal tendency of the people of this century. Russell thinks that the pessimistic people of this century must be taught the spirit of optimism. He does not want the receptive minds to be teemed with many ideas, but extends only the quintessence of optimism.

Russell says that optimism is not sentimentalism and that it has to be the offspring of reason and logical thinking. It is not about being blindly confident or speculative, it is being cocksure out of something practically believable. To be optimistic about something must sound feasible and gettable and says that it is only constructive thinking that will safeguard the people at any exigency and not being poor lamentations or having rash beliefs.

The humanistic spirit of Bertrand Russell feels an excruciating pain at the suicidal tendencies of the people. He strongly censures suicidal tendency and says that those who have it are irresponsible and incapable of facing the inbuilt challenges of life and attacks the self-encouragements and justifications that those who with this psychological imbalance give themselves, even though he says that the pain of such decisions are completely understandable, but calls the tendency immature and weak. Russell begs such people that they must think of suicide in relation to the sacredness of life.

Russell believes that the regular and sincere readers of every society must be properly guided so as to make them become productive to their society and mankind in general. He thinks that the readers must protect themselves from lingering in the utopian world that the habit of reading gives them, since it is extremely distracting from reality. To stay in the world of imagination unproductively is just killing time and causing a considerable distance from the world of responsibilities. But to stay in the world of imagination for creative purpose is a dynamic and productive act like that of the spirit of Mozart for his eternal music compositions. To stay in the world of fancy to do something precious of this sort is what is recommended for readers so that they all can become astounding contributors of many fields.

Huxley wants the people and the general readers to be watchful about their desire to be up-to-date with information and knowledge to impress others and be appreciated, there by feeling of a great standard. This is a time-wasting carefulness according to Huxley. He says that he had to be in the unnecessary painful process of staying up-to-date with information from all the fields, which he regrets. He says that he felt truly liberated only when he extricated himself from that particular habit to turn back to being at his own desire to things according to the necessity.

Huxley comes out with the moral prescription that people must stay away from the societal expectation that they must be up-to-date.

Huxley also warns people not to believe that doing something that the majority in the society is their true assignment, without which life is meaningless. He says that the typical example is people's attitude that being a government officer is superior to any position in a private concern. Huxley promotes the concept of equality and says that the sense of equality has given birth to the concept of democracy, which is the cradle of humanitarianism. Huxley speaks for democracy and talks of the various comforts and benefits of the people of a democratic country when compared with the situations in a tyrannical society.

Russell says that the educational system is not compatible with the real meaning of education. The strategies and rules practiced in the field of education in the modern world are not capable of producing children of original thinking and creative ability to make them become independent and solvents. He says that the present system creates thraldom through emphasizing on passive obedience. Russell says that the Kindergarten and Montessori system of education were invented by those who were ignorant of both advanced styles of instructing the children and the ultimate fruits of education.

Russell says that the powerful role of education is to form and shape the character of children and their opinion. The impressionable nature of children should not be swindled to enslave them to an inferior social system. Education is for promoting original thinking and decision making, which is out of the wishful operation of intelligence in a particular situation and not being efficient about doing something mechanically, but what is imparted in the name of education is to respect the establishments of life and the instructions of the teachers without any questions.

The perspectives of Russell resemble the educational views of Huxley. Huxley says that the actual concept of education is applied psychology and heredity and applied psycho-physiology and so the modern world must meditate on these subjects to establish an ideal system of education. He says that the real fruits of education are observational capacity, associating skills and digesting ability to be clear and confident about one's understanding on a subject. Russell says that a teacher with reverence for children feel accountable, with humility, for taking responsibility to imagine the growth, strength and the accomplishments of the children.

The teacher will have dreams about the children and belonging to help them win the battle of their aspirations. He wants to help the children explore their potentiality and operate at its height, and experience the fulfilment of self-actualizing and reaching inspiring heights in their life. But unfortunately teachers are pressurized with loaded official responsibilities and orders due to which they are not able to devout an ideal quality time with students and says that ideal teaching is possible only with a class of students small in number.

Russell says that the national greatness of a country has a dominant role in the positive attitude of its citizens and so every nation must try to be in the good books of its people and that it is good to be inspired by the national greatness of their country, but must understand that they should not expect an external superior source to depend on like Mozart and Beethoven who came musical genius which has nothing to do with the greatness of their countries.

Russell says that politicians are unpatriotic and that a good person who is popular in his area or community would never think of getting electoral votes and even if he endeavours, he would be a miserable failure and those who win do not deserve it. He says that the field of politics has become extremely corrupted. Russell says that the people should not vote for anyone without making a reasonable enquiry about the character, ability and the merits of the person concerned. Russell says that people vote for a person mechanically, because their fathers did it in the same manner, following their fathers.

Russell says that it is very difficult to break this abominable habit and until it happens good people will have no place in politics. Russell says that this state, which is dominated by the force of habit from a very long distance of ancestral attitude has to be mitigated, at least, though not uprooted and that people should understand that the sort of criticism that they have on politics in democracy is actually a criticism on themselves, because they ultimately have politicians they deserve to be ruled by.

Huxley says that a true leader has animal magnetism in terms of expressing his mind. The people are enchanted and inspired with the formidable magnetism that commands a natural obedience on the part of the onlookers. He has the combination of this animal magnetism and eloquence of speech that covers a large gathering. Huxley says that such a leader has got a prompt practical intelligence with cunningness. He says that the modern beneficial leader must be a philosopher and scientist. Huxley says that just one leader of this kind is not enough to make any changes because if the majority is the opposite to the ideal type, even the most desirable personality cannot do anything against their collective effort to make him ineffectual. So cooperation is needed from the leaders of other countries.

Russell says that the rash and insurmountable hostility of increasing military strength and lethal weapons has pushed the present world to the limits of insecurity, restlessness and hopelessness, and the only reason for this unfortunate state is the tension between the East and the West, especially America and Russia. He says that the existing enmity between East and West is capable of bringing the catastrophic possibility of ending in nuclear war that would reduce both to ashes. The bitterness for each other is so deep-rooted for many generations with haunting thoughts about each other's wickedness that even a slight flexibility from any side would be surrendering to absolute evil.

Both Russell and Huxley think that the reason for the existing enmity even in the minds of the people is due to the official propaganda of both US and USSR. Huxley says that the frailty of the gullibility of the people is effectively utilized by the powerful nations to prepare their minds against their enemy country. Huxley says that this weakness is very effectively manipulated in religion and morality. The cunning techniques of being assertive and unflaggingly repeating something in or to make people believe in some ideas or constructed principles has been in those spheres for ages.

Huxley says that what is unacceptable, unjust and atrocious about the outbreak of war is that it is not the collective decision of a country or the two countries involved, but the two heads of the nations, along with the powerful military authorities, but unfortunately they do not fight among them to prove each other's. They are safe and comfortable, even if the two respective countries encounter severe damage, but it is so cruel that the innocent civilians, who have nothing to do with the decisions, are victimized and decimated. Gustave Gilbert, in his book, Nuremberg Diary, says, "Naturally, the common people don't want war ... but after all it is the leaders of a country who determine the policy, and it is always a simple matter to drag the people along, whether it is a democracy, or a fascist dictatorship, or a parliament, or a communist dictatorship." (34) The bloodshed, painful cry and pathetic tears of the people of the two countries, who are toiling well to lead a comfortable life, are attacked to severe damage and death. Those who are truly responsible for waging war against a country or countries do not come to battling with each other.

Governments use language to hide the cruelty of war and through personifications of decisions, army, soldiers and war, they try to perpetuate the existence of war in the world. The glorification of violence and killing is what happens through using convincing words and phrases to sugar-coat the merciless act of smashing people. George Orwell says, "Political language... is designed to make lies sound truthful and murder respectable, and to give an appearance of solidity to pure wind." (3) War is a contest of domination and destruction, not morality and any moral considerations are retroactive justification and rationalization.

War predates and pervades civilizations and yet is simultaneously antithetical to civilization. Russell and Huxley say that there must be a controlling body for disarmament and peace keeping, for which the formation of World Government is the only solution. Russell and Huxley are very confident that sufficiently a large majority of human species will understand the wastefulness of war in future and shall strive towards the construction of a single government for all the countries of the world so that war can be extirpated from the world eternally.

246

WORKS CITED

Primary Sources

Huxley, Aldous. Between the Wars. Chicago, Ivan R. Dee, 1994. Print.

---. Complete Essay. 1 Vol. Chicago: Ivan R. Dee, 2000. Print.

---. Collected Essays. London: Chatto and Windus, 1960. Print.

Russell, Bertrand, Fact and Fiction,

---. Mortals and Others. 1Vol. London: George Allen & Unwin, London, 1975. Print.

---. Unpopular Essays. London: George Allen & Unwin, 1950. Print.

---. The Basic Writings of Bertrand Russell. London: George Allen & Unwin, 1961. Print.

---. Human Society in Ethics and Politics. London: George Allen & Unwin, 1954. Print.

Secondary Sources

Aiken, L.W. Bertrand Russell's Philosophy of Morals. New York: Humanities Press, 1963. Print.

Black, Kenneth and j Harry Ruja. Bibliography of Bertrand Russell. Vol. London: Routledge, 1994. Print.

Black well, K. The Spinojistic Ethics of Bertrand Russell. London: Allen and Unwin, 1985. Print.

Barker, Chris. The Sage Dictionary of Cultural Studies. London: Sage Publications, 2004. Print.

Black, Scot. Of Essays and Reading in Early Modern Britain. New York: Palgrave Macmillan, 2006. Print.

Bloom, Herold. Bloom's Modern Critical Views, Aldous Huxley. New York: Infobase Publishing, 2010. Print.

Bone, Andrew G. Détente or Destruction, 1955-57. Vol. 29. London: Routledge, 2005. Print.

Carr, Brian. Bertrand Russell, An Introduction. London: George Allen & Unwin, 1975. Print.

Carrington, Erasmus. Encyclopedia of Educational Theory and Philosophy. 1 Vol. 2014. Print.

Charles, Holms M. Now More Than Ever: Proceedings of the Aldous Huxley Centenary Symposium. New York: Routledge, 1994. Print.

Chomsky, Noam. Towards a New Cold War, US foreign policy from Vietnam to Reagan. New York: The New Press, 2003. Print.

Cooper, David E. World Philosophies, an Historical Introduction. Second Edition. New Jersey: Blackwell publishing, 2003. Print.

Davies, Tony. Humanism. New York: Routledge, 2008. Print.

Davies, C James. Human Nature in Politics the dynamics of political behaviour. New York: John Wiley & sons. 1963. Print.

Deery, June. Aldous Huxley and the Mysticism of Science. London: MacMillan, 1996. Print.

Daedalus. Science and Technology in Contemporary Society. London: The MIT Press, 1962. Print.

Dyson, A.E. Aldous Huxley and the Two Nothings. London: George Allen & Unwin Ltd, 1975. Print.

Egner, Robert E. Russell's Best. London: Routledge, 2006. Print.

Eulau, Heinz. Political Behaviour Reader in Theory and Research. New York: Amerind Publishing Co. Pvt. Ltd, 1956. Print.

Firchow, Petre. Aldous Huxley Satirist and Novelist. Minneapolils: University of Minnesota Press, 1972. Print.

Fromm, Erich. Man for Himself. London: Rouledge, 2003. Print.

Grayling, A C., Russell. A Very Short Introduction. Oxford University Press, New York, 2002. Print.

Harris, William. The New Columbia encyclopaedia. New York: Columbia University Press, 1995. Print.

Huxley, Julian. Aldous Huxley, A Momoral Valume. London: Chatto & Windus, 1965. Print.

Huxley, Aldous. The Science News-Letter, Vol. 55, No. 13 (Mar. 26, 1949), pp. 199-202. Society for Science & the Public, 1949. Print.

---. Brave New World. London: Cahatto & Windus, 1959. Print.

---. Improving College and University Teaching. 6 Vol. Taylor and Francis Ltd., 1958. Print.

---. An Encylopaedia of Pacifism. London: Chatto & Windus, 1937. Print.

Honderich, Ted. The Oxford Companion to Philosophy. Second Edition. Oxford University Press, 2005. Print.

Jha, Animdha. Social Philosophy of Bertrand Russell. Delhi: A Janta Publications, 1978. Print

Jebb, R.C. The Romanes Lecture, Humanism in Education. London: Macmillan & Co., Limited, 1899. Print.

Johnson, Samuel. Dictionary of the English Language. First Edition. London: Studio Edns, 1994. Print.

Jalalul ha. Bertrand Russell's Philosophy of Perception. Delhi: Amar Printing Press, 1984. Print.

Kindersley, Dorling. Chronicle of the 20th Century. London: 1988. Print.

Krishnamurti, Jiddu. To Be Human. Chennai: Sri Venkareshwara Printing House, 2007. Print.

---. On relationship. Chennai: The Indcom Press, 2010. Print.

Marion Young, Iris. Political Theory: An Overview. New York: Oxford University Press. 1998. Print.

Mandelbaum, Michael. The Ideas that Conquered the World, Peace, Democracy, and Free Markets in the Twenty-first Century. New Delhi: Viva Books Private Limited, 2004. Print.

Mises, Von Ludwig. Omnipotent Government: The Rise of the Total State and Total War. New York: Libertarian Press, 1985. Print.

Monk, Ray. Bertrand Russell, The Spirit of Solitude. London: Jonathan Cape, 1996. Print.

Moorehead, Caroline. Bertrand Russell, A Biography. London: Sinclair-Stevenson, 1992. Print.

Murray, Niccolas. Aldous Huxley, An English Intellectual, London: Little Brown & Co, 2009. Print.

Marovitz, Sanford E. Aldous Huxley and the Nuclear Age: "Ape and Essence" in Context. London: Indiana University Press, 2016. Print.

Nietzsche, Friedzsche. Thus Spoke Zarathustra. New York: Penguin Books, 1995. Print.

Parsons, Talcott. American Journal of Sociology. 5 Vol. Chicago: The Chicago Press, 1938. Print.

Pigden, Charles R. Russell on Ethics. London: Routledge, 1999. Print.

Radhakrishnan. Science, Culture and Man, Impact of scientific progress on culture and human evolution. Delhi: Sri Jainendra Press, 1963. Print.

---. The Concept of Man, A Study in Comparative Philosophy. Delhi: Motilal Banarsodass Publishers Private Limited, 1992. Print.

Raju, P.T. The Concept of Man, A Study in Comparative Philosophy. Chennai: Sri Venkareshwara Printing House, 2007. Print.

Rhind Joy, Charles. Albert Schweitzer: An Anthology. Boston: Beacon Press, 1947. Print.

Roberts, W. George. Bertrand Russell Memorial Volume. George Allen & Unwin, London: 1979. Print.

Russell, Bertrand. Authority and the Individual. New York: Routledge, 1985. Print.

---. Autobiography. New York: Routledge, 2010. Print.

---. The Ancestry of Fascism. Let the People Think. London: Watts & Co, 1941. Print.

Ryan, Alan. Bertrand Russell: A Political Life. Harmondsworth: Penguin, 1988. Print.

Russell, Bertrand. Power: A New Analysis. Hyderabad: George Allen & Unwin, 1938. Print.

Sainsbuty, Mark. Bertrand Russell. Philosopher of the Century. London: George Allen & Unwin, 1979. Santayana, George. The Birth of Reason and other Essays. New York: Columbia University Press, 1968. Print.

Satre, Jean Paul. Existentialism Is a Humanism. New Haven: Yale University Press, 2007. Print

Schmerl, Rudolf B. Chicago Review, 1Vol. Chicago: Chicago Review Press, 1959. Print.

Shashi. Encyclopaedia of Humanities and Social Sciences, Volume 49. 1992. Anmol publications, 1992. Print.

Singh, Amita. The Political Philosophy of Bertrand Russell. Delhi: Mittal Publications, 1987. Print.

Slater, John G. Bertrand Russell. Bristol, England: Thoemmes Press.1994. Print.

Spinks, Lee. Friedrich Nietzsche. New York: Routledge Taylor & Francis Group, 2003. Print.

Smith Glenn. The Phi Delta Kappan, 9 Vol. Phi Delta Kappa International, 1968. Print.

Swami Vivekananda. The Complete Works of Swami Vivekananda. 9 Vols. Kolkata: Advaita Ashrama, 2009. Print.

The Essay Review: A Journal for Literary Criticism of the Nonfiction Essay, Volume I Issue I Spring Action Printing, 2013. The Quarterly Review of Biology, 4 Vol. The University of Chicago Press, 1946. Print.

Vellacott, Jo. Bertrand Russell and the Pacifists in the First World War. New York: St. Martin's Press, 1981.Watt, Donald. Huxley, Aldous. The Critical Heritage. New York: Routledge, 1997. Print.

Watts Estrich, Helen. The Sewanee Review. Vol. 47. Johns Hopkins University Press, 1939. Print.

Worley D. Robert. Bertrand Russell's Power: A New Social Analysis. New York: Johns Hopkins University, 2021. Print

Journals Boswell, James. 'The Life of Samuel Johnson' (1791) vol. 2, p. 219 (13 April 1773) 1930, The Conquest of Happiness by Bertrand Russell, Chapter 14: Work, Quote Page 208, George Allen & Unwin, London.Chmerl, Rudolf B. "Aldous Huxley's Social Criticism." Chicago Review, vol. 13, no. 1, 1959, pp. 37–58. JSTOR, https://doi.org/10.2307/25293502. Accessed 10 Jan. 2023.

Eagleton, Clyde. "The Demand for World Government." The American Journal of International Law, vol. 40, no. 2, 1946, pp. 390–94. JSTOR.

https://doi.org/10.2307/2193199. Accessed 30 Dec. 2022

Kavka, Gregory S. "Nuclear Weapons and World Government." The Monist, vol. 70, no. 3, 1987, pp. 298–315. JSTOR, http://www.jstor.org/stable/27903036. Accessed 30 Dec. 2022.

Meclier, Jerome. "Aldous Huxley: Dystopian Essayist of the 1930s." Utopian Studies, vol. 7, no. 2, 1996, pp. 196–212. JSTOR, http://www.jstor.org/stable/20719517. Accessed 19 Jan. 2023.

Meckier, Jerome. "Prepping for Brave New World: Aldous Huxley's Essays of the 1920s." Utopian Studies, vol. 12, no. 2, 2001, pp. 234–45. JSTOR,

http://www.jstor.org/stable/20718327. Accessed 19 Jan. 2023.

Remphel, Richard. Pacifism and Revolution (1916-18), Collected Papers, Vol. 14, Routledge, London and New York: ,1995.

Roosevelt, Franklin D. (1950). "Public Papers of the Presidents of the United States: F.D. Roosevelt, 1944-1945, Volume 13", p.615, Best Books on. Smith, Glenn. "Aldous Huxley: Analyst and Prophet for Twentieth Century Man." The Phi Delta Kappan, vol. 49, no. 9, 1968, pp. 507–10. JSTOR, http://www.jstor.org/stable/20372148. Accessed 19 Jan. 2023.

Yunker, James A. "Evolutionary World Government." Peace Research, vol. 44, no. 1, 2012, pp. 95–96. JSTOR, http://www.jstor.org/stable/23607919. Accessed 30 Dec. 2022.

Electronic Resources

So You Want to Read Bertrand Russell.pdf

ON SUFFERING AND COMPASSION.pdf

file:///F:/MY%20goal/article%20pacifism_brief.pdf

http://theessayreview.org/

file:///F:/MY%20goal/TheEssayReviewVolume1Issue1.pdf

https://www.spokesmanbooks.com/Spokesman/PDF/140Russell.pdf

https://humanists.uk/wp-content/uploads/ExploringHumanism-Course.pdf

https://americanhumanist.org/

file:///C:/Users/HAPPY1/Downloads/1277-Article%20Text-4247-1-10-20201125.pdf